Anticipation Science

Volume 10

Anticipation Science encompasses natural, formal, and social systems that intentionally or unintentionally use ideas of a future to act in the present, with a broad focus on humans, institutions, and human-designed systems. Our aim is to enhance the repertoire of resources for developing ideas of the future, and for expanding and deepening the ability to use the future. Some questions that the Series intends to address are the following: When does anticipation occur in behavior and life? Which types of anticipation can be distinguished? Which properties of our environment change the pertinence of different types of anticipation? Which structures and processes are necessary for anticipatory action? Which is the behavioral impact of anticipation? How can anticipation be modeled?

The series is interested in receiving book proposals that:

- are aimed at an academic audience of graduate level and up
- combine applied and/or theoretical and/or philosophical studies with work especially from disciplines within the human and social sciences broadly conceived.

The series editors aim to make a first decision within 2 months of submission. In case of a positive first decision the work will be provisionally contracted: the final decision about publication will depend upon the result of the anonymous peer review of the complete manuscript. The series editors aim to have the work peer-reviewed within 4 months after submission of the complete manuscript. The series editors discourage the submission of manuscripts that are below 150 printed pages (75,000 words). For inquiries and submission of proposals prospective authors can contact the editor-in-chief:

Roberto Poli: roberto.poli@unitn.it

David J. Staley

Anticipatory Biographies

Personal Histories of the Future

Springer

David J. Staley
History
The Ohio State University
Columbus, OH, USA

ISSN 2522-039X ISSN 2522-0403 (electronic)
Anticipation Science
ISBN 978-3-032-08911-3 ISBN 978-3-032-08912-0 (eBook)
https://doi.org/10.1007/978-3-032-08912-0

This Springer imprint is published by the registered company Springer Nature Switzerland AG.
The registered company address is: Gewerbestrasse 11, 6330 Cham, Switzerland

For Alexa Marie Reck

Competing Interests

The author has no competing interests to declare that are relevant to the content of this manuscript.

Contents

Chapter 1
Preface

Anticipatory Biographies is a mash-up of different genres and literary influences. Grounded in design fiction, futures research, anticipation science, and scenario writing, this collection envisions a world reshaped by artificial intelligence, economic automation, climate change, political fragmentation and technological upheaval. These forces, familiar to us today as emerging challenges, have reached full maturity in the futures imagined in this book. *Anticipatory Biographies* reveals how this future might be lived, felt and adapted to by individuals navigating their way through this world.

Anticipatory Biographies presents an alternative way to write scenarios. Scenarios are a management tool, defined by Jay Ogilvy and Peter Schwartz as

> narratives of alternative environments in which today's decisions may be played out. They are not predictions. Nor are they strategies. Instead they are more like hypotheses of different futures specifically designed to highlight the risks and opportunities involved in specific strategic issues. To be an effective planning tool, scenarios should be written in the form of absorbing, convincing stories that describe a broad range of alternative futures relevant to an organization's success. Thoughtfully constructed, believable plots help managers to become deeply involved in the scenarios and perhaps gain new understanding of how their organization can manage change as a result of this experience.

Ogilvy and Schwartz emphasize that a scenario is not a prediction, and this is not just playing academic word games. A prediction is a scientifically grounded statement of certainty of some future outcome or occurrence. A scenario is a proposal, a statement of possibility used by managers to anticipate the future world their organizations will have to operate in. Each of these anticipatory biographies should be read as the narrative of the life of an individual living in the world represented by that scenario.

As they are traditionally written, scenarios focus on vast, impersonal forces—technological innovation, economic systems, political structures, global trends—that shape the world in broad strokes. Yet, in writing about these macro-level shifts, the texture of how individuals will experience these shifts remains underexplored.

D. Staley, *Anticipatory Biographies*, Anticipation Science 10,
https://doi.org/10.1007/978-3-032-08912-0_1

Anticipatory Biographies seeks to fill this gap by presenting 16 speculative biographies, each set 20–40 years into the future. The individuals imagined here span the breadth of human experience—from the privileged to the marginalized—and across diverse cultures. By their actions and beliefs, some individuals help to bring about global change. Others have their lives defined and dictated by these changes. I have attempted to style each speculative biography in the manner of Ann Wroe, who writes the insightful obituaries for *The Economist* newspaper, who is able to distill a complex life in a few thousand words with acuity and elegance.

This collection of essays is a work of design fiction, which Anne Burdick describes as the merging "design's focus on human-made settings and stuff with literary fiction's focus on inner lives." Alessandro Fergnani's advocacy for future personas—fictional individuals created to explore the implications of scenarios—further informs this book's approach. Fergnani views personas as valuable supplements to scenario planning, tools for making abstract possibilities more concrete and relatable. *Anticipatory Biographies* expands on this idea, treating individual stories not as bullet-pointed add-ons to a scenario but as primary vehicles for exploring complex scenarios. By centering the narrative on these speculative lives, the book offers a way to think about the future viewed through the lens of biographical experience.

Anticipatory Biographies draws creative inspiration from several notable works that have explored societal change through individual stories. George Packer's *The Unwinding: An Inner History of the New America* examines social and economic disruption in the United States between 1970 and 2010 through a series of personal narratives, capturing the interplay between large-scale forces and intimate experiences. Similarly, this book uses individual stories to explore the future of automation, climate migration, and technological upheaval. Another key influence is John Dos Passos—specifically his *USA Trilogy*—who employed a multitude of characters to depict the grand tableau of American society during the early twentieth century. *Anticipatory Biographies* resonates with Dos Passos's fragmented, multi-voiced approach, and presents a diversity of perspectives to reflect the multifaceted nature of the future. Tony Fry's *Writing Design Fiction,* a speculative account of life in an environmentally threatened delta city, explores social and technical challenges through varied voices.

Each chapter offers a glimpse into a life lived in this speculative future. Some protagonists confront the challenges of environmental displacement, living in a world transformed by shifting climates. Others navigate the consequences of the widespread adaptation of artificial intelligence, grappling with the dislocations that arise when human capabilities are surpassed and rendered obsolete. Here is a brief summation of the 16 biographies:

Annika Stern reports from Srinagar, the site of the world's first fully autonomous weapons battle. Scarred by the horrors she witnesses, she channels her trauma into painting a twenty-first century *Guernica* and becomes a leading advocate for banning autonomous warfare.

South African sprinter Chioma Amaechi redefines what it means to be an athlete. Her prosthetic legs, far superior to biological limbs, propel her to win the first Olympic gold medal by an "enhanced" athlete. Amaechi's triumph inspires others to embrace voluntary limb replacement for performance gains, sparking ethical debates about the nature of competition and the definition of being human.

As climate change reshapes the Arctic, Inuit farmer Tekkeitsertok helps turn northern Quebec—now the province of Nunavik—into Canada's new breadbasket. Using bioengineered grains designed to thrive in the warming climate, he helps ignite the agricultural potential of the region. He is also part of a movement that reasserts Inuit rights and dignity, especially to control and benefit from the new industries the warming of northern Canada has unleashed.

Late in life, renowned physicist Lawrence Schumann reveals that he was born female and had gender-affirming surgery, transitioning at a time when gender dysphoria was pathologized in the United States. His decision to remain closeted during his career sparks both praise for his eventual candor and criticism for his silence.

Raised by anarchists, Jennifer Nanabah becomes the mayor of Austin, Texas, leading the city's successful legal secession from the state. Her actions mark the beginning of the "city rights" movement, a push for urban autonomy in a fragmented political landscape.

Emily Woodward's life symbolizes the United States' partially successful pronatalist campaign. As the mother of 15 children—more than half conceived and incubated in artificial wombs—she becomes a national icon, celebrated as "Mother America." After her death, "Mother America" becomes the very symbol of the country, displacing Uncle Sam, reflecting the United States' changed position in global affairs.

A pioneer in traffic management for autonomous vehicles, Matthew Shaw applies his expertise to a darker purpose: developing systems of cybernetic population control for authoritarian regimes. His work underscores the dual-edged nature of technological innovation, his decisions raising questions about the responsibilities of designers and engineers.

The CEO of a literary production company, Lindsay Davidson is not an author but a *muse*: the prompter of an AI that produces a Pulitzer Prize-winning novel. This award highlights the evolving definition of creativity in an age of machine-generated art, scrambling traditional notions of authorship and artistic merit.

As automation accelerates, Richard Blankenship finds himself among the growing class of the "unproductive:" workers continually displaced by technology despite their frenzied efforts to adapt. He joins a Luddite collective attempting to dismantle the automation economy, a futile act that underscores the human costs of remorseless innovation.

In a future where internal migration within the United States is restricted, Jayden Meyrick becomes a climate immigrant, seeking to move his family from parched Arizona to the relative environmental safety of Ohio. His illicit journey, aided by a "coyote," is thwarted and he is deported back to Arizona, exemplifying the challenges faced by millions displaced by environmental collapse.

As President of the People's Republic of China, Zheng Jiehong oversees the world's most brutal eco-authoritarian regime. China's climate policies achieve remarkable ecological gains, but at the cost of the repression and the forced re-education of its population.

Amar Chaudhri, an Indian-Australian meteorologist, becomes captivated—and ultimately consumed—by a persistent Indian Ocean cyclone that wreaks havoc for over 200 days. His obsession with this unprecedented phenomenon reflects the escalating extremity of climate events.

Saitō Miku's unremarkable yet long life—spanning over 121 years—demonstrates the societal transformations of twenty-first-century Japan. From her work as a microplastics removal technician to her second and third retirements, her biography explores the nature of aging, labor, and purpose in a society of supercentenarians.

An Ecuadorian prosecutor at the International Criminal Court, Martin Solis achieves global renown by successfully trying the first case of "arbicide:" the deliberate destruction of forests as an act of ecocide. His opponent is the neo-Bolsonarist president of Brazil, a figure emblematic of deforestation as political ideology. Solis's legal theory is rooted in the recognition of trees as sentient beings, capable of communication and worthy of rights. His work is aided by a technology he helps develop that allows humans to interface with trees, an invention that reframes humanity's relationship with the natural world.

London ambulance driver George MacGowen uses a brain interface to operate his autonomous vehicle, but the social instability of his world leaves him anxious and adrift. Through dream-capturing technology, George's therapy sessions reveal the psychological impact of living in a society where one's unconscious thoughts and emotions have been extracted and commercialized.

On a bleak Moon-based compound, Taniya Hughes tutors the child of a billionaire family who have escaped Earth's devastation. Her story provides a critique of the inequality and escapism that characterize the privileged few who have abandoned the planet they have helped to despoil.

At its core, *Anticipatory Biographies* rejects the notion of a single, monolithic future. As a futurist, I am often asked to speculate on the quality of the future. "Are you an optimist or a pessimist?" "Neither…or both," I usually say. At this moment, we are living in somebody's idea of Utopia; at the same time, we are living in somebody's idea of Dystopia. The future will be neither good nor bad, or rather, it will depend on who is living in and experiencing that future. Tomorrow's world will vary widely across different people, cultures and circumstances. This diversity is not just a narrative choice; it reflects a fundamental truth about the future of the human condition. Just as today's global challenges affect individuals differently based on their identities, locations and resources, the future imagined in this book unfolds through this spectrum of experiences.

By focusing on what Burdick terms the "inner lives, actions, and consequences" of its characters, it is my intention that *Anticipatory Biographies* redefine how we anticipate the future.

Chapter 2
Annika Stern: War Correspondent

Already a well-respected commentator and war correspondent, Annika Liese Stern was the first journalist to report from the Battle of Srinagar, the site of the first fully autonomous war.

She was born in Frankfurt am Main, Germany. Her father, Volker Stern, was a respected diplomat and government minister. When the Green Party won its first clear majority in the German Bundestag, Volker was tapped as the interior minister. When the government was forced into coalition, his cabinet post was given to the SPD as part of the coalition agreement, and in exchange, Volker was appointed UN ambassador. Anika travelled with him to the United States and to other posts in India and Australia. Her education was, necessarily, peripatetic, but she was especially drawn to figurative painting, languages and, of course, geopolitics. She was good at football, handball and basketball, and for a short while seriously considered training as an athlete, although this would have required her to settle someplace with a sporting club. Her father quietly discouraged this path, his eyes affixed on a political career for his only daughter. And, if truth were told, Anika enjoyed following her father around the world, and relished the chance to follow in his footsteps.

She admired and respected her father, but she did not worship him. She recalled the first time—she was about 15 years old—when she first disagreed with him at a family meal. It was over the Green Party's foreign policy, and especially their dealings with Moscow. Annika rejected what she called the Green's "pacifism" in the face of persistent threats. Although she did not court war, she said that the party's long-standing anti-militarism was old-fashioned, and more dependent upon the Americans than Green leadership cared to admit. Her father was furious, or as furious as an anti-militarist was capable of mustering. Besides, he could hardly fault his daughter's independence, as he had always encouraged her to state her beliefs clearly and seriously. Volker found their dinner-time conversations valuable in helping him sharpen his own positions and convictions.

D. Staley, *Anticipatory Biographies*, Anticipation Science 10,
https://doi.org/10.1007/978-3-032-08912-0_2

Where Anika would attend university was a difficult family decision. Her father had hoped she would attend Heidelberg University, his alma mater. Heidelberg had reclaimed a position in the Times Higher Education global rankings as a world-class institution, the result of a deliberate government policy and investment. She was also accepted at Oxford to read in Politics, Philosophy and Economics—her father would have grudgingly approved of this—but she decided to attend the newly formed Institute for Dynamic Change.

Colloquially called "Davos University," the Institute for Dynamic Change was chartered with the intention of training the next generation of global leaders. At a gathering of the World Economic Forum, Aseem Joshi, the tech billionaire and philanthropist, gave a talk that criticized the modern university, and especially the education and training of the kinds of leaders who would annually meet in Davos. Their educations trained them as narrow technical specialists, when what was needed was a broad education in the behavior of complex systems of many varieties. In addition to being siloed in disciplines, too many elite students were learning how to manage in a static world.

What if the intellectual exchange of a World Economic Forum gathering occurred not just every year but every day, Joshi asked? In addition to delivering a talk or participating on a panel, WEF attendees would be invited as "visiting professors" who would lecture for a term at the proposed Institute. There would be a single curriculum, with students taking courses on the history and behavior of various complex systems: economic, social, cultural, political, financial, technological, environmental, architectural, military, aesthetic, epistemological, and legal systems. Governments, multinational corporations and the United Nations contributed funds to establish an endowment, the World Economic Forum paying for a building (then for a campus) and an operating budget. Unsurprisingly, Joshi was appointed its first chancellor—especially given his own investment of $500 million in the venture. Students admitted to the program were assumed to be the next leaders in business, government, higher education, international philanthropy, and the non-profit sector.

Volker Stern attended the World Economic Forum to participate in a roundtable on climate mitigation strategies, now that the global temperatures had surpassed the 1.5 degree threshold identified by climate scientists as a climate crisis tipping point. Having failed to decisively take climate action, how might the world's leaders learn to live and cope with flooded coastal areas, more intense, frequent and longer-lasting storms, drought and high temperatures. Volker Stern spoke specifically about designing a climate-adaptable infrastructure in Germany. Annika sat in the front row of her father's talk and attended other sessions at her first World Economic Forum. She was especially drawn to discussions of conflict and geopolitics. At Davos, she met Celine Brayson-Walsh, professor of international political economy at the London School of Economics and columnist for the *Financial Times*. Here, Annika first articulated her desire to become an international though leader.

After IDC, Stern earned a PhD from the Johns Hopkins University School of Advanced International Studies. Of all the wicked problems she studied at IDC, the specter of "autonomous weapons" drew her particular interest. She was interested in the tactical use of drone armies in warfare, but also the geostrategic and ethical implications. Her dissertation explored the implications of autonomous weapons in the continuing European confrontation with Russia, and specifically the strategies Europe could employ to stave off further Russian incursions into Europe. After the Russo-Ukrainian War, and licking its wounds from the European response, Russia turned its strategic attention eastward toward its former Central Asian territories. Many observers saw this as an effort to reestablish a Eurasian empire; Stern argued that this so-called "Pivot to the East" was a temporary phenomenon, a strategic pause so that Russia might redesign its military to one day move westward again. Having lost a generation of soldiers in Ukraine, Russia was retooling to create a modern autonomous fighting force, aided by resources, technology and expertise from India and China.

Contemporary warfighting was already highly mechanized and automated, with the effect of pushing human fighters to the physical and tactical periphery of the battlespace. Stern's dissertation had noted that there had been previous conflicts in what had been termed "asymmetrical battle spaces," which pitted drones versus soldiers or armies of drones and soldiers working in concert. Drone aircraft had long been a fixture of the operational environment, no longer used only in asymmetrical conflict. Today, the logic of drone warfare was extended to ground forces. Companies such as Boston Dynamics annually rolled out startling video footage of their robots performing human-like physical feats. Years before, Boston Dynamics and their competitors pledged not to develop for or sell their creations to the military, that robots would not be used as weapons of war. That gentlemen's agreement did not even last until the end of the decade. The mercenary company Ares Automatons sold specially designed "machine guns with four legs" to the Chinese, and shortly thereafter an arms race followed among both state and non-state actors.

At her dissertation defense, Stern observed that governments had long relied on the specter of bloody human combat losses to rein in their impulses to resort to war. The sight of soldiers returning home in body bags made leaders reluctant to deploy ground forces. Air drones took human pilots out of the battle space and out of harm's way, but military theory and actual experience demonstrated again and again that air power alone was insufficient to ensure victory in most operational environments. Only ground forces could secure victory, and ground warfare always produced morale-sapping casualties. These early combat drones were not yet autonomous. Like their airborne counterparts, the "machine gun with legs" was operated at a distance by a soldier. One operator would control the actions of two, then four, then eventually a dozen ground drones, increasing their presence in the battle space. In these conflicts, drones acted as advanced troops, not unlike the dogs that sniffed out and cornered the Islamic State leader Abu Bakr al-Baghdadi from his bunker.

With a reliable weapon in the ground drone, national governments were no longer hesitant to escalate hostilities into full-blown wars, sending in "machine guns on four legs" into more and more conflicts. Loss of capital investment in any drones downed during conflict was much easier to justify than young men and women dying. Ground drones were a fact of modern warfare, and Stern was one of the world's leading analysts.

After her PhD she considered an academic appointment, but then decided to accept a position with the European Defense Ministry in the Capability, Armament and Planning Directorate. Her portfolio concentrated on autonomous warfare, with particular attention paid to developing Europe's defense against Russian use of autonomous weapons. After the United States left NATO, Europeans elevated and redesigned the former European Defense Agency into a transnational defense infrastructure, the EDM. She would be appointed the Undersecretary for Autonomous Warfare in the EDM, focusing on policy development, strategic planning, research and development, collaboration, regulation and standardization, awareness and education, and assessment and evaluation in the context of autonomous warfare. She contributed a critical memo on Europe racing to achieve parity on autonomous weapons. She gave voice to many within the Directorate and across the Agency that, in the post-American reality, EDM should be more than NATO-lite. NATO should remain a defensive organization (NATO had been integrated into EDM), and Article 5 should remain in force, she argued, even without the American's participation. But Europe also needed to be able to project power, to fill the vacuum left by the retreat of the United States, which had neither the appetite nor the stamina to maintain world order, especially in the face of the Indo-Pacific as the new locus of geopolitical power. It was in this context that she first encountered a briefing on the increasing tensions in Kashmir.

Her memo was not universally accepted, but among her supporters she was a rising star. Some observers wondered aloud if she might return to Germany in a ministerial position, even to achieve what her father could not: Chancellor of Germany. She found the parts of the job she liked the most were the researching and reporting and writing of memos and white papers. She disliked the bureaucratic infighting and backstabbing, which made it difficult to affect policy, to make a difference in the world. She would eventually leave the EDM to become the thought leader she dreamed of becoming as a first-year student at the Institute.

She would spend a year writing a book on the place of Europe in the world, which advocated for a more muscular foreign policy, one which autonomous weapons would play a critical role. The book drew the attention of Reuters, whose executives were about to greenlight a new public affairs program to be streamed globally. They approached Stern about hosting the program. Each week, she would be interviewing statesmen, policymakers, academics, thought leaders and other influential people. Additionally, Stern would write a weekly column on her observations. These were largely about global politics and military affairs, but she displayed a broad interest in the arts and culture, social trends and economic affairs, a testament, perhaps, to the broad training she received at the Institute for Dynamic Change. In agreeing to host the program, Stern also negotiated for time away to report on site from hot spots around the globe. She would report from Taiwan where autonomous drone ground forces were deployed for the first time and, notably, from the war between Morocco and Western Sahara, a war that was almost fully autonomous, though largely fought in relatively unpopulated regions. The Reuters platform gained Stern a worldwide celebrity.

The long-simmering conflict in Kashmir had recently heated up in a disquieting manner. The region was being inundated with next-generation autonomous weapons, meaning that this conflict had the potential to become the first war without human soldiers in the battlespace, just technology, one where the machines were making all of the tactical decisions. That is, the drones operated independently, not via the commands of a distant soldier/operator. Strategy was still nominally a human affair, although that role was shrinking as well. Because the conflict was centered in the city of Srinagar, there were still humans in the battlespace, which is what compelled her to report from the war zone.

As she was flown to Kashmir, she read briefings that reported that there were at least three sides in the conflict: India and China, both of whom had long laid claim to the region, and the Kashmir Liberation Front. The latter was the unknown in the equation. It was not clear who were supporting them, maybe Russia, probably Iran. Others claimed that they were receiving aid from the Indians and Chinese, and were playing the two larger powers against each other. In any event, the Battle of Srinagar was emerging as a modern war with three combatants, each with similar technological capabilities. Stern remarked that it was a kind of three-body problem of the kind she learned to understand at the Institute.

Because it was urban warfare, in this conflict ordinary citizens were caught in the middle between competing armies—and air forces—of machines. There was little warning for the civilians to flee, and indeed, as is the case with many conflicts, there were many who were reluctant to leave homes and lives behind. For the most part, the machines, or rather their algorithms, were designed not to deliberately target humans. Another thing that made the Battle of Srinagar unique was that the ground drones were, for the first time, untethered from complete human decision-making. Earlier drones were piloted by humans, but these next-generation drones were programmed to follow a strategic course but were free to improvise their own tactical decisions. Humans remained "in the loop" inasmuch as they continued to direct the overall strategy. And the drones were programmed to "learn" as they fought, gaining experience at each encounter. The tactic was to allow the drones to battle each other until one side had secured the operational environment. Only at that stage would human ground forces arrive to administer the secured territory. Because no soldiers were dying, both sides felt unconstrained about continually filling the region with ever more deadly autonomous weapons, as long as they had the capacity to continue to manufacture them. Stern would later wonder if the autonomous weapons developed judgement or even wisdom. She asked this only in the context of the seeming refusal of the drones to initially fire at civilians. And so the residents of Srinagar—and the reporter—were consigned to the role of terrified bystanders, as the machines waged a war of attrition indifferent to the suffering of the people around them.

In one memorable report, Stern strolled down a sidewalk outside a café with residents seated inside. She stared into the camera, patiently and with characteristic wry delivery described an evening battle which forced the civilian population into their homes and underground shelters. Unlike other forms of urban warfare, the infrastructure had yet to be targeted. Killing civilians had no effect on the results on the battlefield: reducing the other side's technical capacity was the strategy of the day.

Stern's "Café Report" occurred during a lull in the fighting, although this was not the result of fatigue on the part of the "soldiers." The strategists, from all three sides, merely pausing to consider new "orders" for their remorseless soldiers—for they were incapable of remorse.

Once she understood the battle conditions, Stern ventured out from her safe house. Over the objections of her production team and in direct contradiction to the protocols of the network, Stern decided that she would report from the midst of a firefight, if for no other reason than to test her hypothesis. These next generation ground drones had been trained to discern combatants from non-combatants, homing in on other autonomous weapons first, human warfighters second, while avoiding civilian casualties. Using a hand-held camera to avoid bringing a cameraperson along—a very sophisticated selfie—Stern was going to report from the middle of the conflict, to dramatize the new kind of urban warfare occurring in Srinagar.

One morning, Stern departed from the hotel in which she had taken shelter with her crew. At first, she walked along the sidewalk that abutted the apartment blocks on Residency Road, past the cafes and shops that remained open throughout the conflict. On this morning, the bullets and other ordinance were concentrated in the area of Lal Chowk, and so she confidently, if cautiously, walked in that direction, holding her camera aloft.

What followed is considered one of the most striking moments in the history of war journalism. As bullets whizzed past her ears, Stern walked in the middle of an autonomous firefight, as if she were underneath a bullet-proof umbrella. Ordinance did not touch her, even as explosions and automatic weapons fire nearly drowned out her commentary. She said little, allowing the video footage to speak for itself, but she did note that what was claimed of these weapons proved to be true, at least for the moment: that warfighting could be carried out autonomously of any human intervention.

The episode lasted a minute and 49 seconds; she crossed the square and hastened a retreat to a restaurant she frequented in the days leading up to the Battle of Srinagar. From there, she concluded her report by wondering if other civilians might carry out some semblance of daily life even in the midst of a brutal war. Indeed, after her report some residents did venture out if only to secure food and supplies, and even to hustle to jobs. It seemed out of the question that schools might reopen, but nevertheless at least two schools began to hold regular classes.

Stern wondered if she had made the right decision. She only believed her own life was at risk in reporting from the middle of the battle. But her actions had invited others to attempt to resume some semblance of normality. She was lucky to have not been hit by weapons fire or shrapnel: the more she considered her statements, she wondered how lucky other citizens might be.

Two weeks after her broadcast, a woman was killed by what the three belligerents described as an accident. She did not appear to have been directly targeted: her injuries were caused when part of the cornice of a building fell on top of her. After her death, the city went into hiding again, allowing the Battle to rage around them, while they sheltered in place. As the Battle continued over the next several weeks, more civilians were killed, others leaving the city. It was clear that, although not directly targeted, civilians remained in danger even in the era of "smart weapons."

People huddled out of sight of the weapons, but without access to food and supplies, they sat by helplessly as the autonomous weapons raged around them. Eventually, more civilians were killed by accident, necessitating the establishment of a humanitarian corridor. Stern stayed, however, continuing to report for the Reuters platform. She took video, wrote dispatches, and produced a new kind of news content: video, text, spoken word. Neither mawkish nor sentimental nor exploitive, not exactly documentary or cinema verité, hers was a kind of reporting unseen in the media for some time. She humanized the plight of the residents, while carefully explaining the technology, its significance and the larger geopolitical situation.

Stern remained in Srinagar but had retreated into a deep depression. Her reports became shorter, less frequent, gruff and impertinent. Her journals revealed that she blamed herself for the loss of civilian life, that her "walk on water" reporting had been ill-advised, failing to take into consideration the effects of her behavior on others.

She returned from Srinagar broken and sullen. Her analysis of autonomous weapons had always been an abstract, academic, emotionally distanced pursuit, written from the vantage point of the operators of the drones and the strategists who deployed them. She had been in war zones many times before, but never one where the machines obliterated the presence of humans. She did not return to her Reuters program. She could only sit in the dark of her Paris apartment, eating sparingly, sleeping irregularly.

Fabien Duguay, her mentor at Reuters, finally convinced her to undergo art therapy. He introduced Stern to Dr. Stéphanie Montagne, the world's leading art therapist. She once appeared on Stern's program, although at the time Annika thought her little more than a quack, a charlatan. Montagne had a medical (psychiatry) degree and an art history PhD, and had developed Surrealist automatism into a therapy, featuring little or no words exchanged between therapist and patient. After their first session, Montagne asked Stern to draw her experience at Srinagar, using no figurative drawing and no words. "Then how am I to draw it?" Stern asked incredulously and slightly defensively. Montagne was using a technique Rudolf Arnheim first explored, drawing or expressing feelings or abstract qualities without recourse to familiar objects or words. The technique was almost Jungian in that the patient was to draw their experiences, only rather than dreams Montagne had her patients draw their waking experiences. "And no," Montagne said, "the goal is not to capture the collective unconscious or some sort of archetype. The goal is to discover your unconscious."

In addition to pen and paper, Montagne provided her patients with a tool kit of materials, shapes, pipe cleaners and so forth. At first Stern was at a loss about how to depict her feelings and anxieties. Montagne suggested she begin by taking a clean white sheet of paper and a pen. Stern drew some lines, straight at first then bent and twisted like calligraphy. They were not letters, more like abstract glyphs or runes that she scattered across the page. She then began making broader, courser strokes, darkening the upper half of the paper. She grabbed a new piece and continued the theme, the upper half of the paper swirling with ink dervishes. Below this ensemble, she started dotting the lower half of the paper. As she drew, Annika felt a kind of calm and sense of meaning she had not felt since before her trip to Srinagar. Scribbling on paper gave her focus: "Don't struggle to put your feelings into words," Montagne counseled. "They would probably be inadequate anyway."

After two sessions, Montagne asked "Tell me what you've made." "Indifference," Stern announced with conviction. "Not only did they not fire upon us, they seemed oblivious to our presence. I felt, not so much powerlessness, as I did invisibility. As if I had been erased."

Using the drawings as a kind of blueprint, Stern worked with the materials, creating what she would later describe as a textured scene. Stern would experiment with a new material, kinetic acrylic. The dynamic pigment included nano-engineered shape-memory and light-sensitive polymers, allowing the paint to change its form and texture. The material could dynamically shift colors and physical position on the canvas in response to environmental conditions like sound, movement, or time. A painting using kinetic acrylic might transform from subdued tones to vivid hues when exposed to different temperatures or lighting or might move across the canvas like a video in response to viewers. Kinetic acrylic blurred the distinctions between traditional painting, sculpture, and digital art, and Stern was eager to play with the seemingly sentient material. She confided to Montagne that it allowed her to represent the "dynamic change" she was unable to explain in words.

Stern would depict human beings in her painting as ghost-like. The machines—or, rather, an abstract representation of machines swirling at the top of the composition—were boldly depicted. Among this fury of pigment huddled the afterimages of people. It was as if two conscious entities occupied the same physical space, one certainly sensing the other's presence, the other oblivious.

Over the course of several months, she would produce a monumental painting that critics would describe as a twenty-first century *Guernica*. In working out her own trauma, she depicted the horrors of the new kind of warfare. She detested the comparison to Picasso—"that lecherous misogynist"—and yet the media feeds could see no other comparison. For Stern, her inspiration, her muse was Kathe Kollwitz. In preparing *Out of the Loop*, she found herself reading every word, looking at every charcoal drawing and sculpture from the German artist.

Out of the Loop was exhibited around the world, drawing attention to the horrors of this new kind of warfare. It was first displayed at the Venice Biennale, for which she was awarded a special Lion for "conscience of the world." Her acceptance speech noted that *Out of the Loop* was as much about the implications of the Battle of Srinagar for the future of warfare. War was always and everywhere destructive, obscene, a violation. This kind of warfare was unlike all before it: it was indifferent. Machines fighting machines with little regard or notice of human beings. She envisioned a future of perpetual warfare oblivious to the humans unlucky to be caught in the conflict. In this bleak future of autonomous warfare, humans truly were "out of the loop." Without her intending it, she was declared an artist and slowly came to accept this new designation. After touring the world's major art capitals, she established a studio in Berlin where she would produce more works on autonomous warfare, but with an expanded focus on peacemaking.

She was invited to deliver a keynote at the World Economic Forum. She had sat on panels before but had never taken center stage at the gathering. *Out of the Loop* was displayed at that year's event, but her keynote would go further. Evoking the moral philosopher Paul Lederach, she admonished the assembly that her invitation to speak came too late. Artists are often called upon to commemorate or lament war and other horrors but only after they occur. She recited Lederach:

> What would happen if leaders of national and global politics invoked the artist, particularly at times when violence is present or its use is about to be justified?...Too often, artists are called at celebrations, inaugurations and victories, or when leaders decisions' need to be blessed, or when group and national ethos need to be solidified and sentiments of loyalty and allegiance affirmed, or when national grief needs to be expressed. Rarely, if ever, when faced with large scale life and death issues, do leaders invite artists...to respond imaginatively from within their disciplines, to the challenges they face as leaders.

Stern stared at the assembled group: artists should be included in peacemaking efforts as leaders, not as commentators after an atrocity. Kathe Kollwitz drew her memorable charcoals after the Great War had ended. What if she had the prescience to depict suffering mothers before the shooting began? What if the artist were consulted by the world's leaders? What if artists *became* the world's leaders? Stern concluded her keynote by demanding that artists, writers, poets, composers—and not just celebrity musicians—be invited to Davos each year, not as observers but as active participants in the deliberations. She argued that without their participation, artists and intellectuals should form their own World Economic Forum. She left the stage to a thunderous ovation.

Because of the effect of *Out of the Loop* on the world's consciousness—but also because of her expertise in geopolitics and her celebrity—subsequent World Economic Forum gatherings had several sessions and exhibitions from painters and sculptors and fiber artists and choreographers and architects and actors and graffiti artists, all of whom addressed war, poverty, unproductivity, climate mitigation, human dignity.

After her keynote, Stern was invited to return to her alma mater as a professor at the Institute for Dynamic Change, where she founded the Lederach School for the Moral Imagination, serving as its dean. Her work concentrated on the elimination of autonomous weapons, and she would work closely with the United Nations, urging them to establish rules and protocols and conventions banning the use of such weapons, not unlike the agreements previously reached on landmines. But like those previous conventions, the use of autonomous weapons declined a little, but did not cease, and every year, new conflicts dotted the planet with ever more sophisticated "weapons on four legs."

In Stockholm, as she accepted the Nobel Peace Prize, as autonomous war reigned over 20% of the Earth's surface and 15% of its oceans, she lamented that all the exhibitions in the world had yet to deter autonomous warfare. Art did not yet have the power to emotionally move artificial intelligence, that entity without a moral imagination.

Key Futures Themes

- Autonomous Warfare
- Geopolitical Shifts
- Civilian Experience in War
- Media and War Journalism
- Trauma and Art as Response
- Role of Artists and Intellectuals in Global Leadership
- Climate and Systems Thinking
- Future of Peace and Security

Bibliography

Arnheim, Rudolf. 1972. *Visual Thinking*. Berkeley: University of California Press.

Crootof, Rebecca. 2015. The Killer Robots Are Here: Legal and Policy Implications. *Cardozo Law Review* 36 (5). https://cardozolawreview.com/the-killer-robots-are-here-legal-and-policy-implications%E2%80%A8/.

European Defence Agency, Capability, Armament and Planning Directorate. https://eda.europa.eu/who-we-are/organigram/capability-armament-planning-cap.

Hernandez, Joe. 2022. Some leading robot makers are pledging not to weaponize them. *NPR*, 6 October 2022. https://www.npr.org/2022/10/06/1127227605/boston-dynamics-robots-pledge-against-weapons.

Human Rights Watch. Losing Humanity: The Case against Killer Robots. https://www.hrw.org/report/2012/11/19/losing-humanity/case-against-killer-robots.

Lederach, John Paul. 2005. *The Moral Imagination: The Art and Soul of Building Peace*. Oxford: Oxford University Press.

Scharre, Paul. 2018. *Army of None: Autonomous Weapons and the Future of War*. New York: W. W. Norton & Company.

Staley, David J. 2022. An Education for Dynamic Change. *Ingenious*, 6 January 2022. https://ingeniousu.wpcomstaging.com/2022/01/06/an-education-for-dynamic-change-by-david-j-staley/.

Tumber, Howard, and Frank Webster. 2006. *Journalists Under Fire: Information War and Journalistic Practices*. London: Sage.

Chapter 3
Chioma Amaechi: Athlete

From the time she was five years old, Chioma Amaechi knew what she wanted to be when she grew up. Her parents took her to a performance of *Ubuntu Drift* by the Cape Convergence Collective, and she was transfixed. The coordination of the bodies, the rhythms, the athleticism. "Music without instruments," she would later call it. "Human architecture." Chioma was going to be a dancer.

She returned home after the performance and raced to her room, twirling and leaping and emoting with her eyes, her fingers. She convinced her parents to provide her with lessons, which they did on the condition that her schoolwork not suffer, which it did not. Indeed, as she grew older dance unlocked thoughts and visions and questions. She believed herself destined for a dance academy, thoughts of university distant from her mind.

Chioma was a better dancer in her head than in reality. She eventually began to understand this: she was not winning leading roles in the recitals, her auditions were unsuccessful. She was pondering her latest failed audition, the words of her teacher encouraging her that she was only 16, that there was still time for her to grow and develop. Her technique was flawless, her teacher enthused, her style athletic, as damning an evaluation as any she might ever fear to receive.

She was contemplating her future as a dancer as the family chauffeur drove her home one afternoon, when they were hit head on by a truck. The driver was instantly killed and Chioma was crumpled in the back of the car. When she regained consciousness at the hospital, her devastated parents informed her that the doctors were forced to remove her left leg below the knee, and the other just below the hip.

She was fortunate that her family resided in Cape Town, the symbol of modernity and "the new Africa." Cape Town was an attractor for many Africans from the north. Chioma's grandparents were among the first to leave Nigeria and emigrate to South Africa, just before its government set up walls and barriers to climate migration, but not until Cape Town ballooned four-fold in population, now around 20 million

D. Staley, *Anticipatory Biographies*, Anticipation Science 10,
https://doi.org/10.1007/978-3-032-08912-0_3

residents. Cape Town was entrepreneurial and chaotic and technology-driven and awash in venture capital.

She lay in her hospital bed, fully aware of the challenges she was facing. She would have to learn to walk again once her prosthetic limbs were attached to her body. She counted herself lucky that Cape Town was an innovation hub for start-ups advancing artificial limbs and other types of human enhancement. She even allowed herself to dream that she could continue her dance career after surgery.

Kinetic Horizon viewed Chioma as a perfect test subject for a new kind of artificial limb they were developing that not only gave the wearer increased strength but was as natural and balanced as an organic human limb. Its artificial skin was not a convincing substitute, but the ensemble nevertheless had a reasonable likeness to a human leg. Kinetic Horizon wanted to demonstrate that their artificial limbs performed better than a natural human limb. The CEO John du Plessis was always searching for test cases for their more advanced technologies. (Some observers thought this practice was ghoulish.) Du Plessis was especially on the lookout for young, athletic amputees to field test some of their next generation designs and when he learned of Chioma's accident, he showed up at her bedside to convince her to go with Kinetic Horizon prosthetics. Her family would not have to pay for her new legs—the surgery, though, was another matter. In lieu of payment, and after she had regained the ability to walk, Chioma would be asked to test out her new legs in a competitive setting. Kinetic Horizon was not simply building prosthetics for amputees. They were developing high performance artificial limbs to be used in athletic competition. Ultimately, the decision to work with Kinetic Horizon was her family's choice. No one would force her to participate in the experiment. In her mind Chioma thought she might be able to dance again and be an even more athletic dancer, even if that is not what the dance companies wanted. She agreed to be fitted with experimental artificial legs that were designed to provide more speed, agility and power. She would eventually be dubbed the "bionic woman" not only because of the artificial legs but the seemingly superhuman ability that came along with it.

Once she had gone through therapy and had learned to walk again, she was eager to return to the dance floor. The terms of her agreement with Kinetic Horizon were that she would train as a sprinter, at both 100 and 200 meters. Chioma had never raced in her life, outside of physical education classes at school, and du Plessis would have preferred an athlete to test out the new prosthetic model. But being dancer, especially an "athletic" one, would be a more than adequate substitute. Kinetic Horizon had one of the few advanced training centers for para-athletes outside of the United States, where para-athletic training had long been established. One year after her new legs were attached, she attempted her first run around a track. After more training, her trial runs were already approaching paralympic records in the 100 and 200 meters. A year later, her times matched those of Olympic competitors such that Kinetic Horizon executives began to wonder if she might not be competitive against able-bodies athletes. Their artificial legs had more than demonstrated their mettle.

Once she had discovered that she had an aptitude for athletics, Amaechi found that she liked sprinting, liked the competition. It was different from dance, which was a collaborative effort. On the track, she performed alone—alongside others, perhaps—the solo artist. Amaechi entered several African para-athletic meets and was a consistent winner at the 100 and 200 meter events. Her ambitions had elevated such that she accepted a scholarship to the University of Oregon in the United States, which had remained one of the leading track and field programs in the world, placing elite athletes at all the top meets.

Before she even arrived on campus, she was going to be a different kind of athlete. Amaechi decided to pursue a degree; she would ultimately leave Oregon with a Bachelor's in cognitive psychology and philosophy. It was unusual for athletes at American universities to take classes and work toward a degree. Most were full-time athletes, lured to the university by name-image-likeness contracts. Amaechi was no different, of course, her NIL deal with Nike being another reason for her being at Oregon. Athletes were given the option of taking classes and earning degrees at no charge, but most ignored the invitation.

Hers was a controversial admission, as she was the first paralympic athlete who sought to compete alongside able-bodied college athletes. At first, no one seemed especially concerned about her appearing at intercollegiate meets, for they had not yet witnessed what Amaechi's advanced technological legs allowed her to achieve. As she won event after event at the 200 and 400 meters, protests dogged her at subsequent meets. Some athletes grumbled to the press that Amaechi's legs gave her an unfair advantage. These discontented competitors were joined by a group of Christian athletes allied with the Morality Guardians who were less concerned about Amaechi's results as they were with Amaechi the person, that her artificial limbs were "not how God made us." Two generations of military veterans, however, vigorously defended Amaechi, and would even appear at meets to cheer her on and to display their own prosthetic limbs and to deflect the protesters. Finally, Merideth Foster from the University of Southern California—the college record holder in the 200 meters and easily beaten by Amaechi at a meet in Los Angeles— sued Amaechi, the University of Oregon and the NCAA. She contended that Amaechi's artificial limbs gave her an unfair advantage, detrimental to the performance and self-esteem of other athletes who must compete without a similar advantage. The suit would ultimately be mooted by the actions of the NCAA.

Her reputation preceded her appearance at the prestigious Prefontaine Classic. She reached the finals of the 200 meters, and won the race by nearly a second ahead of the closest competitor. The complaints became public: the artificial limbs gave Amaechi too much of an advantage over the able-bodied field. Bowing to pressure, the NCAA stepped in and ruled that going forward Amaechi could only compete against other para-athletes. They were, the NCAA insisted, conforming to international rules. The Olympics, the Athletics World Championships and the Diamond League all held separate competitions for para-athletes like Amaechi. This was not because athletes like Amaechi were perceived to have an advantage, only that para- and able-bodied athletes had always competed separately, and no one saw any reason to alter this state of affairs. Amaechi sued in Oregon state court, but lost the case and an appeal. She lost her NCAA eligibility to compete against the able-bodied, but was welcome to compete in para-events.

At a press conference after her last appeal had been rejected, Amaechi denounced the decision, calling the NCAA's policy "segregationist." Chastened, Amaechi completed one more year of college eligibility in the para-athletics category, all the while seething at her being denied the chance to run and prove herself against the able-bodied. She would leave Oregon—after completing her degree—in order to compete professionally.

Nike muscled to the front of the line of companies looking to sign Amaechi to endorsement deals. Indeed, it was a name-image-likeness package—probably backed by Nike—that had initially lured Amaechi to Oregon. Nike were keen to have the symbol of the future of track and field wearing their designs. Nike had other motives in signing Amaechi: they were looking to expand into the "enhanced athlete" space ahead of other athletic equipment makers. Amaechi faced a dilemma: working with Nike on the next generation of athletic artificial limbs would be fascinating and lucrative. But she maintained a steadfast loyalty to Kinetic Horizon who designed and built her legs, and so only agreed to wear and promote Nike shoes and sportswear, and nothing else.

There were an increasing number of para-athletes whose performances were approaching those of the able-bodied such that a growing chorus of athletes, activists and sports administrators were wondering why these athletes should be so segregated? Amaechi's use of the word at her press conference was soon widely adopted to describe the policy of separate competitions for para- and able-bodied athletes. Kerem Yılmaz, the president of the IOC, objected to Amaechi's use of the word "segregation" to describe the separate but equal competitions they sponsored, but the term would not disappear from the feeds.

The first moves toward an integration of these two categories of athletes started in regional competitions. The African Games was the first athletics competition that brought enhanced and un-enhanced competitions together, although they would not compete directly against each other until 4 years later. The Olympics had long ago established the precedent: for 2 weeks, the able-bodied would meet in the host city for competitions; then, a week after the conclusion of the Games the Paralympic athletes would arrive for their competitions. The African Games were the first to bring the two competitions together, still separate but occurring simultaneously.

At the first "combined" African Games, Amaechi ran a 21.41 in the 200 m, winning the gold medal and comfortably setting a para-athletic record. Her time was only about .3 of a second off of best time at the previous Olympics, making Amaechi ever more confident that she would be ready to compete in an Olympic games, if only given the chance.

Bowing to the pressure, the IOC finally allowed for a combined Olympics, although initially limited to a few select events. Track and field was one such category, and Amaechi won gold in the 200 meter, silver in the 400 meter and served as the powerful leg of the bronze-winning 4 × 400 relay team. Some competitors grumbled that the patented legs provided her with an unjust advantage. Some athletes even began to compare what Amaechi was doing to doping. Others defended her by arguing that she was simply being assisted by a new technology. One could hardly accuse a bicyclist of cheating if they employed a new bike with better design and lighter materials, or if a footballer wore a new kind of high-tech boot. Amaechi's legs ignited a very old argument about "purity" in sport dating back to the disgraced sprinter Oscar Pistorius. Like swimmers in the 2016 games who used a technologically engineered form of swimwear—and broke practically every record in the process—Amaechi was using technology to extend human ability, to exceed limits once thought impossible to break. Others were quick to point out that that swimwear design was outlawed at the next Olympics, and times dropped back down to "acceptable" levels.

At this point, especially given the media attention that was drawn to her, Amaechi went on the offensive. "Why shouldn't we enhance our abilities!" she thundered. Segregating para-athletes from the able-bodied perpetuated an outdated, nineteenth century obsession with "purity." As long as we have been a species, humans have been augmenting our abilities. The bow and arrow, writing, the wheel all allowed humans to extend our abilities beyond our "natural" bodies. Should an athlete be banned because they wear eyeglasses or contact lens, technologies which afford improved eyesight? Why should sport be any different from any other human endeavor? For most of her athletic career, controversy would follow Amaechi. For every medal she would win at the Olympics, for every convincing win at a Diamond League meet, athletes would grumble about "Amaechi the cheater." Following her trailblazing example, other para-athletes were entering races such that more and more enhanced athletes were standing on the winners' podium, supplanting able-bodied competitors.

After her retirement, she established a center to train elite enhanced athletes. After her triumphs in the Olympics, upon being a Diamond League fixture and upon leading a parade of so-called para-athletes to compete and medal at the major competitions, Amaechi's performances and advocacy meant that enhanced athletes from around the world flocked to the Amaechi Center to train. Her initial business plan was to train enhanced track and field athletes, especially those from Africa who may not have had access to the kind of elite training methods and state-of-the-art facilities as she had at the University of Oregon. And indeed, African athletes arrived at her Cape Town campus in such numbers that she had to institute a selective screening process. Many of the athletes who trained at her center became elite-level competitors, which only added to the demand for admission. She would open a second training center in Eugene, Oregon.

She also found that not just track and field athletes were interested in training with her. Footballers who had once played amputee soccer were seeking out the kind of prosthetic legs Amaechi had made famous and were clamoring to be allowed to join able-bodied clubs. CONCACAF was the first regional association to permit para-athletes to play for club teams, and indeed players with one or two bionic legs played for some Caribbean club teams and in the lower divisions of the United States system. UEFA followed suit. Karl Falkenrath was the first enhanced footballer to be admitted to the Cape Town Amaechi Center, and the first to be picked up by a major club (Bayern Munich) and to play in a Bundesliga match. Amaechi found she had to hire more coaches and trainers as her enterprise expanded from track and field to include football, handball and basketball. Other sports followed, and Amaechi opened new training centers in Barcelona, Toronto and Mumbai. At her original center in Cape Town, Amaechi also established a studio to train enhanced dancers.

The legitimacy of Amaechi's training centers was rent asunder by accusations that some otherwise able-bodied athletes were electing to have their limbs severed and replaced with advanced technology. Taavi Mägi, an Estonian javelin thrower, won a bronze medal at the Olympics, and was held up as yet another example not only of Amaechi's excellent training methods but that enhanced athletes belonged as full participants at the Olympics. It was only after his laurels that Deutsche Welle, acting on a tip from an unnamed source—presumed to be his girlfriend—started an investigation into Mägi's life before he arrived at Amaechi's center.

It turned out that Mägi had been a javelin thrower of mediocre talent. He maintained that his arm had to be amputated following a skiing accident, after which he received an Amaechi-style prosthetic right arm. After recovering from his skiing injuries, Mägi returned to the javelin pit where he markedly—and not unexpectedly—improved his throwing distances. He was soon competing in the Diamond League, then qualified to represent his country at the Olympics. Deutsche Welle discovered that this backstory was a fabrication: Mägi had feigned the ski accident and instead underwent a voluntary amputation of his "inadequate" throwing arm, to be replaced by the sleek technology. (The name of the surgeon was never revealed, but concerns developed about whether he represented the tip of a black market iceberg.) To this day, there is no evidence that Amaechi was ever aware of the Estonians' deceit.

The reaction was swift. First the Diamond League barred Mägi from competition. This was initially a lifetime ban, which was later rescinded to a five-year ban. After a week's deliberation, the IOC stripped Mägi of his medal. At the same time, the IOC announced they would begin an inquiry into other athletes who had trained with Amaechi, to determine if any others had had elective surgery to replace otherwise healthy limbs. This inquiry ultimately yielded no further cases like Mägi's, a conclusion that failed to satisfy many who were convinced that "body hacking" was systematic and widely practiced in sports. The episode nevertheless led many to question the legitimacy of all enhanced athletes.

To the surprise of many, but not to those who knew her well, Amaechi delivered a vigorous public statement in support Mägi. She maintained that she was unaware of the circumstances of Mägi's surgery, but that even if she had known it would not have mattered to her. Mägi would have been admitted to her center on the basis of merit, not on how he came to his prosthetic. Millions of people around the world have artificial hips, shoulders, and knees replaced each year, she exclaimed. Millions who undergo cataract surgery each year receive an artificial lens. Like others, Mägi had simply chosen to replace a defective body part. She welcomed Mägi and anyone with prosthetic enhancements to her centers.

For this public support of Mägi, she was widely criticized. Detractors exclaimed that excusing the javelin thrower's actions would result in young people electively manipulating their bodies. She preferred to think that they were "improving" their bodies. What are eyeglasses, she bellowed, if not an enhancement? Were we going to disbar athletes who wear contact lenses? Her critics quickly countered that wearing corrective lens was hardly comparable to having an eye-transplant.

The IOC was having nothing of it: athletes who were discovered to have been able-bodied but nevertheless amputated healthy limbs in order to receive technological implants were banned from competition. This ban, however, would not even see the end of the decade, the IOC and other elite competitions having found that determining the provenance of prosthetic surgery was a nearly impossible task, and so reluctantly rescinded the ban. But the entire episode resurfaced the debate about athletic enhancement such that some were calling for a "resegregation" of the Olympics.

A collection of Amaechi's advocacy, public statements, interviews, and op-eds were collected together with the assistance of a generative AI to produce the spoken-word book *Enhanced*. She argued that the history of sport (and of humanity) was that of technological improvement of our bodies. Athletes used to run on cinder tracks; polyurethane tracks contributed to ever-improving times. Cyclists—when they stopped doping—rode carbon-fiber bikes, lighter, sturdier and thus contributing to better performance. Advances in shoe technology, in the design of footballs have all altered and enhanced athletic performance. Artificial limbs were but the next frontier.

While she certainly had legions of detractors, Amaechi's advocacy for Mägi and others who made similar choices endeared her to many around the world, not only those with artificial limbs. There were calls in some quarters for Amaechi to become the next president of the IOC, given her advocacy for the "enhanced." It should also be noted that many others rejected her on the same grounds. Indeed, Amaechi's advocacy for Mägi led to notable criticism from the Director-General of the World Health Organization. If Mägi's actions were encouraged by influential celebrities like Amaechi, the result will be a rash of young people electively manipulating their bodies. Some will do this in the mistaken belief that they can instantly become an elite athlete, some for no other reason that they want stronger arms or more muscular appearance. Indeed, one effect of the Mägi incident was that, coupled with the decreasing price of artificial limbs, some young men were having their arms amputated and replaced with augmented biceps, not necessarily to win gold medals but to impress women. These were knockoff artificial limbs not powerful enough to give Olympic-level strength but still attractive to a growing number of consumers.

A year after the Mägi scandal, the BBC ran a weeklong expose on the fears of social critics, medical doctors and economists on the rise of "the new enhanced elite." The documentary identified a new class fault line between those with the resources and the access to the technology and the medical talent to perform the surgery. In athletics, at least, the BBC reported that enhanced athletes were crowding out the able-bodied, and that competitions like the Olympics would one day feature only the enhanced, the unenhanced unable to qualify. And indeed, this vision of the future came to pass. Given the success of enhanced athletes at the Olympics, one result was the creation of a new sporting competition that allowed only unenhanced athletes, a kind of Invictus Games in reverse. Amaechi's support for elective body hacking helped to turn what had been a black market, back-alley criminal enterprise into a reputable medical practice.

She did not win the presidency of the IOC. Her name was also advanced for the Secretary General of the United Nations, although it is not clear how seriously the nomination was actually considered. Closer to home, there were calls for her to run for the Presidency of South Africa, though politics did not appeal to her. Her training centers remained the global standard in the preparation of elite athletes and dancers, now covering 14 sports. Her enterprises grew larger and more varied, moving away from sports.

Given her argument for enhancement as a human aspiration, Amaechi was invited to become a co-founder of a company that developed technologies for cognitive enhancement. The United States Pentagon—specifically through its DARPA agency—finally released the technical specifications for a new technology aimed at speeding up the learning process by electronically stimulating a specific part of the brain through a direct implant. The brain could be manipulated to be like a younger version of itself, more plastic and supple, and thus better able to either learn more rapidly or in greater amounts than in an unstimulated brain. The military saw this as a tool for speeding up language acquisition when troops or diplomats were stationed overseas. The brain enhancement meant that it took 30–40% less time to achieve mastery in any subject. Amaechi recognized the implications of this technology for education and her company developed a commercial grade version that was marketed to schools and universities. With the device, a student could move through a curriculum in half the time or alternatively, could fit more knowledge into a four-year course of study than the unenhanced. With the device, a student could major in four or five subjects or receive two or three degrees while spending the same amount of time at university as an unenhanced student.

The marketing team worried that consumers might balk at having an implant directly attached to the brain, but they needn't have worried. First, Amaechi herself had one of the implants placed at the base of her skull, which she proudly displayed to the international media only hours after the surgery. With Amaechi as a spokesperson and given the wave of elective body hacking she helped unleashed, there was a ready and eager market for students—really, their parents—who were prepared to pay around $150,000 for the implant, although that price dropped rapidly over the course of the next decade such that electronic brain stimulation was within easy reach of most middle class families. The BBC followed up on its enhanced elite reporting with another documentary that highlighted what it called the growing "cognitive divide" between those with brain implants, and those so unenhanced, with implications for job prospects, earning power and success in life.

Her athletic career, her advocacy, the success of her training centers and the media attention she generated made Amaechi one of the world's wealthiest, influential and recognizable individuals. Very few people in the world remembered Amaechi's life as a dancer and might have been surprised when she debuted *Ballet (Im)possible*. For years, Amaechi had been cultivating a company of dancers at her training centers. Although she never became the principal dancer she had dreamed of as a young girl, she decided that she could become a choreographer. She designed

Ballet (Im)possible expressly for dancers with Kinetic Horizon prosthetics, with grands jetés and tour l'air reaching heights no able-bodied dancer could ever hope to achieve. Dancers could lift four and five dancers at a time, tossing them into the air and catching them in ways never before seen on a stage. *Ballet (Im)possible* could only be performed by enhanced dancers. The Chioma Amaechi Dance Company toured the world, and critics largely approved of its innovative choreography, surprised by its flawless technical proficiency and athleticism.

Key Futures Themes

- Human Enhancement and Prosthetic Technology
- Redefinition of Sport and Fairness
- Social and Ethical Divides
- Commercialization and the Power of Corporations
- Cognitive Enhancement and Education
- Global Inequality and Governance
- Changing Narratives of Disability

Bibliography

Clark, Andy. 2004. *Natural-Born Cyborgs: Minds, Technologies, and the Future of Human Intelligence*. Oxford: Oxford University Press.

DARPA. TNT: Targeted Neuroplasticity Training. https://www.darpa.mil/research/programs/targeted-neuroplasticity-training.

David Howe, P., and Carla Filomena Silva. 2016. The Fiddle of Using the Paralympic Games as a Vehicle for Expanding [Dis]ability Sport Participation. *Sport in Society* 21 (1): 125–136. https://doi.org/10.1080/17430437.2016.1225885.

Loland, Sigmund. 2009. The Ethics of Performance-Enhancing Technology in Sport. *Journal of the Philosophy of Sport* 36 (2): 152–161. https://doi.org/10.1080/00948705.2009.9714754.

Mayer, Craig. 2024. Why Are Full-Body Swimsuits Not Allowed at the Olympics? What to Know for Paris Games. *USA Today*, 29 July 2024. https://www.usatoday.com/story/sports/olympics/2024/07/29/full-body-swimsuits-olympics-swimming-paris-2024/74591854007/.

Chapter 4
Tekkeitsertok: Farmer

The name of the course intrigued him, “Inuit Agriculture.” It seemed like an oxymoron. The Inuit had had been farmers, but not for centuries and only along the coast of Greenland, not in Nunavik. Some Inuit, decades ago, incubated a kind of agriculture, really an agriculture of the greenhouse or hydroponics in the snow and ice. In Canada, farmland had long been associated with the prairie provinces, with Manitoba and Saskatchewan. Tekkeitsertok wondered if the course was some kind of historical or anthropological survey, but it turned out to be a modern environmental design course. Until that moment, Tekkeitsertok’s course in life had not been determined. As a boy, he thought he could never hope to achieve the status and respect his father enjoyed, one of the architects of Nunavik. So no one was more surprised than he was when he became an executive at the agri-business giant Richardson International.

His father was an engineer, having been educated at First Nations University of Canada before transferring to the University of Guelph to study mechanical engineering. His father’s was an especially politically active generation, pushing back against decades of economic domination and cultural assimilation. His father was born Ethan Fields, a name given to him as a result of the government’s Project Surname. Activists in Field’s generation returned to the Inuit practice of taking single names as an act of political defiance. Traditionally, Inuit did not take family names; these were imposed by the Canadian government and for activists like Fields were of a piece with the religious schools and land seizures that had eroded Inuit culture, identity, and sense of worth. Ethan Fields took the name Amaqjuaq—“the strong one”—and when his son was born named him Tekkeitsertok, meaning “master of caribou,” the god of hunting.

It was not at all uncommon for some Inuit to leave the north to settle in cities like Toronto and Montreal. At first, it appeared that Amaqjuaq would follow this pattern: earn a degree and then take a position with an engineering firm in Toronto. However, he had no intention of remaining in Guelph, but to return to Kuujjuaq to, in his words, “build Nunavik’s future.”

D. Staley, *Anticipatory Biographies*, Anticipation Science 10,
https://doi.org/10.1007/978-3-032-08912-0_4

Amaqjuaq returned to help launch the "blanket project," but was also one of the council leaders involved with securing provincial status for Nunavik. Neighboring Nunavut had been named a Canadian territory in 1999 and had achieved provincial status thirty years later. The goal of the change in territorial status was to enshrine Inuit political rights over their land, and to provide a mechanism for preserving Inuit society and culture. There had been stirrings for decades of a secessionist movement across the Inuit Circumpolar Council, that the people of the northern regions of the United States, Canada, Russia and Greenland would simultaneously break away from their respective countries, in order to create their own political-legal entity. Among other reasons the secessionist movements stalled were questions as to the economic and population base necessary to sustain the polity, to say nothing of the challenges of a simultaneous independence from different countries. (Russia was never going to permit this.)

After years of negotiation, and intermittent calls for Quebecois secession, Ottawa had learned that a certain amount of provincial autonomy quelled such ideas. By making it a province, Nunavut would simultaneously allow Canada to retain its territory within the Dominion and at the same time empower the Inuit.

Given what had occurred in Nunavut, leaders of the Kativik Regional Government similarly petitioned Ottawa to become a territory. At first, Ottawa proposed having the northern third of Quebec join with the province of Nunavut, but this was rejected by Quebec. The irony was lost on no one: that Quebec, of all places, was arguing against a part of its territory becoming independent. (Austinites in Texas could not help but to voice their solidarity.) After a lengthy series of debates, largely drawing on the long history of exploitation of Canada's First Nation citizens, a plebiscite voted to break away to form a territory and shortly thereafter pressed for provincial status. Amaqjuaq and others of his generation of university-educated technocrats were especially active in securing provincial status. Tekkeitsertok and his generation never knew a world where Nunavik was not a province. From nearly having their culture eliminated, Inuit were reasserting their identity, and the province of Nunavik was one expression of this.

Nunavik's political independence was wrapped up with the dramatic ecological changes occurring. As Northern Canada's tundra melted, a host of problems emerged, not the least of which was the release of long-trapped methane into the atmosphere. This had long been predicted by climate scientists, but when the reality finally confronted the world's governments, there had been few plans of action imagined, let alone implemented.

The provincial government in Nunavik was a notable exception. Engineers like Amaqjuaq had devised a strategy of covering vast acres of land with polymer blankets. These would capture the escaping methane, allowing it to be converted to liquid fuel. The original idea for the blankets came from a professor at First Nations University and perhaps for that reason was overlooked by the world's scientists and policymakers.

To institute the blanket program required capital investment that the provincial government could not muster. There were still only a small handful of engineering companies in Nunavik, and no investment capital. To engineer the blanket solution would require expertise from Toronto and Ottawa, and this was of great concern to political leaders in Kuujjuaq, now the capital of Nunavik. This was setting up to be the next chapter in the continuing history of exploitation of the people of Canada's North. An economy and culture of hunting and fishing was to once again be displaced by the extractive industries—in the past it was oil and gas and timber and minerals—where companies would remove what was determined to be economically valuable, leaving behind poverty, alcoholism and despair among the indigenous populations.

That Nunavik was now its own province made this scenario less inevitable. Further, the Canadian government was more sensitive to this history. Ottawa and Kuujjuaq worked closely to develop a plan to address the methane problem, with assurances that the economic benefits would not be leeched from Nunavik. Because this was an issue of global importance, the United Nations played a mediating role in ensuring that the blanket solution was a First Nations initiative that would benefit the whole of humanity.

And so around one million acres of Nunavik were at various points covered in bioengineered blankets, looking like an enormous Christo installation. No one was under the illusion that all of the escaping methane could be captured via this process. But scientists measured that about 40% of the methane that might have seeped into the atmosphere was stored and converted into fuel. The Piujuq Corporation, a public/private entity, became the largest employer in Nunavik. Amaqjuaq was a chief engineer for the company. The liquid methane was indeed shipped via pipelines to southern Canada, but there was no capital drain following in its wake. The success of the Piujuq Corporation provided Nunavik with a tax base and economic infrastructure that it had lacked since its days as a territory. It also meant that Canadians from across the Dominion were migrating to Nunavik, meaning the composition of the province was changing. Inuit still made up the majority of citizens, but that majority had dropped to around 55%. Fifty years before, the population of Kuujjuaq had been around 3000; it had swelled to 200,000.

One effect of the melting permafrost that whatever transportation infrastructure that did exist, built largely to service the mining industry, was now cracking and buckling. Ottawa earmarked funds to build new roads to service the methane recovery industry, of course, but that also established a high-speed rail from Kuujjuaq to Montreal. A small airport was constructed that could serve as flights to cities in Eastern Canada.

As one way that the benefits of the methane project might be shared with all Inuit, the provincial government established a universal basic income scheme. As a public/private entity, the Piujuq Corporation would pay tax—that there would be no tax abatements was a key provision of the agreement. All citizens of Nunavik would receive $20,000 a year. This allowed many to supplement their income and diets and maintain hunting and fishing as a way of life. It also meant that consumer goods from the south rushed into Kuujjuaq. Target, Tim Hortons and Walmart infiltrated, moving as far north than they ever had, though this was a temporary phenomenon, as a small group of Inuit entrepreneurs established their own businesses to compete with these global brands. As a boy Tekkeitsertok rode his bike into the "old village" of Kuujjuaq, which was now its downtown core. Construction cranes rose like church spires across what had once been a fishing village, the buildings made of corrugated metal having been razed and replaced with apartment blocks built in an indigenous style. He would spend idle hours at Aklaq, a combination coffee bar and gallery, where Tekkeitsertok would see Inuit carvings and textiles on display. He would take the occasional class in print making and liked expressing himself through traditional forms, although he never produced a work suitable enough to be hung, let alone purchased.

Culture clash was inevitable. Although nothing like a cosmopolitan city, Kuujjuaq nevertheless had more white Canadians living there than even twenty years earlier. They were largely engineers and other professionals of the Piujuq Corporation, but also included doctors, teachers and business owners. Tekkeitsertok's first job was as a server at a Tim Horton's. He couldn't help but notice that Inuit tended to take these kinds of jobs, as waitstaff or cashiers, with only a few professionals like his father to be found in the city. Some of the older residents welcomed the newcomers, and the wealth and the new buildings, as long as it did not disrupt traditional pursuits. The UBI helped to sustain the traditional ways, although racist incidents persisted.

Tekkeitsertok was subjected to such racism, as when one afternoon a customer apparently did not like his service and muttered "dumb Eskimo" under her breath to her companion. Tekkeitsertok had learned from his father that "the E-word" was the name imposed on the Inuit by the colonial oppressors. His father was incensed that anyone would still use the slur today and pressed Tekkeitsertok to identify the speaker so that they might be publicly shamed. Tekkeitsertok begged off his father's wrath and debated with himself whether he should have even told his father of the incident. Tekkeitsertok did not think it a big deal, didn't feel particularly offended by the slur, although he was miffed at the customer's arrogance. But it was true that despite the best efforts of the provincial government, a two-tiered class system had emerged in places like Kuujjuaq.

There were three types of schools in Nunavik. There were a small number of traditional schools, institutions whose orientation was toward the traditional sources of Inuit culture and epistemology. Traditional knowledge, Inuit Qaujimajatuqangit, or IQ, governed the curriculum. Core subjects included ᐃᓅᖃᑎᒌᑦᓯᐊᕐᓂᖅ—*Inuuqatigiitsiarniq, r*especting others, relationships and caring for people; ᑐᙵᓇᕐᓂᖅ—*Tunnganarniq, f*ostering good spirit by being open, welcoming and inclusive; ᐱᔨᑦᓯᕐᓂᖅ—*Pijitsirniq, s*erving and providing for family and/or community; ᐋᔩᖃᑎᒌᓐᓂᖅ—*Aajiiqatigiinniq,* decision making through discussion and consensus; ᐱᓕᒻᒪᒃᓴᕐᓂᖅ—*Pilimmaksarniq, d*evelopment of skills through observation, mentoring, practice, and effort; ᐃᑲᔪᖅᑎᒌᓐᓂᖅ—*Ikajuqtigiinniq, w*orking together for a common cause; ᖃᓄᖅᑑᕐᓂᖅ—*Qanuqtuurniq, b*eing innovative and resourceful; and ᐊᕙᑎᑦᑎᓐᓂᒃ ᑲᒪᑦᓯᐊᕐᓂᖅ—*Avatittinnik Kamatsiarniq, r*espect and care for the land, animals and the environment.

There were a number of college preparatory academies. The families of the white Canadian professional classes sent their children to these schools, if they were not paying for private tutors or sending their children off to boarding schools in Ontario or Quebec. Then there were newer hybrid schools that would teach IQ but also prepare students for university, and Tekkeitsertok's parents opted to send him to one of these hybrid schools. The school was majority Inuit, but there were also a sizable number of non-Inuit students who attended. The hybrid schools were born in the aftermath of Nunavik becoming a province. Leaders felt that it was important that such schools be founded to help ensure the next generation of leaders of the province, a strong cohort of Inuit children who were both educated in traditional ways, and who could serve as the technocrats governing the nascent province.

Tekkeitsertok liked the school, and he made many friends who called him Tek. He gravitated toward both biology and traditional ecological knowledge and was a well-above-average snowshoer and goaltender. For a short while, he wondered if he had ice hockey in his future, maybe with a junior club, probably at university.

Amaqjuaq had hoped that Tek would attend the University of Guelph and play goalie there, but his mother Alasie had hoped he might stay closer to home. Indeed, Tek had only ventured out of Nunavik once in his life. He and his father once took the train to Montreal, Amaqjuaq to conduct business and Tek to take in the city. Experiencing a city of three million people was overwhelming, and he couldn't wait to return home to a more manageable city. If he was to attend university, Tek was increasingly coming to the opinion that it would be at a branch of First Nations University. It was a measure of the size and importance of Kuujjuaq that FNU had recently opened one of their branches there. Tek was drawn to the institution, both because of its proximity to home and that its mission was centered on IQ, and during his schooling Tek had become very interested in indigenous epistemology.

Tek arrived at FNU-K full of wonder and curiosity, but with little vision for what he wanted to study or what direction he wanted for his life. He had a vague notion that his education was preparing him to become a productive member of Inuit society, and that there were expectations that he emerge a leader in the community as his father was. He took courses in Inuktitut and philosophy and *Aajiiqatigiinniq*, as was expected of him. Tek would have been content to take as many courses as he could, voraciously consuming knowledge, even if he were not properly digesting it all. And then he saw the notice for the Inuit agriculture course.

The professor, Toklo, was a polymath, with an interest in philosophy, ecology and engineering. Like Amaqjuaq, he was of the generation of Inuit activists, and as many of that generation, he matriculated at the University of Toronto to study landscape design, but was very keen to not only preserve Inuit culture, but to advance it. He was identified as one of the "progressives." He did not wish to see Inuit culture preserved as a museum exhibition but imagined what a vibrant and thriving culture might look like in the future. At FNU-K, he taught philosophy and landscape design, although he had developed an interest in agronomy. The "Inuit Agriculture" course was of a part with his philosophy of what was being called "Inuit Futures." His theory was that as the planet warmed and as the permafrost melted away—and after the release of methane was complete—the soil, now freed from its frozen imprisonment, would be rich and inviting for agriculture.

Tek was interested in the course but was warned by several of his classmates not to get sucked into Professor Toklo's orbit. There arose at FNU-K a lively debate between the traditionalists and the progressives. Traditionalists felt that only Inuit culture, or broadly indigenous culture, was the only true knowledge of the college. They accused progressives of privileging modern Western ideas, imposing these on and crowding out indigenous knowledge. Indeed, progressive ideas were the very antithesis of indigeneity, a capitulation to modernity and Western neocolonialism. Agriculture, especially the autonomous farming practice today, could not be further from Inuit indigeneity. Further, there was a small but vocal faction that rejected agriculture entirely, not only as a Western import, but as the greatest calamity humanity had ever unleashed. After agriculture came hierarchical society, task specialization, gender disparity, rapacious cities, to say nothing of the environmental degradation agriculture leaves in its wake.

Progressives parried back that their ideas were indigenous, even if they appropriated some Western ideas. Inspired by Afrofuturism, Inuit Futures was an intellectual program that imagined the Inuit alive and thriving and vibrant in the future, and that this future could be and should be directed by the Inuit themselves. Inuit Agriculture was but one manifestation of this program. Agriculture, in this view, was the most productive human activity outside of bearing children. Producing food, domesticating nature is the basis of all other economic and social activity. UBI gave all the citizens of Nunavik the ability to purchase good, nutritious food. Rather than relying on food producers in Western Canada, the Inuit could be self-sufficient. Further, solving the problem of "agriculture after permafrost melting" would be an Inuit solution. "Permafrost reclamation" was the name the progressives gave to it.

All throughout his life, Tek demonstrated that he was someone who could be easily swayed, whose ideas and view of the world could be directed by others, his father in particular. Many of his friends were traditionalists, and he could have easily fallen into their camp. At their urging, he was ready to abandon the course, until he learned that a key feature would be working on an actual—albeit experimental—farm in the southern region of Nunavik. The thought of getting his hands dirty, of working outside, of learning a new set of skills held great appeal to him. To hear Professor Toklo describe it, the class would be helping to forge a new Nunavik, a way to the future. And so, he signed up for the course, and fell under Toklo's influence.

Like everywhere else in the world, farming was a capital-intensive enterprise. The long-ago image of the small farmer plowing his 100 acres on the plains of Saskatchewan had long given way to a highly technological enterprise. Toklo had applied for and won a grant from the National Sciences and Engineering Research Council of Canada. NSERC had always funded "visionaries, explorers and innovators who are searching for the scientific and technical breakthroughs that will benefit the country." Toklo had to negotiate the last part to ensure that the Inuit agricultural project was not viewed as a purely indigenous enterprise. Toklo argued that the first goal was to make the province self-sufficient, but that ultimately, once the efficacy of agriculture in northern Canada was demonstrated, that agriculture for export would be the ultimate goal. The NSERC were persuaded—and also eager to fund an Inuit initiative—and so, provided Toklo with the seed funding he needed to build an experimental farm, this proof of concept.

Preparing the soil was the first order of business, and this activity took up most of the time Tekkeitsertok spent in that Inuit Agriculture course. His first job was to till the soil, to turn whatever organic material that sat on the surface into the ground. Although risky, he applied nitrogen and phosphorus to the turned soil. This combined effort would give the sandy, pebbly soil the nutrients it would need.

The grant allowed Toklo, Tek and the team to work with only 200 acres. And so, this first planting would be more of a test case than a productive enterprise. Tekkeitsertok was in charge of planting rows of so-called "green manure," plants that gave the soil the nutrients needed before it could accept other plants in the future. He planted beans and peas, rye grass and oats, and winter wheat and buckwheat. Although the climate was warmer, the growing season in Nunavik was still shorter than in southern areas.

The Inuit agriculture course lasted only a year, but Tekkeitsertok signed up for a second year, so he might see his efforts through. That first yield was "promising," Professor Toklo declared, but Tekkeitsertok could see that only about a third of what they planted germinated sufficiently to be harvested. Toklo was undeterred. The point of this first planting was to build the quality of the soil. Success would come in the future.

Five years after the first planting, the experimental farm was producing 5000 bushels of winter wheat, buckwheat and oats. This was nowhere near the productivity of farms further south, but the results were nevertheless hailed, a demonstration of the efficacy of Inuit agriculture.

If the Inuit's future was clear, Tekkeitsertok's personal future was not. He entered the college to seek clarity and guidance as to where his path lie. He found that in agriculture, or rather in the program to reclaim the permafrost. He wrestled with his conscience. After the methane had been captured, after the blankets had been removed, perhaps we should have allowed this land to reclaim itself, he asked himself. Maybe allow forests to grow for a time. He wondered if not allowing the forest to grow was a form of arbicide. Toklo would disabuse him of all of these thoughts.

That first year had been labor intensive. Tekkeitsertok piloted a tractor and deposited nitrogen in a way that would have looked familiar to farmers on the Canadian plain decades earlier. These methods were not what agriculture meant today. If the idea of the tundra farm were to take root, it would eventually have to become automated.

After the soil had been designed to be fertile, after five successful growing seasons, Professor Toklo would need to secure more funding, to make the capital purchases necessary to expand the enterprise. Despite his bravado, Toklo had only a vague sense of how the experimental farm might make money, or even to be self-sustaining. The NSERC provided funding, so long as this was an experiment. Their results demonstrated, NSERC no longer wished to fund the project. Toklo created a business to continue operations and hired Tekkeitsertok as his chief operations officer. For two years the Katilvik Corporation operated as a break-even enterprise, servicing Nunavik as well as customers in a few southern cities.

Toklo was growing disinterested in running an agricultural business. He yearned to focus on his teaching and research, and so informed Tekkeitsertok that he would be stepping down. This was another of those pivotal moments in Tekkeitsertok's life. Would Katilvik dissolve? Would Tekkeitsertok be looking for a new life's mission? In announcing his departure, Toklo simultaneously urged Tekkeitsertok to become the new CEO. He never imagined himself in any leadership role. He was not his father, nor was he professor Toklo. Proximity to the soil, working with his hands had been his passion, not glad handing for grants and seed capital. But neither did he want to see Katilvik come to an end after all they had accomplished. Tekkeitsertok reluctantly agreed to take over the company.

His first controversial decision as CEO was to begin talks with Richardson International. The agribusiness firm had approached Toklo 18 months earlier with a proposal to acquire the company. Toklo refused, fearful that Richardson would leech any Inuit influence out of the enterprise, or worse, would siphon the value off of the firm and away from Nunavik.

Tekkeitsertok was certainly aware of the dangers, but absent an infusion of capital could not see a path forward for the company. The agreement that was signed made Katilvik a subsidiary of Richardson. The leadership team would stay in place, and Katilvik would be organized as a benefit corporation, for the benefit of Nunavik. Richardson agreed to these terms largely because they saw the potential of what they called "northern agriculture," not only in servicing new markets, but also serving as a testing ground for new technologies. Tekkeitsertok was not fully aware of Richardson's intentions when he signed the agreement; it would ultimately lead to his departure from the company.

Richardson introduced agri-automation technology to the Nunavik farms. Tekkeitsertok was very much against this idea. He held that working and tilling the soil with one's hands—metaphorically—was the only way to farm, and was a key feature of Inuit agriculture. Further, he insisted on hiring Inuit employees, and automation of any kind took away jobs. Tekkeitsertok would lose this argument. Agriculture everywhere Richardson did business was an automated enterprise. The combines that traversed the land were controlled by a GPS system. Real time analysis of the soil meant that seeds, fertilizer, nutrients and water could be precisely targeted. Harvesting, too, was largely automated. Katilvik Farms now accounted for 500,000 acres, employing around 90 people.

For his part, Tekkeitsertok sat in an office in Kuujjuaq 100 km away from the farms, looking at monitors, analyzing and interpreting agricultural and ecological telemetry, directing agri-bots in the field. Katilvik Farms had become so productive that in addition to serving much of eastern Canada, Richardson began plans for exporting grain; sub-Saharan Africa was an emerging market. Richardson built a terminal in Kuujjuaq to ship grain via the Hudson Strait and the Labrador Sea to ports to ports in West Africa.

Richardson were also eager to test a new kind of seed they were developing in their labs in Winnipeg. This involved redirecting the chirality of molecules. Most molecules spiral in a specific direction, its chirality. Researchers had been experimenting with changing the direction of those spirals, creating what amounted to a new, "mirror image" life form. Richardson scientists had developed mirror images of oats, wheat and barley, grains with new flavor profiles, a mirror-image wheat that was high in protein. The company decided that at least a portion of the acres at Katilvik Farms would be given over to the new seed types. This was done over the objection of Tekkeitsertok. He had swallowed his pride at working in an office, feeling as if he were not really engaged in farming, but the introduction of these seeds ran counter to *Avatittinnik Kamatsiarniq*, respect and care for the environment. When his objections were ignored, Tekkeitsertok submitted his resignation. Despite this grand gesture, the mirror-image seed project went on apace.

For the first time in many years, Tekkeitsertok was without a purpose in life. He remained in Kuujjuaq, guest lecturing at FNU-K. He had remained in contact with Toklo, even as his mentor's attentions were turning away from agriculture and toward "Inuit social media." He eventually became active in politics, serving first on the city council of Kuujjuaq and later representing the city as a member of the Canadian parliament. In his 50s, he was he was elected premier of Nunavik, where he oversaw a province that had a population nearing one million, and that had managed to balance tradition and vision. In his memoirs, Tekkeitsertok wondered if it had been at all beneficial to the Inuit. He wondered what if there had been no intervention in the thawing permafrost. What if the experimental farm had never been introduced? Would the Inuit be just as well off today, or considerably worse? He soothed himself with a thought that he had played an important role in making northern Canada verdant and productive.

Key Futures Themes

- Climate Change and Environmental Transformation
- Indigenous Self-Determination and Political Futures
- Economic Development and Risk of Neo-colonialism
- Cultural Identity and Social Tensions
- Agriculture After Permafrost
- Corporate Power
- Biotechnology
- Social Futures
- Governance

Bibliography

Alia, Valerie. 2006. Chapter 3 Renamed Overnight: The History of Project Surname. In *Names and Nunavut: Culture and Identity in the Inuit Homeland*, 65–90. New York/Oxford: Berghahn Books. https://doi.org/10.1515/9780857458490-009.

Ball, Philip. 2023. Mirror-Image Life. *Nautilus*, 9 October 2023. https://nautil.us/mirror-image-life-412729/.

Barton, Katherine. 2020. What's in a Name? How a Government Project Forced Surnames on Inuit. *CBC News*, 6 October 2020, https://www.cbc.ca/news/canada/north/project-surname-inuit-names-nunavut-1.5747040.
Bracken, Amber. 2023. In Gjoa Haven, a Greenhouse Creates New Possibilities. *The Globe and Mail*, 30 April 2023. https://www.theglobeandmail.com/canada/article-gjoa-haven-inuit-greenhouse/.
Cover Crops & Green Manures. *UMass Extension Fruit Program*. https://www.umass.edu/agriculture-food-environment/fruit/ne-small-fruit-management-guide/general-information/cover-crops-green-manures.
Cyca, Michelle. 2024. Vancouver's New Mega-Development Is Big, Ambitious and Undeniably Indigenous. *Macleans*, 11 March 2024. https://macleans.ca/society/senakw-vancouver/.
First Nations University of Canada. https://www.fnuniv.ca/.
Hillemann, Friederike, Bret A. Beheim, and Elspeth Ready. 2023. Socio-Economic Predictors of Inuit Hunting Choices and Their Implications for Climate Change Adaptation. *Philosophical Transactions of the Royal Society B* 378 (1889): 20220395. Theme Issue 'Climate Change Adaptation Needs a Science of Culture' Compiled and Edited by Anne C. Pisor, J. Stephen Lansing and Kate Magargal, 1–9.
Inuit Qaujimajatuqangit. *Nunavut Impact Review Board (NIRB)*. https://www.nirb.ca/inuit-qaujimajatuqangit#.
Sacco, Joe. 2020. *Paying the Land*. New York: Metropolitan Books.
Schuur, E., A. McGuire, C. Schädel, et al. 2015. Climate Change and the Permafrost Carbon Feedback. *Nature* 520:171–179. https://doi.org/10.1038/nature14338.
Simpson, Audra. 2014. *Mohawk Interruptus: Political Life Across the Borders of Settler States*. New York: Duke University Press.
The Natural Sciences and Engineering Research Council of Canada. https://www.nserc-crsng.gc.ca/index_eng.asp.
Turetsky, M. R., B. W. Abbott, M. C. Jones, M.C., et al. 2020. Carbon Release Through Abrupt Permafrost Thaw. *Nature Geoscience* 13:138–143. https://doi.org/10.1038/s41561-019-0526-0.
Vonk, J. E., et al. 2015. Reviews and Syntheses: Effects of Permafrost Thaw on Arctic Aquatic Ecosystems. *Biogeosciences* 12:7129–7167.

Chapter 5
Lawrence Schumann: Physicist

Until recently, it has been difficult to write about the early life of Lawrence Schumann, since almost every documentary trace of his life appeared to have been purged. But we are only now in a position to write the real biography of this Nobel laureate.

Although he became world renowned, he worked in an esoteric field. Physics, the queen of the sciences at the start of the previous century, had fallen out of many university curricula. Even at the remining high prestige institutions, there were few people working in physics. A handful of European institutes still boasted physicists, largely working in solitude, not in an academic department. In the United States, MIT was the most prominent place for physics.

Physics seemed an impractical subject—where would one find a job?—and even among elite institutions, it was not evident how preparation in physics could help future leaders. Besides, most physicists would concede that all of the major problems in physics had been examined to the point of exhaustion. There was nothing new to discover. The world needed thinkers to tackle wicked problems like climate acclimatization or to negotiate the interface between human and artificial intelligence. Studying the fundamental properties of reality struck many as an aristocratic luxury.

Perhaps it was the challenge of upending these assumptions that drew Schumann to the subject. Schumann arrived at the recently-moved Massachusetts Institute of Technology. Coastal flooding had wound its way up the Charles River such that The Great Dome was regularly flooded. President Rajeev Singh had convinced a reluctant Board of Trustees that the Institute could no longer keep the rising Charles at bay. Levees and other interventions had proven costly and not nearly as effective as was hoped. Singh proposed physically moving the campus further inland; an abandoned campus in Framingham, Massachusetts would serve their purposes well. And so, over the course of five years, MIT moved 20 miles away, outside the I95 beltway.

D. Staley, *Anticipatory Biographies*, Anticipation Science 10,
https://doi.org/10.1007/978-3-032-08912-0_5

Attached to Aron Pethes' quantum computing laboratory, Schumann studied boundaries and thresholds, both conceptual and physical. Everyone—even schoolchildren—understood that the world around us was expressible through the laws of Newtonian physics. At very small scales, quantum physics described this subatomic realm. What interested Schumann was the boundary between those two realms, the threshold between the Newtonian and quantum universes. The boundary was, of course, not hard and fast and not at all a clear straight line. One could not say on this side is the Newtonian and on that side is the quantum. He thought the boundary looked something like that produced in the Mandelbrot set, an intricate interweaving of Newtonian and quantum.

Schumann devised the mathematics of this boundary, noting that in this threshold space the laws of physics were "both-and." In this space, quantum rules applied in one place, but in a very adjacent space Newtonian laws operated. Schumann determined that the distribution was not random but ordered, regular if complex. He compared it to the threshold between the states of matter. Something was a liquid until enough heat and pressure changed it into a gas. But there was a region where matter was both-and or more typically both-neither. Schumann postulated that such a complex boundary existed between quantum and Newtonian worlds. This transitional space—liminal—could be described as a kind of edge effect. He borrowed the concept from ecology, where the point of interface between two biomes exhibited edge effects, a space of great creativity and generation. The world between quantum and Newtonian was liminal, in the same way psychologists sometimes described an uncertain or a disquieting place of transition. *Limen*, the Latin from which liminal is derived, means "threshold," and Schumann identified a transitional physical and conceptual space. This threshold required new theories, both-and theories about the physical universe, but also new experimental methods to verify. Schumann was a theoretical physicist; he left it to others to perform the experimental work. Indeed, his theories led to a brief renaissance of physics as a vibrant field of study.

Schumann came to physics, and to this particular area of research, from various directions, from various analogies. His approach was almost polymathic. He had experienced life in a liminal space, a threshold space when, as a young man, he travelled Europe with his mother. They eventually spent six months in Strasbourg. The history of the Alsace–Lorraine region of France was the story of its alternation as a territory of either France or Germany. Alsace–Lorraine was, of course, both-and, a liminal transition between two cultures. Today French was the dominant language spoken there, but Germanic terms and placenames remained scattered about the region (the name of the principal city, Strasbourg, was as much German as it was French). Like all French people, Alsatians enjoyed good wine, but this was also the chief beer-brewing region of the country. At bars and restaurants patrons were just as likely to be consuming both. Residing in Strasbourg, Schumann did not feel as if he were in either Paris or Frankfurt, or rather it felt like a combination of the two. That feeling, that phenomenological experience of both-and was the metaphor Schumann used to mathematically describe the threshold between the Newtonian and the quantum.

He stayed at MIT for his undergraduate and graduate degrees, as well as for a two-year post-doc. He was somewhat unusual in that he arrived at MIT as an undergraduate at age 20, after his stay in Strasbourg. Although a less prestigious subject, physics was still a young man's discipline, and its practitioners were almost entirely male. There were few faculty openings anywhere in the world for physicists, and so Schumann was fortunate to have received an appointment at the Max Planck Institute at Heidelberg, one of the few places in the world where there remained an active physics research program.

The location of the Institute and the revival of its university meant that Heidelberg was a vibrant, cosmopolitan city and an excellent place to incubate new ideas. This idea-rich environment attracted new businesses, venture capital and eclectic thinkers. Schumann left the Institute to head up a R&D think tank/skunkworks at The Neckar Group. Like corporations in the past, such as Bell Labs or IBM, Neckar was one of a cohort of new companies that produced basic research, not just commercializable products. It was at Neckar that Schumann wrote many of the papers that spelled out his threshold theory. He brought in talent from the Institute and the University such that Neckar was mentioned in the same breath as those older, academically prestigious institutions. If physics experienced any sort of renaissance, it was largely centered in the once sleepy university town of Heidelberg.

The Nobel Prize in Physics had been awarded sporadically over the last two decades, and there were discussions about whether to cease offering the award. At the age of 62, Schumann was awarded the Prize, both for his specific contributions but also for the revival of physics his work engendered. Now a laureate, Schumann continued to work, writing books on the philosophy of physics. In his late 60s, he became an unlikely influencer with a series of lectures delivered on the feeds on physics, philosophy, the nature of reality, the history of the universe. Contemporaries remarked that he was the modern Richard Feynman: both a gifted scientist and one who could easily and clearly communicate complex ideas to a wider public.

As far as contemporaries could determine, Schumann's life began around age 18; very little of his life before then—where he was born, where he went to school, which sports he played—could be conclusively proven. His acceptance into MIT was most improbable: his academic record was largely undistinguished, mostly having been home-schooled in the United States, with some time spent studying in Europe with his mother. Some researchers had claimed that there had been deliberate tampering with the record: there were notable gaps in the few social media accounts attached to his name. His application to MIT was unusually loose and informal. While staying in Strasbourg, he serendipitously met Pethes, the quantum physicist, at the hotel which both were staying. The hotel restaurant became the site of their almost daily seminar, Schumann listening intently to Pethes describe some of the work being done at quantum levels. Quantum computing had by then become an established discipline such that the world's leading companies jockeyed for leadership of the QC market, the theoretical work that drove this industry had ceased being cutting edge years previously. In his youth, Pethes had been a leader in the field, but he was nearing retirement when he happened upon Schumann. By the end of that summer, Pethes had convinced his young pupil to come to Framingham to work in his lab. The personal recommendation from Pethes was the chief reason Schumann matriculated at MIT.

We are only able now to write the biography of Schumann's early life. At age 85 he held a press conference where he announced that Lawrence Schumann had in fact been born Adele Johnson. Schumann had no intention of ever revealing his early life, that he was born female, and that he had transitioned to male during a trip to Europe with his mother. Olivia Carson, a journalist and academic, was about to publish a monograph on the network of groups who had, decades earlier, performed the necessary surgery and, importantly, forged new credentials and identities, especially for American clients. This was not intended as an expose but more like a commemoration of the heroism of those living in a darker time. Carson had uncovered as part of her research that Lawrence Schumann was one such client. Schumann was mortified that he was about to be outed and so decided to take his press conference ahead of the publication of the book. He agonized over this choice, angry that his secret was about to be revealed. What did it matter anyway; at his advanced age, he had nearly forgotten details of his life as female. As far as he was concerned, he had always been a man. Whose business was it otherwise?

Adele Johnson was born in Muncie, Indiana. At an early age, she had an interest in and showed an aptitude for bioengineering, but also music and basketball. At age 12 Adele began to express to friends that she felt unease; she was too young to fully articulate her feelings, that she didn't feel like a girl. Later, before her transition and as she gained more confidence in naming her emotions, she confided to friends that she felt "perpendicular to herself." She told a trusted teacher/mentor, who told her to tell no one of her feelings of displacement, of perpendicularity.

Her interest in science might have been a red flag for the Morality Guardians, who took a dim view of girls engaged in any activity they identified as "masculine pursuits." Because bioengineering involved the study and manipulation of life, only the most reactionary of Guardians objected to women engaged in this pursuit, since women were equated to life-giving. The interest in basketball, on the other hand, was more problematic, as the Morality Guardians thought that "athletic girl" equated to lesbianism. They had tried, unsuccessfully, to convince state legislators to ban women and girls from certain sports as unfeminine, but these were largely rejected.

The Morality Guardians were a self-appointed sect who railed against what they saw as the moral degeneracy and decadence of American society. Born out of tattered remains of the evangelical Christian movement, the Guardians aspired to be a political force. There were attempts in some states to create a Morality Guardians Party, but they found more success as a kind of pressure group allied and aligned to traditional conservative governments. Indiana was a typical case: the governor appointed a prominent Guardian to a newly created cabinet position as Secretary for Public Morals. More frequently, Guardians would summarily discipline anyone they saw as deviant. Discipline usually meant public displays of ridicule, where a transgressor would be captured—kidnapped—paraded around in shackles, typically with a sign hung around their necks listing their moral failings. If a man had unacceptably long hair, the Guardians would conduct public hair cuttings, the offending man shackled and forcibly shorn of his locks, the hair ritually set ablaze. The

Guardians would invite the mob that would inevitably gather to denounce the unfortunate mark, all of which was captured for the feeds, which drew millions of hits. "Capture and release" was the name the Guardians gave to this practice. The authorities in many locations would look the other way at these violations of civil rights. In some cases, local leaders openly applauded. Part Taliban, part Red Guards, part Sturmabteilung, the Morality Guardians became a powerful cultural and political force in many parts of the country.

The Morality Guardians were recognizable by their white garments, emphasizing purity. Many were masked or hooded, especially for the public exhibitions. But as they gained influence, the hoods came off and their displays more brazen. They made a deliberate effort not to appear fanatical. In fact, they made very few public statements, preferring action over rhetoric. They projected the appearance of being devout and disciplined.

Adele's father, Malcolm, was not a moralist or a conversative nationalist and certainly was not in league with the Morality Guardians. But he was a rule-follower, and did not approve of Adele's flirtations with boy's clothing or hair styles. Adele's mother Sophia, on the other hand, was sympathetic and supportive. In the relative secrecy of her bedroom, Adele would put her hair up in a ball cap, wear a flannel shirt and blue jeans. This all seems so innocent and unremarkable today, but when Adele was a girl sexual and gender roles were severely policed. Many states, Indiana included, enforced a sort of dress and behavior code; although not an official part of government, the Morality Guardians sniffed around seeking anyone who transgressed sexual and gender roles. Sex equated to gender in their eyes. One time in public, Adele insisted on being called Emerson, but her parents immediately silenced her, hustling her into their car. Even having an ambiguous name, one that did not conform to gender stereotypes (boy names for boys, girl names for girls) could be met with apprehensions by the Morality Guardians.

One afternoon, Adele and her mother went to Indianapolis to shop and enjoy lunch. The Morality Guardians were more effective and tended to be found in small towns and rural areas. But there were some chapters that attempted to exert influence in larger metropolitan areas. Indianapolis was one of the few big cities where the Guardians were active. As the state capital of a conservative state which housed a Public Morality agency, Indianapolis was a vision for what the Guardians had hoped would spread across the country. It should also be said that as a large city, Indianapolis did not afford the Guardians complete and unfettered freedom of action. Most citizens ignored their public stunts. Even though the Public Morality agency was headquartered downtown, most Indianapolitans assumed that it was charged with enforcing public morality for the rest of the state. Citizens of Indianapolis looked at cities like Austin and yearned for its autonomous status.

On this particular afternoon, Adele witnessed the Guardians kidnapping a young woman dressed in a boyish manner: short cropped hair, flared jeans and a shapeless hooded sweatshirt. Adele watched in horror as the Guardians—after denouncing the "transvestite"—forcibly disrobed the woman, dressing her in an "appropriate" skirt, blouse and flats. A wig was forced upon the bound woman's head, makeup smeared on her resistant face. Those who gathered largely heckled the Guardians and at least a few attempted to free the woman from her shackles. Only in Indianapolis might the Guardians have been so publicly rebuked without consequence. For her part, Adele stood in silence, tearing up at the sight of the bound captive. Adele had often dressed in a similar manner in the privacy of her room. Seeing this very violent public humiliation might have discouraged her from thinking the thoughts she had. Adele witnessed only a few seconds of the spectacle, her mother bustling her away. She had seen the Guardians in Muncie, of course. They were very active there, but they mostly targeted abortionists, free thinkers and fornicators. There were no trans folk in Muncie—none, at least, who might appear in public—and so to see someone who looked so much like her brutally targeted might have easily frighten her. Instead, it spurred her into action.

There was, of course, an underground of trans folk in the US who congregated in New York, Miami, and San Francisco. She wondered if she might one day move to one of these cities. Living as a trans person, even in these oases of progressivism, was not an easy life. Living an in-between existence was uncomfortable in the United States at that time. Trans people had higher rates of suicide, were less likely to be hired in the professions, and were forced to live at the margins of even the most forward-looking cities. She could also take the step of transitioning, crossing the threshold completely and living as a man. To do this meant finding a way to Europe, Copenhagen specifically, where transition surgery for those with gender dysphoria was still openly and actively practiced. Nowhere in the United States offered such services.

Malcolm Johnson would never have permitted this. A gentle soul with a kind face, Adele knew that he would have bellowed "Out of the question!" at the suggestion. Indeed, Adele was not sure if her own father would have reported her to the Guardians had she ever broached the subject with him. Two weeks after the incident she witnessed in Indy, Adele summoned her mother into her room and raised the question for the first time if she would be permitted to one day live as a man.

At his coming out announcement, Lawrence Schumann would state categorically that Sophia Johnson was the best and most supportive mother anyone could ever have. She was born and raised in a utopian community in upstate New York, by parents—by an entire village, really—that lived according to Emersonian principles. Dubbing themselves the Neo-transcendentalists, they rejected American culture and American institutions as decadent and fascistic, a miasma poisoning the individual soul.

Sophia left the community shortly after she turned 18, always wondering if she could live as a Neo-transcendentalist outside of the village, out in American society. She met Malcolm in Cleveland, where he was interning as a minister—one profession that had yet to be automated. Sophia worked as a docent at the Cleveland Museum of Art. They met at an outdoor festival, another example of the adage "opposites attract." At the conclusion of Malcolm's internship, he found an associate pastor's position in Muncie, and Sophia followed him there. They married a year later.

As a Neo-transcendentalist, Sophia despised the Guardians. To her, Adele had the soul of a man and it was society that was impinging on the release of that soul.

Sophia did not use this terminology when talking behind the closed doors of Adele's room. She only gently indicated that she would support her decision to transition to a man.

The opportunity came a year after the bedroom confidential. Malcolm was diagnosed with an aggressive cancer and was dead eleven months later at a tragically young age. After burying her dad, Adele and her mother sat together on her bed and began planning a trip. Using the life insurance money, Adele and her mother traveled to Europe where they eventually appeared in Copenhagen for the surgery. They opted, as many others in this circumstance, to not only elect a new name but a new identity: birthplace, parents, upbringing. All the vestiges of her life as Adele Johnson were wiped away, as if she had never existed. Such extreme measures were a necessary deterrent from the prying eyes of the Morality Guardians, whose networks even extended overseas. Adele and her mother posed as tourists, on a river cruise of Europe. At one of the designated ports along the journey, the two left the cruise and did not return, making their way to Copenhagen.

Sophia was also given a new identity. She would return to the United States and live out her days in Bozeman, Montana, like someone in witness protection. Sophia—now Charlotte Daniels—and Lawrence would reunite briefly in Denver, where he was ostensibly traveling on business. Maintaining their discretion, they warmly embraced and spent four days together. Before departing, they would reunite two more times before her death. Such was the fate of many trans people in the United States at that time: transsexuality was closeted through these extreme measures.

Gender dysphoria had at one time in the United States been recognized as a psychological condition and many people decided to undergo sex reassignment therapy. Indeed, this became a relatively common procedure well before Adele's birth. But owing to the increasing regressive nature of political and cultural life in America, many states had re-classified gender dysphoria as a pathology. Indiana was one such state that produced its own Diagnostic and Statistical Manual of Mental Disorders, meant to counter the DSM produced by the American Psychiatric Association. DSM had years before reclassified "gender identity disorder" to "gender dysphoria." The Indiana guide returned to that earlier designation, emphasizing that this condition was an affliction. The creation of the Indiana Diagnostic Manual of Mental Disorders (IDMD) was not only the work of politicians: the state drew conservative mental health care professionals educated at state-administered, ideologically-directed universities. Similar manuals were drawn up in nearly two dozen other states, each reflecting some reaction to the more inclusive language of the DSM. At one time, the DSM was the global standard for mental health clinicians. Its decline as the standard-setter mirrored the decline in scientific soft power the United States once wielded. For Adele Johnson, the IDMD was just one more reason that coming out as trans in Indiana was simply not an option. Adele's gender identity disorder would have been met with enforced "treatments."

There were no trans folks after genetic engineering, or so it was to be believed by the Morality Guardians. In the same way that CRISP-R and other advanced gene editing technologies had eradicated Huntington's disease, sickle-cell anemia and other scourges, gender dysphoria was placed in this same category, of a "disease" that technology can "fix." Many trans folk had once claimed that they were "born this way," and that the desire to have their biological sex align to their gender identification was not merely a "lifestyle choice." Reactionaries finally accepted this argument but now enshrined into law policies that said those born that way—with the mistaken notion that they feel they are a man rather than the women that they are—would undergo genetic therapy to eliminate these tendencies in-utero. (The same went for homosexuality, altruism and other "undesirable" traits.)

After his press conference, Schumann wrote a memoir, which turned out to be his last published work. Here he explored the link between his transition from female to male and his work on transitions and threshold conditions in physics. In describing the latter as a liminal space, Schumann surmised that he had experienced a similar disquieting liminal space between two biological sexes.

After the press conference and the revelation of his origin story, there was disagreement in the trans community about how Lawrence Schumann should be remembered. There were an unusually vocal number of trans folk and the recently transitioned who denounced Schumann. Given the fame and renown he had attracted as a young physicist, why had he not come out earlier? Schumann was an influential executive at the Neckar Group, and could have been a prominent voice in trans rights. At the very least he could have advocated for the decriminalization of transitioning, even from his perch in Heidelberg, where gender dysphoria was broadly accepted. There were some European countries, especially those under the thumb of Russian occupation, that were intolerant of trans folk. Schumann could have saved thousands of lives and reversed discrimination years ahead of time, had he used his influence for good. Why was Schumann so cowardly, these activists demanded to know?

There was another faction who defended Schumann. Transgender folk of that generation lived in fear, in silence and alone. He still held the trauma of how the underground trans community was treated and vilified. Today's generation had no memory of the Morality Guardians and their tactics. They had not experienced discrimination and humiliation. Schumann had every right to have trust issues, and it was cavalier of the other faction to think that he would have come out so easily.

Indeed, immediately after Schumann's announcement, scores of men and women came out as having transitioned. Some were prominent people, but just as many were ordinary, otherwise unremarkable people, grandparents whose children and grandchildren had no hint at all of the lives they once lived. The number of such incidences grew across the United States. Families were reacquainting themselves with a grandfather who was born a girl or a grandmother once named Richard.

Schumann's announcement had reopened a chapter in American history that had hitherto passed in silence. Lydia Barlow, an oral historian, began collecting these stories, which were eagerly read by a younger generation who had no sense at all of this dark and forgotten chapter of an even darker recent history. For most people, Schumann's announcement barely registered. It is, of course, safe to identify as trans today. For most people living today, Robert Schumann is simply a well-known scientist.

Key Futures Themes

- Future of Physics and Knowledge Production
- Climate Change
- Gender Identity
- Biopolitics
- Reactionary Movements
- Cultural Memory and Historical Reckoning

Bibliography

Barres, Ben. 2020. *The Autobiography of a Transgender Scientist*. Cambridge: The MIT Press.

Chapter 6
Jennifer Nanabah: Mayor

When Jennifer Nanabah was in the fourth grade, her learning center was locked down because an armed intruder strolled into the building and walked into the cafeteria and began spraying several rounds from his AR-15. The gunman was a recently fired high school custodian and he was seeking revenge. This was a story repeated endlessly across the country. Jennifer recalled the incident and while she was terrified, she and her classmates and her learning coordinator were all well-trained on what to do when this situation would inevitably arise. She remembered the learning coordinator dashing to the whiteboard, which she pulled away from the wall, creating a small cubical shelter that everyone was to rush behind. The resulting structure was a bullet-proof safe room that provided protection, even if it was small and cramped. While the learning coordinator was assembling the safe space, the students had been piling their desks and chairs against the door, to halt the intruder's progress should he try to enter the classroom. As a final measure, Jennifer's learning coordinator was armed with her own handgun, which she would use as a last resort should the gunman breach their defenses. The learning coordinator had used firearms on her family's ranch growing up, and had received some minimal training in firearms use, but had no training on using the weapon in a tactical situation like an active shooter in a school building. Jennifer and her classmates crouched behind their shield for what felt like hours, and indeed the entire episode lasted about an hour and a half. The gunman never made it to Jennifer's classroom: after the carnage he unleashed in the cafeteria, he made his way toward the administration offices—his real target—and killed two administrative assistants before the principal shot the man. For this, the principal was declared a hero.

Jennifer and her classmates were led out of the school, a drill they had practiced countless times before that it was almost routine. Public shootings were such a fact of daily life that, on the outside at least, the students were not in the least affected.

D. Staley, *Anticipatory Biographies*, Anticipation Science 10, https://doi.org/10.1007/978-3-032-08912-0_6

The lesson Jennifer took away from this and other such experiences was that the adults will not protect you, that they will do nothing to prevent this violence from happening, as it happens again and again and again. In response, she joined an online forum of children across the country who had lived through mass shooting events. For some children, this was their third or fourth such incident. What these children were experiencing was beyond trauma.

As with every other case, the Texas legislature did nothing in response to this school shooting apart from mouthing platitudes and bowing their heads and praying for the victims. Not that anyone expected this incident to be any different from the countless other mass shootings that occurred across Texas every year. Jennifer had always assumed that she would be traumatized by mass violence at some point in her life. In the midst of the shooting, as she scrambled behind the shield, she felt a kind of resignation, her body no longer her own, swept along by an invisible riptide.

One would suppose that this was a formative moment for Jennifer Nanabah, but in truth other issues would crowd out gun violence in her mind, which was but one piece of a mosaic of concerns about the world. Austin, and the entire state, had been hemorrhaging population after decades of seemingly endless growth. Summertime temperatures reached into the 110°s and stayed there for the entirety of the season. As a child, Jennifer rarely played outside. Water was at a premium—literally, as it must be paid for—with desperate people willing to steal it and even kill for it.

Jennifer was probably more sensitive and aware of these larger issues because her parents were prominent activists and community organizers. Dinnertime conversation frequently veered toward homelessness, climate, dwindling water. Jennifer fantasized about attending the University of Texas, but knew that goal was far out of her reach. Like many of the universities that survived the purges, Texas had become ridiculously exclusive—no one bothered to say "selective" anymore—becoming a kind of finishing school for the elite. Besides, Jennifer was interested in sociology, philosophy, social justice, literature, all of which was forbidden knowledge at The University of Texas, knowledge unbecoming the future leaders of society.

Jennifer's parents began a "folk college" modelled after the radical folk school established by Myles Horton. There she read Pyotr Kropotkin, treated like the kabbalah in contemporary Texas. She also learned about organizations, about anarchism. Among Texas' leadership class the word still incorrectly meant violence against the state, and the folk college was often labeled a terrorist organization, even though they never committed a violent act—indeed abhorred violence. The Folk College practiced nineteenth century anarchism, meaning a rejection of higher authority and the cultivation of self-organized authority from small associations.

The Folk College itself was a case in point: Jennifer's parents received no permission to start the college, simply deciding one day to convene a group in their living room. In its early days, the college met in coffee shops and artists' studios and in the homes of students and teachers, although the distinction between the two was often blurred. A "student" might be a 60-year-old community organizer, a "teacher" a 23-year-old who had written an underground comic. The Folk College—even writing it in capital letters seems overblown—did not bother with accreditation or a curriculum or admissions or even tuition. Members traded and bartered food, hand-made goods, services ("I'll clean your house or look after your kids"). The Folk College was the model of a workers' association so central to anarchist thought, and the experience had a powerful effect in shaping Jennifer's views on politics, of the organization of society, the exercise of power. No one matriculated or graduated from the Folk College; people arrived and left as their circumstances allowed. Jennifer never really left the College, even when she embarked on a political career.

Because anyone could lead a discussion or start a class at the folk college—self-organization rather than top-down administration or burdensome committees were the order of the day—when Jennifer turned eighteen she began a small group devoted to the theory and practice of insurrectionist anarchy. The Italian immigrant anarchist Luigi Galleani became her guiding light, and she read everything she could find that he had written. She started a newsletter called "Subversive Chronicle," named after Galleani's anarchist newspaper. While Jennifer's parents identified as anarchists, they adhered more to the ideas of Proudhon or David Graeber, anarchism as the politics of local autonomy. They abhorred violence and were concerned about their daughter's infatuation with it. Having grown up in a society where low-level violence was a constant hum, punctuated by frequent episodes of mass violence, Jennifer wanted not just to react to violence but to harness it toward her own ends. The political party that dominated national politics—certainly the politics of the state of Texas—enshrined political violence as a legitimate form of policymaking. "Why should they have a monopoly on violence?" she asked her seminar.

It is difficult to say where Jennifer Nanabah's infatuation with political violence came from, although her childhood experience with gun violence must have played a factor. Her seminars drew a considerable number of students and her parents feared that she might be forming a revolutionary cadre within the Folk College. This necessitated a community gathering on the subject of violence as a political methodology. In the end, the Folk College collectively decided to become more heavily armed—not unusual in the state of Texas—but to eschew the export of political violence. The episode would prove formative for Nanabah. Galleani was a writer, and she asked herself whether his words were a more effective weapon than his actions, that he talked about violence more than he practiced it. Long after her interest in Galleani had subsided, that rhetoric of political violence would continue to shape her thinking.

While simultaneously teaching at the Folk College, Jennifer Nanabah began organizing in District 10, focusing on homelessness, police reform and equitable water access. Very soon after she was appointed to Austin City Council.

Nanabah learned—or, rather, was reminded again—that the state government was weak and ineffectual and would do nothing to address the myriad issues facing Austinites. Those issues would have to be taken up by city government. City Council passed stringent gun laws—to help prevent the recurring tragedy of mass shootings—but were repeatedly rebuffed by a state law that forbade municipalities from enacting their own laws that counteracted state law. Texas lawmakers burnished their limited government credentials when attempting to lure companies to the state, but were all too eager to bring the full weight of government down on misbehaving cities like Austin. Nanabah grew ever more frustrated and her anarchist hackles were raised. Austin should "go it alone," should ignore Texas law, even nullify those laws.

Nanabah would reminisce several years later about how ironic she found the entire enterprise. American conservatives had long fantasized about secession, using it as a cri de coeur for decades. And the first political entity to secede since the Civil War was led by a radical anarchist mayor.

Nanabah continued to propose—and have passed—scores of laws that were repeatedly struck down by the Texas legislature and upheld by its supreme court. She finally sought appointment as Austin's mayor, and there was great support for the move. After six years in politics, Nanabah had acquired the art of political rhetoric, burying the language of anarchism underneath more palatable words that sought to achieve the same outcomes. In her mind, Austin was a workers' association, albeit one of 600,000 people. Although it remained a "luxury city"—even if it was no longer a tech hub—many of the city's residents hated the repeated rebuffs from the state and, while probably not anarchists, were filled with enough civic pride that Nanabah's message of fighting back against the state resonated with a population that had always wanted Austin to remain "weird." In her campaign for mayor, Nanabah's clarity was unmistakable: she was going to declare Austin's independence from the state of Texas.

This would require a vote of the citizens and could not be declared unilaterally. Although much of the rest of the country had succumbed to authoritarians, American cities still retained at least some semblance of democracy. Besides, as an anarchist, Nanabah felt that this decision had to be made by the members of the association that was Austin.

Questions arose about the geographic extent of the secession. Would it involve just Austin proper, or would it include Red Rock, San Marcos, Wimberley, Hutto, Lockhart and Taylor. Some even wondered if San Antonio, 80 miles away, would similarly move toward independence and join up with Austin in a kind of "twin city state."

There was no precedent that could be easily followed. She considered a law in Ohio, for example, that allowed a city to officially change its name with a two-thirds majority in a referendum. And she looked to history to learn how the northern counties of Virginia voted to secede to become West Virginia in 1863. Nanabah proposed a referendum: a yes vote by two-thirds of the citizens of Austin would warrant its independence from Texas.

Nanabah campaigned for a year on the referendum, and was watched carefully by the state, by the governor Royce Baker, in particular. Like many US governors, Baker was part high school football coach, part warlord, part feudal baron. After a political career devoted to greater autonomy to states—he was one of the leading confederationists—he drew the line at urban independence. Born and raised in Granbury, he harbored a dislike for Texas' big cities, even as he professed a lifelong affiliation with the Dallas Cowboys. Although neither expected nor wanted it, their names—Baker-Nanabah—would be entwined for decades.

At first, Baker was unconcerned with the independence referendum. But as it became evident that support for the measure was surging, he began to take action. It was not at all ironic that a city-state declaring its independence would be happening in Texas, which had long touted its independence –it was, after all, an independent republic before its admission to the Union.

The referendum passed with 72% of Austinites voting to form their own state. It was made very clear that Austin was not leaving the United States but was going to become the 53rd state of the Union. (Washington, DC and Puerto Rico had been previously granted statehood.) Would other cities follow suit? Columbus, Nashville, the San Francisco Bay area—all were cities that chafed under state regulations or state neglect. She would be sought out by other municipalities as an advisor on how to declare independence. Some European cities were exploring the idea of establishing themselves as city-states, and the mayors of Barcelona and London were eager for her insights.

The United States had flirted with confederacy throughout its history. When it was originally declared, and before the ratification of the Constitution, the US was a confederacy of states. The impracticality of that arrangement was one of the spurs for the Constitution, which established a stronger federal system. Of course, the break-away Confederate States of America—bound together by the immortality of slavery—gave primacy to state governments over any sort of overarching federal authority. The rallying cry of "States Rights!" had long been code for the continuation of apartheid policies.

But the US had drifted into a confederacy. States claimed more and more authority as Washington's influence over national life declined and retreated. As one could have easily predicted, the 52 states bickered and squabbled and accomplished little in concert. The United States began to look like Europe in the late nineteenth century: whatever national government remained was more like an alliance system holding separate countries in a tense equilibrium.

Any move toward urban independence or city secession would have been unthinkable decades before. Under the American Confederacy—a wholly unofficial title—a legal opening was created that hinged on the primacy of the city over the primacy of the state.

Even if not recognized in law, Austin was independent in fact. The city stopped sending sales taxes to the state, keeping it for themselves. There were already local taxes collected in the city: the high sales tax was reduced.

Although there was no specific law banning secession by any of its cities, Texas state legislators nevertheless pointed to a host of laws that made the state paramount over any city ordinance—the very conditions that fueled Austin's secession. Texas legislators introduced bills designed to revoke Austin's independent status, challenging the act in the courts, and enacting constitutional amendments aimed at preventing any other city from seceding. Governor Baker threatened lawsuits, vowing to take this up to the Texas Supreme Court.

Nanabah laughed at all of these efforts. Austin was an economic driver of the state. Whatever state funding the city received was miniscule in comparison to what Austin generated for the state. Nanabah delivered a defiant speech reminding legislators and the governor that "Texas needs Austin more than Austin needs Texas."

The slogan didn't have the same pop as "Keep Austin Weird," but the stickers and memes nevertheless proliferated.

Nanabah repeatedly said she had no concern for any law Texas might pass. She reminded the legislators that for decades the state, and the governor in particular, ignored laws, initiatives and other measures voted on by the citizens of Austin. To return the favor, whatever laws the State might try to pass would also be ignored by Austin. Nanabah's anarchist upbringing was very much in evidence.

Ultimately, the Texas Supreme Court ruled that because it was the voters who had decided—rather than political leaders—Austin's actions were legal. The ruling was widely interpreted to be one consequence of America's turn toward confederacy.

There remained a knotty problem. The Texas Statehouse sat squarely in the middle of the city. Like Cold War Berlin, the square made by W. 15th Street, W. 11th Street, Colorado Street and San Jacinto Boulevard was ceded by the city, where it would remain an outpost of the state of Texas within the state of Austin. Austin City Hall would remain the seat of government for the newly created state. Acting alone, Nanabah decided to retain the title "Mayor of Austin," rather than "governor."

Governor Baker deployed the Texas National Guard to secure the Capitol building, ostensibly out of concern for the safety of the lawmakers and of potential property damage, which resulted in increased security measures, checkpoints, and a very visible military presence within the city. The governor did this as a way to head off the physical act of secession but also at intimidating and discouraging supporters of Austin's independence. He was working from the assumption that Austin was less heavily armed than other parts of the state and that even a small military presence would act as a deterrent, or would convince the citizens to abandon their secession and return to the fold. He offered "amnesty" to any Austinite who asked for it.

Many feared that the presence of the National Guard would provoke clashes between residents and the military. Nanabah challenged the deployment in court, arguing that this act exceeded the state's authority and was a violation of "city's rights." Indeed, some of Texas' other cities did not look upon the governor's actions favorably, seeing it as a heavy-handed response that undermined the diplomacy that was required in this circumstance.

For her part, aside from legal action, Nanabah mobilized the Austin Police Department and other city law enforcement agencies to reinforce security measures and maintain order within the city. Additionally, she moved to create a volunteer militia—soon named the Austin Militia—to assist law enforcement. These volunteers were willing to undergo training and serve in a defensive capacity. Recruitment efforts aimed at attracting individuals with military or law enforcement backgrounds as well as passionate defenders of the idea of Austin's independence. It seems the citizens of Austin were not as disarmed as the governor had assumed. It was ironic, of course, that Nanabah would oversee and encourage the creation of the Militia, however she would see to it that it was well-regulated.

Nanabah engaged in diplomatic efforts and sought the support of other cities, states and international partners sympathetic to Austin's case. These engagements built alliances and garnered political and diplomatic pressure on the state of Texas.

The mayors of Dallas and Houston served as mediators between Ausitn and Texas. There was some help from Washington, in the form of a summit between Nanabah and Baker, leading to a set of negotiations called the Delaney Summit, after the US Supreme Court Chief Justice who mediated them. The capitol building would remain Texas property. Lawmakers were to be given free access (and could move freely about the city) in exchange for recognition of Austin's independence. Texas had thirty years to transition, to locate and build a new state capital.

After the showdown with Baker had subsided, Nanabah became a global folk hero, the embodiment of "city's rights" movement. She was invited to deliver the plenary at the US Conference of Mayors, an organization whose influence was growing. Even before Austin's independence, some US mayors had been staking a wider national and even global role for themselves. Famously the mayor of San Francisco, Milton Ruiz, traveled to Beijing for high level discussions—most saw it as merely a photo op—with the Chinese President. San Francisco's mayor wanted to align himself with the environmental policies of President Zheng, even as the US government itself had a strained—even nonexistent—relationship with Beijing. Mayors could sidestep state or national authorities to stake out their own political and policy paths. Nanabah's arrival at the conference was eagerly awaited; the mayors of Columbus and Nashville were especially interested in her presentation. If not independence, if not statehood for America's cities, then at least a kind of autonomy might be achieved. In her plenary, she coined the phrase "autonomous city-states" to describe America's new political and economic reality.

Evoking Jane Jacobs, Nanabah asserted that it is cities that are the actual drivers of economic growth, not the nation and certainly not the state. These "supraurban" institutions—another term she coined—actually inhibit the beneficent behaviors of cities. Nanabah's speech was carefully monitored by federal and state political authorities, who feared she would use the occasion to exhort the attendees to follow the path toward independence that Austin had cleared away. Indeed, half a dozen cities began their campaigns for independence as soon as the conference ended. Although it must also be observed that another effect of Austin's independence was that many states began negotiations with the mayors of their biggest cities to reevaluate their relationships, to give municipalities more autonomy, allowing them more freedom to govern themselves and thus avoiding the threat of secession. One observer wondered aloud if Texas had taken a more conciliatory posture, perhaps Austin would have remained in the fold. After Nanabah's speech, only three other American cities declared and secured independence. Many, many others gained greater autonomy.

Nanabah's message was especially well received in Europe, where there was an emerging movement to re-design pan-Europeanism. Confined to universities and think tanks—that is, within the realm of ideas rather than actual policy or direct action—political theorists similarly argued for the city as the primary political form, resurrecting the ancient Greek idea of the *polis*. Pan-Europeanism had been in tatters as various far-right governments followed the lead of the UK and exited the European Union. In almost every case, the residents of the major cities of these countries uniformly favored remaining within some pan-European structure, if not the EU itself. Nanabah exhorted in a manifesto that the "Free Cities of Europe" needed to bind together, a political network of cities that echoed the Hanseatic League. Europe had a long history of independent autonomous city as a political unit—Venice, Bremen—a history the United States could not claim. Nanabah encouraged European mayors to assert their independent status and then bind together into a United Cities of Europe as the new form of pan-Europeanism. She was hailed as the new Jean Monnet.

In another manifesto, Nanabah dreamed of a United Cities that would surpass the United Nations as a global governance organization. The idea of a network of autonomous cities would largely remain a dream. After she left her role as Mayor of Austin, Nanabah would write visionary speculative novels of a future where government is both hyperlocal and globally networked. She is compared to H.G. Wells, a realist utopian.

After the showdown with Governor Baker, Nanabah was held in even higher regard by the citizens of Austin, who collectively felt vindicated with their independence vote. But Nanabah's national and global celebrity soon after began to weigh on Austinites. She seemed to be spending all of her time addressing international audiences and less and less time actually in Austin governing. The issues and challenges that precipitated the independence vote had not subsided and remained largely unanswered by Nanabah. Of course, she had announced sweeping gun control measures to govern Austin, banning the ownership of assault weapons and regulating other types of weapons. Austinites were permitted to own guns, but those gun owners owed responsibility to their fellow citizens. The Austin Militia would remain intact, and all gun owners were required to join. Gun violence and gun deaths, while not eliminated, plummeted.

But other challenges remained, access to water the most vital and pressing issue. Austinites demanded that water be free and widely available, but one could not so easily conjure water out of thin air—although researchers at UT Austin were working on technologies to extract water from the atmosphere. Securing water for Austin meant negotiating with those who had access to water, either from Midwestern states or, more expensively, via the desalinization of water from the oceans. Nanabah's administration largely failed in these efforts, probably because she had become a divisive figure in the US. Midwestern governors especially were loath to negotiate with her. Many feared cities like Minneapolis and Des Moines might follow Austin's lead. Nanabah or her emissaries were politely received in state capitals but ultimately refused favored water rights. The already high cost of water rose 37% during her term in office.

Nanabah could not reverse the population decline that afflicted the whole of Texas—and the entire American Southwest—the price and availability of water only part of the problem. Summertime temperatures hovered around 110° for months at a time, which made the city less attractive than cities further north. During her term, Austin lost around 4% of its population. Ten years after independence, some began to wonder aloud if it had all been worth it, that independence had not solved the underlying challenges faced by the city. The independence genie could not be put back in the bottle.

Austin's absentee mayor was finally voted out of office, which happened when Nanabah was speaking at a conference in Australia. She remained a global celebrity for a time, writing manifestos and lecturing at conferences and appearing on global feeds. Even without a university degree, she was hailed as "the world's urban philosopher." She would create a consultancy, Nanabah and Associates, to advise cities on exercising autonomy. After 20 years of consulting, she retired to Austin, to take up residence at—and to attempt to revive—her parents' folk college. No longer lecturing on anarchism, Jennifer Nanabah taught instead that autonomous self-sufficiency is the highest expression of the good.

In the global imaginary she was the embodiment of the free city, although in reality she was the failed mayor of a declining city.

Key Futures Themes

- Gun Violence and Social Trauma
- Climate Change, Water Scarcity and Urban Survival
- Alternative Education and Radical Political Thought
- Anarchism, Violence and Political Legitimacy
- City Secession and the Rise of Autonomous Cities
- Urban Futures and Global Governance

Bibliography

Brian Charles, J. 2018. Breaking Up Is Hard to Do: Why Some States and Cities Want to Secede. *Governing*, 1 June 2018. https://www.governing.com/archive/gov-secession-movements-reshaping-cities-lc.html.

Griffin, Elle. 2023. What If We Split the US Into City-States? *The Elysian*, 30 October 2023. https://www.elysian.press/p/what-if-we-split-us-into-city-states.

Horton, Myles. 1997. *The Long Haul: An Autobiography*. New York: Teachers College Press.

Jacobs, Jane. 1985. *Cities and the Wealth of Nations: Principles of Economic Life*. New York: Vintage Books.

Kropotkin, Peter. 2015. *The Conquest of Bread*. New York: Penguin Classics.

Sender, Gabriel. 2022. Cities Should Have Constitutional Autonomy. *The Brown Daily Herald*, 23 October 2022. https://www.browndailyherald.com/article/2022/10/sender-25-cities-should-have-constitutional-autonomy.

Senta, Antonio. 2019. *Luigi Galleani: The Most Dangerous Anarchist in America*. Chico, CA: AK Press.

Staley, David J. 2022. The Metropolitan States of American. In *Visionary Histories*, ed. David J. Staley, 208–211. Tempe, AZ: Center for Science and the Imagination.

Welsh, John. 2020. City-State Britain: A Counter-Narrative to 'Brexit'. *Geopolitics* 27 (5): 1497–1527. https://doi.org/10.1080/14650045.2020.1856087.

Chapter 7
Emily Woodward: Mother America

It turns out there was a real person behind the symbol that became Mother America.

Emily Woodward produced fifteen children over a span of eight years. Her mission was to inspire others to repopulate a United States that had barred immigration of any kind. The only way for the population to grow and thrive would be for women to birth as many babies as they could.

She grew up in Lynchburg, Virginia. Her father James McCormick was the two-term governor, who attempted with only modest success to enshrine neo-Jim Crow laws for the state. Although it seems incredible today, Governor McCormick frequently described the "mongrelization" of the state and the country. This was not a hot mic slip up. Indeed, he would continue to use the slur to describe a state where he believed the white Christian population was being overrun by the Other.

He especially detested Richmond, still the state capital, although Governor McCormick had tried unsuccessfully to move the seat of government to Lynchburg. Richmond had become the most populous, prosperous and cosmopolitan city in the state. As an earlier generation of young people had migrated to Austin or Brooklyn, many enterprising souls today were drawn to Richmond, to its neurotechnology scene, its arts and music scene, in addition to being the locus of political power in the state.

Lynchburg had emerged as Virginia's second city, a counterpoint to the diversity and vitality of Richmond. Lynchburg was the fount of white Christian nationalism, with barely disguised segregationist laws. McCormick detested residing in Richmond, and if he were able he would have commuted daily from Lynchburg to spend as little time there as possible. But Governor McCormick well understood that he needed Richmond in his state. He was aware of the "city secession" movement led by Austin, Texas that was that was brewing across the country. The loss of Richmond's tax base would have made it difficult for the state to thrive. Indeed, his economic policy might have been summarized as extracting resources from Richmond and redistributing it to the rest of the state. He needed Richmond, but he did not like it.

D. Staley, *Anticipatory Biographies*, Anticipation Science 10,
https://doi.org/10.1007/978-3-032-08912-0_7

Indeed, he insisted that his family spend no time there. Emily, her mother and her two sisters sequestered in the family estate outside Lynchburg. Only occasionally would they travel to Richmond, to be paraded in front of cameras ahead of the State of the State address, for example. It was not that the McCormick family was not politically useful. Indeed, by the time she was a teenager, Emily would travel the state to address high schools and youth groups on the dangers of the feeds, or to lead prayer groups. James was disappointed that his wife had produced for him only three girls. To be clear, James loved and cherished his daughters, but he very much wanted a son, to cement the McCormick name as a political dynasty. James' father was a state senator and one-term Governor. James had wanted to groom a son for a political career.

He found himself in the very uncomfortable position of pinning all of his political plans on Emily. James had been tutored by his father that women had no business in politics, his father even sponsoring a bill to take the vote away from women. Jonathan McCormick wanted to remove women from public life altogether. Under no circumstances could a woman rule over a man.

James's son would have been prepared to be governor. He could not imagine that his daughter could play that role. Once it was clear that Rebecca McCormick was unable to produce any more children—that he was stuck with daughters—James pivoted. Emily, the brightest, most intelligent, most charming, could become a state senator. That she would attend Liberation University was unquestioned.

With her future now mapped out, James permitted Emily to spend more time with him in Richmond. She would attend the Rogers Academy, a private, very exclusive high school where the scions of the Virginia elite would matriculate. As long as she stayed within the brick walls of the Academy, James did not fear for his daughter, both her safety and her experiences of the world.

Emily was not so easily contained. She would often join her friends on excursions to the city, imbibing in the city's dance clubs. A Richmond-style of music had influential, nationwide impact. She even forged a friendship with a well-known African-American DJ, Brianna Parker. Perhaps in an act of defiance, she did not mind what her father thought of the friendship. There were even photos taken and virtually spread, showing Emily hugging her friend outside one of Richmond's dance clubs. The scandal horrified her father and led to a brief riff between the two. But Emily's time among the creatives of Richmond made her blanch at her father's labeling of her friends as "mongrels."

In Richmond she also witnessed poverty, homelessness, desperation. As she was being chauffeured around the city one afternoon, she saw a disheveled homeless person standing at a street corner holding a sign. It was hardly the first time she had cast her eyes on such a person, despite her father's efforts to shield her from this reality. Usually, she would look away but on this afternoon she decided to make eye contact. This man was not drug addled, his eyes suggesting intelligence and depth. Then she noticed his hand scrawled sign: "Please stop automating my job."

She had dinner with her father that evening and asked him about the sign. James gestured absently about the automation economy, that the creative destruction of jobs was an unfortunate side effect, but that this man probably just needed to apply himself and try harder to find work. She asked him whether as governor he had any obligation to assist this man. This was one of those moments when James was proud of his daughter's powers of observation, a skill she would need to be a successful senator. At the same time, he was irritated that a woman would engage him in a complex, if ultimately fruitless, political debate. If only she were a boy.

Emily wondered what role the state should play in helping this man and others like him who were treated as little more than detritus of the automation economy. "Jesus fed everyone," she reminded her father, a practice of Christianity very much at odds with her father's. This was a pivotal moment in Emily's life. She very easily could become the next Jane Addams, a Christian progressive. For a capstone project at Rogers, she imagined a kind of Hull House for Richmond's destitute, those displaced by the automation economy. This place would provide shelter, food, job retraining, and religious instruction. Her teacher encouraged Emily to develop the idea; with the McCormick name behind such an effort, there was no reason this could not become a meaningful success. Her father, of course, vetoed any such idea, leading to more dinnertime debates about the meaning and practice of Christianity. Emily did not recognize the Jesus her father described. She was drawn to Mary, the mother, the Life Giver, the nurturer. She might have been a Marianist. If she were a man.

She arrived at Liberation University and imbibed in the last throes of Evangelicalism. Intent on practicing the kind of Christian service represented by her Hull House idea, she was planning on majoring in social work, much to the chagrin of her father. She also had thoughts of meeting a husband and starting a family as did many young women of that age. This choice of majors was very much in keeping with Emily's approach to Christianity, of care and service to the cause of justice, not that other kind of justice sought by students at the Ivies. At Liberation, social work was a small department attracting only a few students. Those training for positions of power avoided a major that seemed to concentrate on the powerless.

Friends remembered her as serious yet funny, more cosmopolitan than many of them, owing to her life as the daughter of the Governor. Her professors remembered her as intelligent and articulate. While at Liberation, Emily sought to downplay her famous last name, unlike many of the other children of powerful families. She described it as a kind of Christian humility.

She could not help but notice that Liberation (at one time a university of some 15,000 students) was considerably smaller than when her parents attended. As with most other elite institutions—those still in business, at least—there were perhaps only about 5000 students who came to the campus. (As had always been the case, tens of thousands attended online.) The main reason was that there were fewer traditional-age college students, and especially of the white evangelical type who had long matriculated at Liberation. A Global Political Economy class introduced her to the reality that many African countries had young populations, fueling an economic boom south of the Sahara. She considered her own state, noting that Viginia had been hemorrhaging population for decades. Some people moved, many more were elderly who were now dying off, not being replaced by newborns. Outside of Richmond, very few people were permitted to move to Virginia, and hardly anyone in the state was having children. She began to articulate in her classes the belief that population decline was the greatest threat facing Virginia and the country, a sentiment her father very much approved of.

During her junior year, students occupied a large lecture hall after classes had ended and began to sing, to read the Gospels, to testify. Their numbers swelled as they were joined by more and more students. What had begun as an evangelical university—seeking to become the evangelical Notre Dame, complete with a winning football team—had degenerated in the minds of these students into a corporate university. Administrators were more interested in training the next generation of political and cultural warriors in the continued fight against secular society. Liberation presidents aimed to populate the halls of Congress, the Supreme Court, most state houses with Liberation-trained acolytes.

The message of Jesus had seeped out of the university the students said, or rather demonstrated, their singing and stomping and praying and testifying meant to call forth the Holy Spirit, to fill Liberation once again with the Word. They were joined by faculty, a few administrators and then residents of the town.

Hours stretched into days stretched into weeks. What some were calling a revival had spilled out of the classroom and into the quad where thousands assembled. Observers were labeling it another Great Awakening, as the "Liberation Revival" sparked copycat movements across the country. The founders of what became the Morality Guardians sang and danced at the Liberation Revival. The entire episode lasted but 27 days before the students returned to their dorms, the faculty to their offices. Scholars continue to debate today the long term cultural and spiritual effects of the Liberation Revival.

For Emily, the reaffirmation of her faith would last her lifetime. She was particularly moved by one speaker, Matthew Woodward, who before speaking in tongues extemporized on the population decline in the United States. His language was coded but it was clear he was concerned that white Christian civilization was being overcome by unbelievers and "mongrels." His cadences reminded Emily of her parents, perhaps because this handsome, passionate young man was using the slur made it more palatable to her. She would eventually marry him.

During the Revival, the two were inseparable. After the Revival had ebbed, Emily and Matthew began "dating," although at Liberation this was a highly scrutinized and surveilled activity. Attending campus events together, lunches at a local restaurant, even solitary walks around campus were permitted. They would steal the occasional kiss—frowned upon—but never went to each other's dorm room—absolutely forbidden. Sex was, of course, never a consideration.

This was another of those pivotal moments in Emily's life. In so many ways, Matthew was the opposite of Emily. He studied political science and theology, and would stay at Liberation for law school. His ambition was to serve as a Supreme Court justice, probably the most powerful political position in the United States. Emily never did countenance his use of the word "mongrel," although he refrained from using it once they were married and indeed, disavowed the idea years later, although historians doubt that Matthew had any sort of real change of heart.

Matthew had very strict ideas about the relationship between men and women, and especially the roles each were to fulfill. Having been groomed for a political career, Emily now found herself contemplating life as the ward of her husband. Ironically, or perhaps not, James McCormick liked and approved of Matthew very much. Indeed, once it was clear that the two were to be married, her father transferred his political aspirations onto his son-in-law.

To this day, historians are puzzled at the *volte-face* Emily exhibited. Why would an independent young woman, who by all accounts was going to be a Christian progressive, subsume her ambitions to her husband's? Some have argued that Matthew resembled her father, and so she was exhibiting a kind of father fixation. Others have argued that the Liberation Revival so deeply moved Emily that she was made more spiritually pliable, more open to the conservative Christianity represented by Matthew. Others have argued—although this is a minority opinion—that Emily was never really a Christian progressive or that it was merely an adolescent phase she was going through. Indeed, while at Liberation, Emily never went dancing or made trips to Richmond. She lost contact with her music and clubbing friends, but not because Liberation forbade it. It appears she chose to move away from this life. Perhaps confinement in Lynchburg was what caused this change of heart. Whatever the cause, Emily McCormick—soon to be Emily Woodward—graduated from Liberation University with the aspiration to be a mother.

Virginia was already one of the states that had barred almost all in-migration, except under highly regulated, highly exceptional circumstances. This applied to internal migration as well, as Virginia had joined with other states in holding the line on US climate refugees. It came as no surprise, therefore, that Virginia became the first US state to institute pro-natalist welfare state policies designed to increase population. Of course, the US population was actually in a steady state, not really growing, aging precipitously, but not really declining. What Virgina's legislators meant was the white population, which was not reproducing at a high enough replacement rate. Further, Virginia was top-heavy with elderly, and so the population became less fertile, and grew ever more diverse, twin problems in the eyes of the legislators and the governor.

Although she was very much in love with Matthew and their first year together was blissful, Emily soon discovered that she was effectively the ward of her husband. Matthew prevented her from holding a job outside the home. He allowed her to engage in banking and other commercial transactions, but only as these related to the maintenance of the household. Matthew allowed her to vote. And Matthew insisted that she produced babies, lots of babies. Emily was a willing partner in this endeavor. Matthew's plan was for their couple to have 10 or 12 children, Biblical numbers of children.

But in fact, unless he were a CEO—or the scion of a political dynasty—no one person could single-handedly support a family of 12 children, let alone one of three or four or even one. This was one of the chief reasons for the low birth rates in Virginia and elsewhere: couples—even if they decided to marry at all—were not having children, either because they didn't want them, or, more commonly, because they could not afford to. Like many other polities around the world, Virginia's government instituted pro-natalist subsidies and inducements, promises of money to help bear the cost of raising children. But these carrots rarely influenced the birth rate. Virginia's government therefore turned towards sticks. If you were a single woman or a couple without children, your taxes were substantially higher than those with children. It must also be said that the law was designed to impact white couples only. Indeed, black and brown couples were encouraged not to have children. Abortions for the non-white majority were on-demand.

Therefore, couples such as the Woodwards received generous government subsidies, part of the Tucker Act, which guaranteed couples with at least five children what amounted to a universal basic income, $50,000 each year. This was used to hire nannies and nurses, and to feed, clothe and educate their children. In exchange, a couple would need to be married, and the mother had to give up any aspirations outside of motherhood. Alongside these coercive measures to induce births, the state enlisted a neuropersuasion consultancy to build a subliminal campaign for more births. Using the latest research from cognitive science, the consultants blanketed post-modern fertility symbols across all the platforms—abstracted images of enlarged breasts, vaginal symbols, images evoking wide child-bearing hips. The consultants claimed that these images had seeped into the collective unconscious of the state's residents. In combination with the taxation policy and the persuasion campaign, the Tucker Act was a government strategy to incubate babies. And it ultimately proved moderately successful.

Historians have long debated where the idea for Matthew and Emily to use an artificial womb came from. It turns out that Emily was the originator of the idea. While she shared Matthew's desire for plentiful children, she did not relish the idea of perpetual pregnancy, of delivering a child every two years or so. She presented the idea to Matthew one day over dinner, and he agreed. What Matthew—and Governor McCormick—were unaware of was that Emily was a secret investor in Ectogenesis, a biomedical startup that produced artificial wombs. In addition to producing a large family, Emily had hoped that her personal example would demonstrate the efficacy of the artificial womb, increasing Ectogenesis's sales and thus producing hefty profits for herself. Matthew never knew of Emily's clandestine business plan, which he would have certainly forbidden as inappropriate for his ward/wife.

Her use of the artificial womb to birth her own children was controversial. The technology of the artificial womb was originally designed for animals and had been successfully tested on premature sheep years earlier, proving very effective at gestating fetuses such that five years before her own pregnancy, it was first used on a severely premature baby.

An artificial womb was a polymer-based container or "plastic bag" where an infant was suspended in fluid, simulating conditions similar to natural pregnancy. Used in this way, the technology allowed premature infants additional development time—in the early trials as much as 4 weeks—improving their survival rates and reducing complications when they transitioned to standard care. The technology especially addressed underdeveloped lungs, one of the most vital issues facing all premature babies. Instead of breathing air, the device filled the baby's lungs with specially formulated fluid; developing synthetic amniotic fluid was perhaps the key innovation that had to occur to make the artificial womb a viable technology. Oxygen delivery occurred through a system where the infant's blood circulated via umbilical vessels connected to an external oxygenation device, similar to how oxygen exchange occurs in natural pregnancy.

Artificial wombs proved more successful at bringing premature babies to term than any other previous device that had been found in NICUs. Some fertility experts wondered if artificial wombs might be used for infertile couples. Could a fetus be gestated for nine months in such a fashion? A renegade OB/GYN—ignoring the regulations that were supposed to guard against these kinds of experiments—worked with an infertile couple to implant their sperm and eggs into a modified artificial womb, treating the technology as a virtual surrogate mother. The first attempts failed, and the OB/GYN was discovered performing the illicit procedure. But other actors took up the cause, and when a young couple in Washington State successfully carried a child in an artificial womb to term, the hope was raised that the technology could solve infertility. Emily Woodward's controversy came with her use of an artificial womb when she was otherwise capable of carrying the child on her own.

Emily would initially incubate five babies at once, one naturally and four via artificial wombs. The news soon spread all over the feeds. It turned out that Emily was working clandestinely with one site to give periodic updates as to her progress. They conspired to make the content seem like it was being captured covertly by overaggressive paparazzi without Emily's notice. Matthew was unaware of this deception and was outraged at the invasion of the family's privacy. Emily feigned anger, but was delighted that her pregnancies were capturing so much of the country's attention.

In deciding to have children in this way, the Woodwards were adamant that they were going to ask for Tucker Act funds. Both were convinced of the correctness of the legislation, and both were committed to a culture of natalism in Virginia. That their personal joy would have positive political effects was a benefit both Matthew and Emily sought. Emily successfully gave birth to a girl and the four artificial wombs performed flawlessly, giving the couple three boys and another girl.

Perhaps as a result of her prominent and visible position in Virginia society, questions were raised at to the legality of producing children in this fashion, especially when doing so would yield Tucker Act funding. Medically, using an artificial womb to produce children has been clinically proven and demonstrated. But could a couple use the technology—let alone multiple ones simultaneously—to qualify for the Tucker Act funding? No sooner had the suddenly expanded family returned from the hospital were the Woodward's sued. Casteless, a Richmond-based advocacy group, claimed that their use of artificial wombs was not in issue and was perfectly legal, but that producing children with the technology meant they should forego Tucker Act support. Only those who have the resources to employ the technology could reap the Tucker Act benefits in this way, argued Casteless, giving the Woodwards an unfair advantage over couples without such privilege. The Woodward's lawyers claimed that the legislation said nothing about artificial wombs—the legislators largely unaware of the technology as they were writing the bill—and so they were not violating the law.

The Chief Justice of the Virginia Supreme Court, Carter Greenwood, urged the Woodwards to bring the case before him. Mimicking the actions of the Federal Supreme Court—even if its power and authority had diminished—many state Supreme Courts made proactive use of their shadow dockets. After some discussion among the other justices, the Chief Justice would reach out to the parties in a suit of some kind and clandestinely invite them to bring their cases to the court. (In the past, applicants approached the court; now, the court actively, if surreptitiously, approached applicants.) Their quick, unsigned judgments had the effect of inducing new laws, bypassing legislators, or at least forcing legislators to act on the court's rulings. In this way, High Court Chief Justices became powerful political figures in the United States confederation, the equal to presidents and governors. It was little wonder that Matthew Woodward aspired to this position.

The Virginia justices ruled that since the law said nothing about how couples needed to produce children—it did not mention IVF, for example—the Woodwards would be able to benefit from the Tucker Act. After the decision, other couples would follow, such that artificial surrogacy became widely practiced. There was evidence that the use of artificial wombs had a positive impact on birth rates in Virginia, although rates were still only hovered at the 2.1 replacement level.

Emily was a vocal proponent throughout the trial. The Woodwards didn't really need the money, she conceded, and they were more than capable of providing for their large family. But Emily especially wanted to act as a role model, extolling the virtues of motherhood, encouraging other young women to produce children now made more manageable with the use of the artificial womb. That Emily stood to personally profit was never publicly disclosed until two years after her death. On that occasion, it was revealed that Emily Woodward had been using the profits from her Ectogenesis shares to endow a number of community houses, first in Richmond, then in cities along the east coast, and then finally stretching across the country, some 45 cities in all. Jesus Feeds Everyone provided shelter, food, job retraining, and religious instruction for those made unproductive, and served as a temporary refuge for climate migrants. Anyone looking carefully and remembering deeply would have easily seen Emily's fingerprints all over the enterprise, the actualization of her Hull House idea from her high school days.

Matthew and Emily would produce ten more children. Five years after the birth of her first brood, she had her sixth baby, gestated via an artificial womb. For the next four years, they would produce another child via artificial surrogacy. Then the couple had a girl via natural means, and four more children birthed simultaneously in artificial wombs.

The wording of the Tucker Act was not entirely clear on this point, but it seemed that the state would support all of the Woodward's 15 children, not just the five specifically listed in the legislation. The state found itself in a politically awkward position. There were many couples from around the country who wished to migrate to Virginia to raise a family and to benefit from Tucker Act funds. For years, political leaders had erected borders to such internal migration—Richmond largely ignored these—with the goal of regulating the kind of person seeking residency. The government wanted to keep out "unproductive" and also the "mongrels" decried by McCormick and his ilk. The state government—bolstered by the Supreme Court—amended border protection laws to allow married white couples to migrate, but only on the promise that they would produce at least five children. (There were many cases of couples being deported for failing to produce the children they promised.) Many of these couples did so naturally, but a not-inconsequential number relied on artificial wombs, in order to produce more children in a short amount of time.

The feeds were filled with immersive videos of Emily, her servants, her robotic au pair, and her children living through the day. Breakfast and other meals resembled the bustle of a New York City restaurant; a sub-feed focused on Emily's chef and the chaos of the kitchen. (The "angry chef" genre had never gone out of style.) Given the size of her family, Emily schooled the children at home, with herself as head teacher. The Woodwards would build an addition to their house in Lynchburg, specifically for schooling, a one-room schoolhouse. Emily would stream lessons from the home school, encouraging other families to use her content to educate their own kids, although most families, even with Tucker Act funding, could not realistically home school their children, let alone sustain multiple servants, or a restaurant, or even a robotic au pair.

Emily appeared on the feeds, extolling the virtues of motherhood, offering practical guidance for raising so many children. Managing a schedule to ensure individual attention to each child was a particularly poignant and popular feed. She made appearances at school assemblies across the state, educating young girls to prepare for what she called "patriotic motherhood," and instructing boys in paternalistic respect for mothers and in their obligations to family, that they strive to be the single breadwinner in support of the family. Nothing was said at the assemblies of Tucker Act aid. She was mostly silent on the question of children born out of wedlock. When pressed, she seemed to have no problem with a woman raising a child on her own, although the law was clear: that only legally married couples could benefit from Tucker Act aid. She never publicly acknowledged it, but she privately supported the practice of men using an egg donor and an artificial womb to produce their own children, a practice that was growing in popularity in Richmond and in other large cities. The Virginia legislature drew up laws aiming to criminalize the practice.

As her feeds multiplied, a mythology grew around her: that she had given up career and any idea of ambition, or rather, that the only ambition she harbored was to produce children for the good of the country. How much of the mythology was true? Despite the feeds and the public appearances, Emily suffered from a kind of perpetual low-level postpartum depression, even if the majority of her children were produced by artificial means. She loved her children and never regretted having them, but she would periodically fall into a debilitating mournfulness, never revealed publicly.

For his part, Matthew Woodward never achieved anything like the notoriety or influence that his wife attained. He was a competent attorney with an important firm in Lynchburg, but his political ambitions were never consummated, even with the support of James McCormick. The couple remained married for 47 years, until his death. Theirs remained a cordial marriage, not devoid of love, but dominated by obligation. Emily attempted to engage Matthew in the kind of dinner-time conversation she enjoyed with her father, but Matthew was not the intellectual equal of her father—or of Emily, it must be said—and Emily grew tired of one-sided dialogs. Matthew always quietly resented Emily's celebrity, that her cultural influence far exceeded anything he might have accomplished as a senator or Chief Justice. Emily sensed this, understood this about her husband, which was one reason she concealed Ectogenesis and Jesus Feeds Everyone from him.

As she aged, as her children grew into the next generation of leaders of Virginia society, Emily reinvented the role of the grandmother. She becomes Caregiver-in-Chief for the state of Virginia, and eventually the rest of the United States. She advocated for the caregiver as a profession, with the dignity, respect and remuneration appropriate to such a vital profession. The care and nurturing of the young should be made a high-status enterprise. Whether this effort was successful or not remains an open question.

The feeds having made her a cultural influencer, Emily Woodward had morphed into a symbol long before her death. When it was drawn, the meme initially merited very little attention. The editorial cartoonist at *The Economist* made the decision to depict the United States as a woman, as Mother America, as Emily Woodward. Elicia Linton decided that, given its diminished place in world affairs, the United States should no longer be personified as the swaggering and belligerent Uncle Sam, that it was more geo-strategically befitting to return to a symbol more like Columbia, as the United States had been allegorized in the nineteenth century. Emily Woodward was more emblematic of what America had become, and this national personification spread, displacing Uncle Sam in all the memes. Emily, Mother America, appeared embracing Marianne, to show the conmaternity between the US and France. She would wag a disapproving finger to scold the Russian bear and nurture the injured Chinese dragon.

Whatever symbolic effect she had had on the world, whatever impact the artificial womb had on birth rates and natalism, Emily Woodward more than succeeded in giving life to and loving 15 bright, capable children, each of whom were devoted to their mother.

Key Futures Themes

- Population Engineering and Natalist Futures
- Reproductive Technologies
- Gender, Patriarchy and Care Economies
- Religion and National Identity
- Mythmaking and National Symbols

Bibliography

Fox-Skelly, Jasmin. Artificial Placenta: A New Lifeline for Premature Babies? *BBC*, 18 July 2024. https://www.bbc.com/future/article/20240717-artificial-placenta-a-new-lifeline-for-premature-babies.

Black, Harry Isaiah, and Alicia Bannon. 2022. The Supreme Court 'Shadow Docket'. *Brennan Center for Justice*, 19 July 2022. https://www.brennancenter.org/our-work/research-reports/supreme-court-shadow-docket.

Can the Rich World Escape Its Baby Crisis? *The Economist*, 21 May 2024. https://www.economist.com/finance-and-economics/2024/05/21/can-the-rich-world-escape-its-baby-crisis.

Kocer, Alissa. 2025. *EXTENDing Hope: Artificial Wombs for Safer Neonatal Development*. Duke University School of Medicine. 15 January 2025. https://medschool.duke.edu/blog/extending-hope-artificial-wombs-safer-neonatal-development.

Martuscelli, Carlo. 2023. The Populist Right Wants You to Make More Babies. The Question Is How. *Politico*, 11 September 2023. https://www.politico.eu/article/eu-populist-right-want-you-make-more-babies-viktor-orban/.

Stein, Rob. 2024. An Artificial Womb Could Build a Bridge to Health for Premature Babies. *NPR News*. https://www.npr.org/sections/health-shots/2024/04/12/1241895501/artificial-womb-premature-birth.

The Care Collective. 2020. *The Care Manifesto: The Politics of Interdependence*. London: Verso.

Willyard, Cassandra. 2023. Everything You Need to Know About Artificial Wombs. *MIT Technology Review*, 29 September 2023. https://www.technologyreview.com/2023/09/29/1080538/everything-you-need-to-know-about-artificial-wombs/.

Chapter 8
Matthew Shaw: Designer

As a boy on his family's farm in northern Minnesota, Matthew Shaw watched the starlings' murmuration across the empty sky. At first, it was the cascade of shifting formations, the beauty of the movement that held his attention. But then he began to wonder who the leader was, who was guiding the birds through those swirling patterns. He would sit mesmerized watching colonies of ants surround a corn chip he had dropped on the ground, how they organized into platoons to surround the chip and carry it back in pieces to their colony. Who were their leaders, who were their generals?

He would find such idle time among his daily chores, although there were far too many times that chores would suffer as Matthew sat daydreaming. His parents were largely tolerant of their son's fixations. Like many rural families, Matthew was homeschooled and watching birds or ants was justified as simply another lesson. Jason Shaw, especially, encouraged such education via wonder for his only child. Matthew grew up largely friendless and asocial. In another time and place, he would have probably become a hermit.

Kinetics and the organization and coordination of movement fascinated him. As a boy, Matthew watched sheepdogs corral recalcitrant flocks, directing them toward a desired location by a series of thrusts and feints, a lesson in the management of the herd. Matthew spent one summer attempting to control a flock in the same manner as a sheepdog. He had abstracted a series of movements, eleven basic steps the dog would perform. At first, the sheep were mystified that a boy was frolicking among them, and their first instinct was to ignore him, but eventually the sheep realized that Matthew was their new shepherd and responded to his actions. He wondered if he might actually be successful at "herding cats," as the still popular saying put it, but he could never corral a large enough number of cats to test his hypothesis. Indeed, he wondered if the movements he had discovered to herd sheep could be applied to

D. Staley, *Anticipatory Biographies*, Anticipation Science 10,
https://doi.org/10.1007/978-3-032-08912-0_8

other animals. Could he direct a school of fish? His odd hobby became controlling movement.

One summer, Matthew fashioned a small drone to look like a starling. After months of trial and error, he learned how to fly the drone among the flock. He had learned via an online tutorial that the actions of the birds were governed by a few simple rules, their complex murmuration an emergent phenomenon. Matthew learned how to steer the drone in such a way that he could direct the movement of the flock, controlling their collective behavior. He eventually became skilled enough that he could coax organized patterns from the starlings. Crowds would gather to watch, transfixed, like a fireworks display.

He would plant nodes of corn chip crumbs in an effort to construct networks, webs of ants. Matthew carefully broke a corn chip into small pieces and arrayed these in such a way that he could control the direction, flow and size of an army of ants. He learned to craft the right size of chip to affect the change he wanted, not too big, not too small. He rather cleverly arrayed the chips to have the ants spell out EAT. He videoed his achievements and uploaded it to the feeds. He was hailed by some as an environmental artist, although there were just as many that lambasted him for manipulating living beings for his amusement. For a recluse such as Matthew, this attention was overwhelming, too much for him to process. He had made the error of including a picture of himself, a mistake he would not repeat again. Anonymity would be a guiding principle of his life.

An online college was the best his parents could offer their inquisitive son. Matthew was enrolled in the Minnesota Institute, a remote education provider that featured a study-at-your-own-pace curriculum. The Institute had the reputation of being a "homeschool college," attracting many students like Matthew. For the first time in his life, Matthew felt like he had a community, albeit one that was physically dispersed across the state. Unlike other students, Matthew designed his own course of study in movement studies, and especially the management and control of motion. He took courses in logistics, to understand how to organize the movement of things. But he also studied non-linear dynamic systems, kinetic art and choreography, the coordinated movement of bodies in space. The sociology of crowds particularly interested him; he wrote one seminar paper that examined soccer hooligans in the 1970s, marauding through urban streets in a manner similar to starlings in the air: leaderless, following a few simple rules based on reactions to their neighbors, and thus difficult to manage or control. Identifying "a few bad apples" in the crowd in an effort to control the mob was a doomed strategy. Little did he understand at the time that this work in the sociology of crowds would factor into his professional work.

His senior thesis involved both creating and (attempting) to solve for a Königsberg Bridge problem in three dimensions. The famous mathematical puzzle asked if one were able to cross the seven bridges in the city of Königsberg, traversing each bridge only once, a problem without a solution but which helped create the field of graph theory. Shaw created a three-dimensional structure of "bridges" and determined how to move across each bridge only once without doubling back. Rather than seeing this as a problem in mathematics, Shaw saw this as a problem of logistics.

He was apprenticed at the Twin Cities Autonomous Transportation Network (TCATN). Students who designed their own idiosyncratic programs often found it difficult to find work after graduation. Fortuitously, a learning coordinator at the Institute happened upon a listing in a job board for a traffic controller. Like other metropolitan areas, the skies over Minneapolis-St. Paul were littered with drones and other flying vehicles. Managing the flow of delivery drones, surveillance drones, and passenger aircraft—to say nothing of the autonomous vehicles that scurried between the cities—required coordination and control. Shaw was situated at a terminal in a nondescript building in downtown St. Paul and was responsible, along with a team of ten others, for monitoring traffic flows. Working with others proved difficult for Shaw. He rarely socialized with his coworkers outside of the traffic center. He didn't dislike hockey, but didn't really follow it the same way his workmates did. In his introspective moments, he concluded that he didn't really understand people, nor how to communicate with them. He nevertheless worked very hard at communication skills and building a store of social capital—he could never have risen to the position that he did without it. He learned that if he "knew the score" he would have something to talk about. Reaching this stage was a painful and laborious personal journey for Shaw.

Like a nightwatchman, Shaw was paid to largely stare at monitors, occasionally communicating to his fellow controllers about a bottleneck in the traffic flow, or dispatching responders in the event of the occasional accident. But the job also gave Shaw the leisure to think, especially how he might organize and control traffic flow via techniques he learned controlling murmuration and sheep and ants. He saw no difference between vehicles and starlings, delivery drones and ants and began work on the assumption that autonomous traffic flow could be controlled just as he controlled these other flocks. He began to see traffic flow as a ballet, with himself as choreographer. In his after hours, he began designing what would become his Autonomous Transport Coordination Protocol (ATCP).

Shaw reasoned that a city full of autonomous drones and vehicles was no different than a flock of sheep or a school of fish or a colony of ants. To organize and coordinate their movements meant first identifying the rules that underlie their collective behavior and then devising a mechanism to control or otherwise coordinate that behavior, a "sheepdog," if you will. ATCP was an algorithm that encoded the rules of engagement of autonomous traffic. These rules included vehicles staying close to neighboring vehicles—but not too close—each matching each other's speed and direction, avoiding collisions. Unlike schools or flocks, each individual vehicle had a particular goal or destination in mind. They did not simply follow along with others, and Shaw's algorithm had to account for this. A key feature of the control of autonomous traffic was that the vehicles needed to be in communication with each other, and this featured prominently in the ATCP code.

Shaw presented his idea to TCATN executives, who immediately saw the implications of what he was proposing. At this presentation, Shaw did not yet present the underlying source code. He was smart enough to realize that this was potentially valuable intellectual property. Also, he could demonstrate that this work was done as on his own time, and so the city or state could not claim this as part of his work assignment. After some negotiation, Shaw was named Director of Traffic, the intellectual property to be shared between Shaw and the two municipalities. This was a less than ideal settlement for Shaw, who was content to remain a traffic controller and not have the responsibility to manage others. TCATN would not allow him to retain all of the intellectual property, and presented this option as take-it-or-leave-it. Rather than a protracted legal battle, Shaw decided to become director.

If ATCP was to work, all autonomous traffic would need to be fitted with a communications device which could transmit and receive signals from other vehicles. Also, the Twin Cities would need to create their own fleet of "sheepdogs," as Shaw took to calling them. These would be vehicles controlled by TCATN that would roam around the cities, directing traffic flows, organizing movements without the need for traffic lights—which Shaw labeled as "dumb systems"—or other traditional forms of traffic control. Under this system, traffic flow would be self-organizing, except for those moments when a "sheepdog" was required to provide order. TCATN contracted with a company to manufacture the communication devices, and a city ordinance was enacted that required all autonomous vehicles to be fitted with one.

The success of the ATCP program in Minnesota meant that Shaw's talent was in demand. If the world of urban traffic control had a rock star, Shaw was most certainly it. The Los Angeles Department of Transportation (LADOT) hired him away, and soon enough he would oversee a team that sat in traffic towers scattered about the city. Their task was to maintain safe, orderly traffic flows of air-mobiles. LADOT had hired a number of former air traffic controllers from LAX, most of whom had been made redundant, as the number of long-haul aircraft had been dwindling. AI managed most of the remaining flights over LAX, another reason why there were fewer air traffic controllers needed. But even the best systems still required humans in the loop. Airplanes that flew on jet fuel had been discontinued (although the United States was the last major economy to outlaw the planes, a rearguard action to reduce carbon emissions). Airplane travel was still used for overseas flights, but these had been superseded by craft that flew on alternative fuels. These flights were fewer in number than what flew two decades before. Most long-distance travel domestically occurred via e-vehicles or over high-speed rail (the United States was very late in building a small passenger railway network).

And so, the skies over Los Angeles became his new office. The traffic in the air had shifted away from airplanes toward drones and autonomous vehicles, and especially to the management of the movement of air-mobiles. Futurists had long predicted the arrival of "flying cars" for decades, but they never seemed to materialize. The technology of personalized flight was always readily at hand; indeed, most air-mobiles were a scaled-up version of the drone technology that had been around for decades. The first air-mobiles began flying over Los Angeles seven years before Shaw's arrival. These were very expensive crafts, chauffeuring the wealthy about the city. As long as only a few dozen were airborne, there was no real problem. Motorists stuck in 6-lane traffic jams would look up raging with jealousy at the flying cars that soared overhead, up and out of the traffic. Inevitably, the price came down and more and more commuters switched to electric air-mobiles which, of course, created new traffic problems. Drivers of air-mobiles were told to fly at heights below that of helicopters and what little commercial aircraft remained in the sky, but otherwise they were permitted to freely move about in the air. Mid-air collisions became more common such that the Los Angeles mayor decided to act. Air-mobiles would need to fly over existing roads at a height of no more than 12 ft. This amount of order significantly reduced accidents—but did not eliminate them—and had the effect of replacing terrestrial traffic jams with airborne ones, hundreds of air-mobiles hovering over the city freeways. Interestingly, as the skies filled with air-traffic, the streets were largely emptied of automobiles and trucks. For a time, Los Angeles' enormous six-lane freeways were filled with bikes and scooters, and it seemed that LA might become a walkable 15-minute city, something not even futurists of a previous generation could have imagined. But then air-mobiles grew in popularity such that the number of cyclists dwindled, and the freeways were overgrown with weeds. The abandoned freeways became prime real estate for shops, bodegas and other retail, a ribbon of commerce where there once was limitless vehicular traffic.

The number of air-mobiles had grown to such an extent that the city had no choice but to open up the skies to all traffic and to allow air-mobiles to travel freely without being tethered above the freeways. Before this could go into effect, a new traffic infrastructure was required, and Shaw was hired to design and build this. Shaw installed a modified version of the system he designed for the Twin Cities. That system assumed fully autonomous traffic; while there were certainly autonomous drones flying over Los Angeles, many of the air-mobiles were still piloted by human drivers. Shaw proposed that a law be passed requiring all air-mobiles to be autonomous and self-driving—to better control their collective movement—but this proved politically and logistically difficult. Requiring each vehicle to have a government-approved sensor on board was challenging enough but was nevertheless made into law. Shaw's air traffic system was based on a few rules and was assisted by autonomous "sheepdogs." The Shaw Infrastructure becomes the global standard for air mobile and autonomous traffic control for large cities around the world. This time, Shaw insisted that the intellectual property remain in his control. He would set up a company to commercialize the Shaw Infrastructure and to otherwise allow him to benefit from his designs.

His Infrastructure established as the global standard, Shaw began to contemplate a life beyond controlling the traffic over Los Angeles. As he readied a resignation letter to LADOT, a new crisis erupted that city leaders hoped Shaw would be able to solve. Los Angeles had been infested with feral drones, mini-drones designed by the military to flock or school as a way to defeat anti-aircraft detectors. These had been accidently released from an R&D center in Riverside and now dispersed like locust across Southern California. Harmless by themselves—these were unarmed and were smaller than the palm of your hand—in groups they could disrupt traffic flows and interrupt daily life and otherwise make life miserable. Like large mosquitoes or mayflies, they were not dangerous but were exceedingly annoying. Shaw developed a "sheepdog" drone, one that would harness and steer the swarm away from the city, and within a year the drone swarm had been dissipated such that it no longer posed a problem. There was then a move to name Shaw Director of Public Safety, which he accepted. Some thought he was more influential than the mayor or any city council member.

Cities such as Los Angeles had become sites for regular protests, riots and urban unrest. Water riots were a regular occurrence, as were clashes between the city's rival NFL teams. Ultras from the Chargers, Rams and Cheetahs regularly clashed after games involving the teams. One particularly violent clash erupted after the Cheetahs won promotion to the NFL. Shaw idly wondered recalling his study of the sociology of mobs—if those ultras moved according to similar principles as feral drones, or starlings—leaderless, yet coordinated by simple rules of proximity. His first major initiative as Director of Public Safety was to both study the problem and devise solutions for controlling—even mitigating—these rioters.

During his off hours, Shaw began writing down a few thoughts. He did not keep a close circle of friends, did not socialize with work colleagues. Especially after ascending into management, Shaw kept his distance. He rarely attended events hosted by city leaders and largely kept out of the public eye. Instead, he would retreat to his apartment and write. Shaw Infrastructure was lucrative, earning him enormous sums of passive income. He needn't have kept the job as Director of Public Safety, except only that it gave him access to a laboratory to test his theories. His writings were reflections on what he had learned over the last few years, less about traffic management and more about human behavior. Most people were like drones or starlings or ants, with only the illusion of individual will. As such, their actions could be controlled, managed, brought into order. He would bring that order.

To deal with the football riot problem, Shaw decided to conduct an experiment, the same impulse that led him to broadcast corn chips in order to control a colony of ants. He would disguise a police officer as a Cheetah supporter, who would infiltrate a post-match brawl. Shaw trained the officer to coordinate the actions of the unruly mob. In dealing with the feral drone problem, Shaw did not seek to eliminate all the drones, but to scatter them, to dissipate the swarm into harmless individuals. Shaw instructed the officer in techniques to move the rioters. The idea here is that the officer would have a goal different from the rioters, a difference that would make all the difference.

The first attempt did not go well. The officer ran to the front of a gang of supporters and shouted "This way!" No one followed him, most ignored him and headed in the other direction to smash storefront windows, those not already boarded up. Shaw learned that words alone, rhetoric by itself was insufficient. In his journals, he wondered if people could really be moved by words, or if it was actions that were the key to controlling collective behavior.

The next game Shaw took a different approach. Two groups of ultras faced off in a plaza and we're about to engage in hand-to-hand combat—like something out of the medieval battle. Rather than talking, Shaw instructed the officer—via a two-way communications system—to march in between the groups, grab a trash can and heave it through a shop window. At once the crowd cheered and began looting the store and smashing nearby shops, and, thus, not attacking each other.

Via this experiment, Shaw learned that he could redirect the actions of the crowd. From his college studies, he remembered that members of a crowd often give up their individuality, engaging in behavior they would never condone by surrendering to the mentality of the crowd. The trained police officer, the "sheep dog"—the only one present who maintained his individuality—could therefore control that mentality. He advised the city government that sending undercover officers posing as rioters could dampen and dissipate the crowds. He even suggested deploying lifelike robots who would be easier to program. There were not "a few bad apples" who were the ring leaders and who could be identified and arrested. The crowd itself was the leader and could only be managed as a single entity. Shaw proposed that the methods used in corralling rioters could be applied to a host of urban problems, crime being only one. Shaw began to theorize that social problems like homelessness and income inequality were at root logistical and control problems, that each were governed by a few rules. The free market was a kind of self-organizing system, one that could be controlled by an omniscient intellect, directing the actions of strategically-situated "sheepdogs" or "corn chips."

Shaw came to believe that he was a breed apart. In his journals, he was now writing that he had transcended the behavioral rules that govern the mass of humanity, and in so doing had earned the obligation to manage and control the crowd, to bring order, to bring organization to human affairs. Los Angeles was emblematic of a larger, indeed global, phenomenon. Disorder in the world springs from the lack of efficient controls. Although beautiful, the starlings' murmuration was directionless, uncontrolled. The ultras' violence was not directed to any higher purpose, the result being chaos, property destruction and death. Only a select few, like Shaw, were ordained to bring order, control, coordination to the chaos. Like any budding autocrat, Shaw was reading Nietzsche and started thinking of himself as an Übermensch. He realized at first with horror, and then with a kind of serene comfort that his thought sounded like Adolf Hitler, who often talked about the control of the crowd.

Over the past year, Shaw had been sitting in his apartment—he had since moved to a better, more upscale, exclusive neighborhood—puzzling at the code that would prove that human populations could be managed and controlled. He started to describe himself as a "designer of humans," with the designer as the giver of form, he who brings order to disorder, harmony to disharmony. The rules that governed the relationships between people were more numerous and complex than those that formed schools and herds and rioters and would need to regulate more than just the movement of objects in space. But he convinced himself that they were just as discernible. While he figured the underlying code, he also devised a scheme where everyone wears a sensor not unlike the one that he had installed on millions of drones and autonomous vehicles.

He called it cyberocracy, or social cybernetics. His plan was that once he had designed the control system, he would present his work to the mayor and city council. Los Angeles would be the test case, but he knew that eventually social cybernetics would have to expand to an entire country, perhaps even the world. He could bring order and peace to world affairs, if only everyone could be required to wear a sensor. A few Übermensch like him—if there were, in fact, others like him—could bring about social harmony, international peace and universal fraternity.

Under a pseudonym, he wrote a manifesto, "Design of the Crowd." After he released it to the feeds, in anonymity he became a kind of global thought leader discussing a variety of social problems and his solutions to them. Cyberocracy would replace traditional political leadership with cybernetic governance—the control of human beings. If politics was the negotiation of divergent interests, then it was simply another movement problem, logistics on a human scale.

The self-publication of "Design of the Crowd" became an historical hinge moment. Had he found a traditional publisher, these ideas would have been academized, perhaps would have been debated by policymakers, denounced by libertarians and settled into bland public discourse. But in publishing it himself as a kind of samizdat, the manifesto gained a large cult following. Because it was published anonymously, many assumed its author was a Writer, though that didn't stop speculation as to who the "muse" was. As he had learned the hard way, this time he would keep the code to himself, with a plan to sell to the highest bidder.

He published "Design of the Crowd" after he had retired from the Director of Public Safety role. He had moved back to his parents' farm to care for them after their deaths five months apart. Shaw appropriated the farm, built a new house—really a compound—and hid away from the world. Writing his manifesto, he had determined the underlying code and designed a sensor system. He thought that the badges worn by most US citizens could be re-engineered to communicate with other devices, facilitating the "faints" and "nudges" necessary to steer the crowd in the appropriate direction. He also considered the headbands worn by many workers as a more direct form of mind control and interpersonal communication.

He approached Elliot Ross, a Los Angeles city council member with whom he had established a particular rapport, with a proposal for a social cybernetic system. Ross listened attentively—that Shaw was the author of "Design of the Crowd" was now clear to him—but ultimately said that he should scrap these plans, and not to mention them to anyone else. The United States had finally woken up from its attraction to fascism. Maybe if he pitched these ideas twenty years earlier, there would have been a ready audience. Shaw retorted that this was technocracy, not fascism, but Ross would not be persuaded. Ross also feared that retribution might follow Shaw if he were discovered to be the author of the manifesto. "Go back to Minnesota and control starlings," Ross advised.

Chastened, Shaw did return to Minnesota, but only to regroup. For the past seven months, he had been consulting with the US Army on the management and control of autonomous weapon systems. The Pentagon were looking to improve their capabilities in this area, having lost its lead to China and Bharat. Shaw used channels in the Army to test out his ideas for social cybernetics. He was politely declined, although the Pentagon kept secret watch over Shaw's movement and communications, concerned that he might offer this plan to a foreign government. They certainly had reason to be suspicious. Shaw was surveilled meeting with a low-level member of the Chinese Communist Party who apparently had an interest in social cybernetics as a control mechanism for their eco-authoritarian system.

Shaw was returning to Minnesota from a trip to New York—possibly to negotiate with another foreign government, possibly Venezuela or Kazakhstan—when he was shot through the skull with a high caliber rifle. The consensus opinion is that Shaw was assassinated—by whom was never conclusively determined—although there are skeptics who continue to maintain that because he was not a publicly prominent figure, this could not have been a strategic or symbolic murder. These critics maintain that Shaw was the victim of the casual violence that had long infected the United States.

Had he found a partner, either a polity or a company that could have made the idea of wearing a sensor palatable to a large number of people, he might have exercised control over the global population. He might have become the singular Übermensch as he had long fantasized. As such, Matthew Shaw's impact on world history became a counterfactual, a story of what might have been.

Key Futures Themes

- Swarm Intelligence
- Autonomous Transport and Urban Infrastructure
- Social Cybernetics
- Power, Surveillance and Authoritarian Drift
- Design Ethics

Bibliography

Buford, Bill. 1993. *Among the Thugs*. New York: Vintage Books.

Drury, John. 2020. Recent Developments in the Psychology of Crowds and Collective Behaviour. *Current Opinion in Psychology* 35:12–16. https://www.sciencedirect.com/science/article/abs/pii/S2352250X20300221.

Jaffe, Eric. 2014. If Cops Understood Crowd Psychology, They'd Tone Down The Riot Gear. *Fast Company*, 27 August 2014. https://www.fastcompany.com/3034902/if-cops-understood-crowd-psychology-theyd-tone-down-the-riot-gear.

Jayalath, Pramodaya. 2023. Flocking Algorithm: Simulating Collective Behavior in Nature-Inspired Systems. *Medium*, 4 August 2023. https://medium.com/@pramodayajayalath/flocking-algorithm-simulating-collective-behavior-in-nature-inspired-systems-dc6d7fb884cc.

Nitti, Alessandro, Marco D. de Tullio, Ivan Federico, and Giuseppe Carbone. 2025. A Collective Intelligence Model for Swarm Robotics Applications. *Nature Communications* 16:6572. https://doi.org/10.1038/s41467-025-61985-7.

Chapter 9
Lindsay Davidson: Muse

Lindsay Robert Davidson was the recipient of the first Pulitzer Prize in the category "Muse." He was born in San Diego, California to parents Richard, an executive at the biotech firm NeuroGen, and Mikaila, a learning coordinator. His mother instilled a love of literature at an early age. She read of the Icelandic celebration of Jólabókaflóð, the "Christmas book flood" where family and friends give each other books on Christmas Eve, and then everyone curls up with hot chocolate to read into the night. When Lindsay was eight—and even though they were not Icelandic—his mother began this family tradition that was practiced until her death. In contrast to others his age, throughout his adolescence, Davidson had read *The Wretched of the Earth, The Magic Mountain,* and *Their Eyes Were Watching God* before graduating high school.

Inspired by his mother, as a boy Davidson dreamed of becoming a writer. At age 12, he started writing in a journal. These journals contained short stories, biographies, and what he later called "pretend journalism," where he would write commentaries on the state of the world, his opinions on public matters, as if he were a real journalist. These journal entries were largely about the state of his favorite football team and video game reviews, but as he matured he would also comment on global affairs in the style of the analysist, commentator and novelist Moises Naim, one of his idols. Naim's novel *Two Spies in Caracas* was his Jólabókaflóð gift one Christmas. Lindsay kept to his writing in private, sharing it only with his parents. He would have surely been mocked and bullied at school were his hobby known by his classmates. Lindsay was as much attracted to the image of the writer, at least the image in his mind. He once Googled an image of Hemingway sitting at a low table, probably on safari in Africa, since a pair of binoculars and a tent feature in the photograph. He writes by hand in a notepad. There were many other such pictures, usually of the older Hemingway scribbling with pen and paper. Lindsay took up this practice, rather than reciting his words to the audio transcriber or even using an old-fashioned keyboard, he would write by hand in his journal. Luckily, manufacturers

D. Staley, *Anticipatory Biographies*, Anticipation Science 10,
https://doi.org/10.1007/978-3-032-08912-0_9

were still producing ballpoint pens, although his parents had to specially order these; Moleskine was still in business. More than the love of language, more than the satisfaction of the rhythm of prose, Lindsay was drawn to the idea of the writer as hero.

Davidson attended high school at Westbrook Academy, which provided him with an excellent education, but not one in which he could develop his writing. His parents were part of the first generation of students using the widely available open access generative AI tools. Naturally, these students used these tools to write their own compositions, at first as a way to cheat. For example, many of Mikaila's classmates found generative AI a convenient way to write their college-admissions essays. Teachers soon caught on to the deception and railed against yet another technology encroaching into the classroom. Teachers feared a new form of plagiarism, but then later their chief concern was that students would lose the ability to write, off-loading this most elevated of human cognitive abilities to a machine. Professional conferences and journal articles debated generative AI and the fate of the teaching of composition, as an earlier generation of educators fretted about the fate of mathematics instruction when cheap consumer-grade pocket calculators flooded the market. "Should we teach writing?" became the new pedagogical debate.

And indeed, many local school boards wondered if the classroom time teaching students to write paragraphs and essays was really of any use. If they were to teach anything, teachers should teach prompting, the sentence or two that actuates the generative AI program. But even then, how much time should students spend learning to prompt when there were more pressing subjects that required attention, especially the STEM disciplines. By the time Lindsay entered high school, a "Writer" was an algorithm, a tool that generated text. At one time, a "computer" referred to a human who made calculations but was now the name of a device. Similarly, a "Writer" no longer referred to a person, but to an automated device. When anyone opened a Word document, the "Writer" tool would appear in the upper right corner, ready to be prompted. To call oneself a "writer" seemed odd and eccentric, so Lindsay refrained from identifying himself as such in public. Writing as a school subject withered, especially since it no longer appeared to be a "career-ready" skill. If the workforce demands that employees produce emails, memos, and reports, and the Writer was built to do exactly that, then why emphasize the teaching of writing?

Davidson learned to write in his room, on his own, in his journals, a hobby like collecting Pokémon cards or playing basketball. But like his classmates, he also learned how to use a Writer and eventually he learned to enjoy using it. He was not at all enamored of the turgid prose it generated, but he was interested in the intelligence behind the programming. He wondered in his journals if an artificial intelligence might be built that could create actual literature.

Davidson won admission to Harvard, where he would double-major in cognitive science—with an emphasis on artificial intelligence—and English literature. He was grateful to have been admitted, since Harvard maintained one of the few remaining university programs in reading books and writing literature. Had he gone to college elsewhere, he would have likely been forced to join other students like him in forming extracurricular literary societies at their universities, a practice which harkened back to nineteenth century colleges, since so many colleges and universities had dropped English, creative writing and journalism programs from their formal curriculums. By the time he graduated from Harvard, writing code and creating algorithms had become a largely automated industry. Those who wrote code were hired to produce programs that would write other programs. The field of prompt engineering certainly sought graduates with English or literature degrees; given his training in AI and writing, Davidson was a unique case that made him especially attractive to employers. For Davidson, prompt engineering was simply an evolution in coding. He described both instances as "giving instructions to a computer," only the language used was different in each case.

Davidson learned the literary production trade by working for the James Patterson Company. Next-generation Writers had advanced to the stage where the application could reliably mimic the style of Patterson, producing potboilers long after his death. Patterson's brand had grown such that the best-selling author composed the outline of a new story that would then be written by an assistant who would then receive a smaller billing on the cover of the novel. In effect, Patterson was performing the role of a "prompter." Before his death, Patterson had partnered with a technology company to develop an artificial intelligence that could mimic the distinct Patterson style. This was a Writer trained on the scores of books Patterson had published. Already a brand name, Patterson formalized his name as a corporation, one that would not only manage his intellectual property after his death but that would produce new works in Patterson's distinct—if formulaic—voice. Patterson's company contracted with prompt engineers who would write out a 200-word basis of a story, the Writer producing works to please the legion of fans who until this day consume these books. The covers of these new works would be emblazoned with Paterson's name as the author, the prompt engineer mentioned only on the acknowledgement page after the names of the CEO and VP for development of the Patterson Company.

Davidson began his career in journalism, where he prompted for the *Columbus Dispatch*, the *New York Times*, the *Wall Street Journal* and *The Economist*, mostly prompting sports stories, then accounts of political debates in state legislatures, and then later financial reporting. Sports prompting was probably the worst job of all of these, as it mostly involved just data collecting from the court or ball field, the Writer turning this into prose. Financial reporting was not much better.

An old roommate from Harvard, Owen Dawson, became a state senator for New York, and Davidson spent two years as one of his speechprompters. Most politicians had given over their speech writing to Writers. They would bark "write me a speech on healthcare reform" and usually accept whatever results the machine produced. Legislators had access to proprietary software that would be trained on previous speeches, press conferences, op eds, or other such public statements. Dawson was old school in that he hired human prompters to craft well-wrought instructions to the Writer. Davidson had honed his editing capabilities while working as Dawson's speechwriter, writing and reprompting through several iterations. After a turn in government, he considered interviewing for a position at The Cato Institute prompting white papers, research reports and policy recommendations. Think tanks, especially, had pre-established ideological positions that were embedded in their Writers. Any subject then—war in Asia, domestic spending on homelessness, income inequality—had programmed responses, the prompter providing the dimensions and context of a particular issue that the Writer would render into a coherent policy position. Davidson much preferred the work in journalism, as the outcomes of his prompts still had the capacity to surprise him.

After freelancing in journalism and speechprompting, Davidson accepted an offer to be a prompter at the James Patterson Company, although he had looked at other literary enterprises. The success of the Patterson Company meant that other enterprises emerged to re-produce new works of beloved authors. The estates of these authors, especially, set up companies to produce original works. There were revivals of Charles Dickens and H.G. Wells and Emily Bronte as literary companies created new works that joined the canon of these authors' works. He auditioned for a prompter position at the Ernest Hemingway Corporation, and got a second call back to work at Octavia Butler Ltd. before landing at "The Original," as Patterson was known in the business.

For about a decade there was something of a "wild west" in the literary enterprise space. There were companies whose business model was to Write a young adult novel "in the style of" Hemingway or a space opera "in the style of" Mark Twain, but those companies who mimicked Hemingway, for instance, were quickly sued. The estates of literary giants were quick to incorporate as generative AI businesses, although courts were initially not inclined to view AI mimicry of long-dead authors as any sort of copyright infringement, especially when previous works from the authors were in the public domain. At the same time, there emerged a consumer reaction to AI-generated writing and art works. Not unlike the anti-Genetically Modified Organism movement, there emerged a small "read only human writing" movement, a kind of Luddism that rejected anything written by an algorithm, most of which was not particularly good writing beyond its utilitarian value. Activists won concessions from publishers to affix an "AI-generated" label on every written work, whether novel, news story or non-fiction. Never a very large majority, the ROHW movement nevertheless slowed potential sales of AI-generated works.

Eventually, the courts began to favor estates over entrepreneurs without any familial or legal connections to dead authors. Other companies sought to avoid intellectual property battles by mixing different styles and genres and so would produce literary hybrids: Virginia Woolf with Hilary Mantel, George Eliot with George Orwell. Companies that produced hybrids claimed that they were not transgressing the Hemingway or Woolf "brand." Davidson would base his literary company on a variation of this hybrid model.

A particularly alarming and unpleasant court battle ensued when a literary company, The Bard Enterprises, started Writing new works by William Shakespeare. A dozen Oxbridge scholars brought suit claiming the need to protect this national treasure in the same way the Government might protect a manor house or some other treasure of National Heritage. Works claiming to be "neo-Shakespeare" denigrated the original, these scholars argued, and therefore Shakespeare should be off limits to AI mimicry. A similar case raged in Spain, where literary entrepreneurs post-created new works by Cervantes. At stake in this case was who was authorized—the relationship to the word "author" not lost on the litigants—to establish whether an AI-generated version of Shakespeare or Cervantes was canonical. The European Union, always keen to rein in the worst excesses of the tech sector while also protecting European heritage, passed legislation that certain authors' works were protected from being post-produced using AI, even if previous works by these authors were now in the public domain.

After six years at Patterson, Davidson joined with some Harvard friends as a founder of a literary start-up, the Thoth Company, named after the Egyptian god of writing (the company's logo featuring the head of an ibis). Thoth's business plan was not to simply reproduce dead authors or churn out low-brow fiction. Futurists and other sceptics had long maintained that Writers would not be capable of producing literature, writing of great artistic merit. Thoth was going to prove these doubters wrong by producing "the great AI novel."

Thoth's algorithms were more sophisticated than those of other literature companies. Davidson designed the software to simultaneously find patterns in a "data set"—in this case, the canon of world literature—and to also develop the capacity to write via machine learning. Combing the data to find patterns provided the enterprise with a unique syntax. The interaction with the human prompter produced semantics, which Davidson understood to be an emergent property of the interaction between human imagination and code. Philosophers had long debated whether generative AI applications were in fact "creating," especially given the vital role of the human prompter in the process. Davidson's contribution to this debate was to argue that the entire writing process was a complex adaptive cognitive system, which like all such systems is exquisitely sensitive to initial conditions. In the process, Davidson redefined prompting as the art of establishing the initial conditions of the creative work.

As the Writer became more sophisticated, the prompts simultaneously had to become more sophisticated. The first Writers that sparked Davidson's imagination as a student required prompts of only a sentence or two. The software developed here needed more than even a 250-word paragraph that was commonplace among prompting applications. Davidson role within the company was to compose prompts that would evolve into long-form 5000 word evocations, a kind of literature in themselves. After inputting the prompt, the algorithm produced a 120,000 word novel, the process taking about 14 minutes to complete. Composing such an extensive and complex prompt came naturally to Davidson, who one might say had been preparing for this moment his entire life. In his mind, prompting in this fashion was real writing, of the kind he scribbled in his journals as a boy.

Once the prompt satisfied his aesthetic sense, and after the Writer produced the first draft of the novel, Davidson would then edit the results. One of his achievements had been to redefine the process of editing to mean rewriting the prompt in response to and in conversation with the prose the Writer produced. The revised prompt was then once again inputted producing an updated novel, with subtle changes in tone, mood and direction of plot. He would read the results and again rewrite the prompt, an iterative process that might go through four or five cycles. Davidson referred to this writing/editing process as "a dialogue between human intelligence and artificial intelligence."

Like the art produced by artificial intelligence, this process produced a new style of literature unlike any seen before. Davidson titled the novel *The Deification of Adam and Eve*, and it hit the literary world the way James Joyce's *Finnegans Wake* or Walt Whitman's *Leaves of Grass* did decades before. The novel was an "alternative Old Testament," a fable that pondered a "what if?" where Adam and Eve are the corporeal manifestation of Yahweh. They are not cast out of Eden because of their sinfulness but instead were invited to create a new world by bringing the Light of the divine into it. Critics favorably compared the work to Kazantzakis, some dubbing it the Gnostic Testament.

Quite a few religious groups were furious at the blasphemy they claimed the book represented but were uncertain to whom they needed to vent their anger: the Writer or its prompter. Although they exercised little influence in New York City, the Morality Guardians announced that *The Deification of Adam and Eve* was sacrilegious, that it was a performance of violence against Christians and others who were guided by the Old Testament. They had no hesitation about whom to blame: Lindsay Davidson was the author of this blasphemy, and he would have to answer for it. They announced the unusual step of launching a crusade against Davidson—similar to the *fatwa* levied against Salman Rushdie decades earlier, a spiritual bounty on his head. It was not clear whether the Morality Guardians were advocating for Davidson's death. That was not their usual *modus operandi*, but the chilling language of the crusade made it appear that that was their intention.

Davidson was taking no chances. For a brief, but terrifying, few weeks, he went into hiding. He bunked with friends in the City for a few days but, still feeling vulnerable, escaped for an undisclosed location, which turned out to be an apartment in Albany maintained by Owen Dawson. Former Senator Dawson always rejected the Morality Guardians and was very happy to provide his friend's sanctuary. While in this temporary exile, Davidson wrote furiously, eventually producing an essay asking if it was still possible for a (human) writer to be dangerous. Maybe it was the adventure, but Davidson was almost thankful for the Morality Guardian's crusade, since it demonstrated that the writer—or his ideas—still had the power to provoke. All the great writers in history had offended someone at some stage. It was one of the best ways to gauge whether writing still mattered.

Davidson also used the occasion of the essay to criticize PEN America, which had become a shadow of its previous self. PEN had made no statement of support for Davidson, made no attempt to protect him or to challenge the Morality Guardians. Nowadays, PEN protected and championed the Book before the writer, or, rather, the prompter. In PEN's estimation, books are dangerous, but prompters less so. The human writer was invisible to them. *The Deification of Adam and Eve*, on the other hand, was fulsomely supported by PEN.

The furor eventually subsided when the influential theologian Seamus Doyle concluded that it was the Writer—the artificial intelligence—that created the novel and that because the AI does not possess a soul it cannot actually commit blasphemy. Davidson came out of hiding but was diminished by Doyle's defense. He walked freely and openly down the streets of New York for the first time in weeks, wondering to himself that maybe he was not so dangerous. Maybe he was not so heroic.

The critical reception and best-seller status of *The Deification of Adam and Eve* were one of the proximate causes for the creation of a new Pulitzer Prize category: the "Muse." The Pulitzer selection committee to this day have never been able to bring themselves to reward an AI "author," and indeed Pulitzer still makes no such award. Besides, there were already awards for Writer-generated literature: *Wired* magazine, in partnership with the MIT Media Lab, established the first, although it was not recognized by purists as a true literary prize. The Templeton Foundation established its own literary prize for the best work of "biterature." But the big literary prizes—The Booker, the National Book Award, certainly the Nobel committee—studiously and deliberately avoided awarding recognition to non-human authors. Instead, Pulitzer would create a prize for the "human inspiration" of a great work of biterature, becoming the first major prize to recognize human "muses."

Davidson was one of the first prompters to be listed prominently on the book cover, similar to how a translator was listed in smaller print below the original author. Of course, as CEO of the Thoth Company, he could place his name wherever he wanted. But until this point, prompters were largely anonymous: recognizing them would be like giving billing to the typesetter or the book binder.

Davidson was initially troubled by the recognition, specifically that the Pulitzer committee would use the term "muse" to describe his art. Historically, the source of artistic inspiration was typically a woman in a subordinate position to the Great Man, an asymmetrical sexual and creative relationship that he did not initially embrace. It was true that the Writer produced the 120,000 word novel that Davidson's words inspired. Indeed, literary critics wondered anew about "authorship" under these conditions, especially since Davidson was so central to the writing of the code that produced the novel. Davidson would argue that authorship was not embedded in a person but could instead be found in the relationship between two creative entities. He analogized prompting with an algorithm as like the relationship between two song writers. In accepting the Pulitzer, Davidson asked the audience to think of how Lennon and McCartney wrote songs: it was impossible to disentangle John's contribution from Paul's. Although it appeared there was an obvious division between the 5000-word prompt and the final output, much transpired in that black box of creative generation. The human prompter had his own style, and the human voice was as evident in *The Deification of Adam and Eve* as the algorithmic voice. The Writer could not have created the novel of its own volition, for it had none. The Writer still required the spark of creativity and insight that the human prompter provided.

Receiving a literary prize for prompting seemed like second place, an anxiety Davidson harbored in secret. In public, of course, in his role as CEO, the Thoth company thumped its chest at the award, with its promise of future sales as readers would eagerly await the next masterpiece. Indeed, Davidson had already started thinking about the company's next work the day after receiving the Pulitzer. He found the process of prompting very much like writing—convincing himself that it *was* writing, amplified into literature in partnership with the Writer.

Part of Davidson's unspoken private concerns included how he would be viewed by "writers," those few remaining heroes who continued to write literature the old way, unaided by AI. He had been in love with the written word since childhood, with aspirations to be his generation's Hemingway. When interviewed—and with great conviction—Davidson announced himself and believed himself to be a writer. Did William S. Burroughs' cut-up poetry make him any less a poet because he assembled word fragments? Is the writer the one responsible for composing every single word in a composition?

After the success of *The Deification of Adam and Eve*, Davidson allowed himself the opportunity to write outside of the Thoth company. Even as he built the technology of his literary enterprise, Davidson kept a pen and notebook in his office, the tools of his prompting. But he would also write commentaries, reviews, short stories and even a novel. Most of these were self-published through Thoth, as there were few such opportunities for human writers. Because his company was successful, he did not need an advance or big royalties, which, in any event, were quite meager anyway. Reading had become automated, much of what is written is produced by bots and read by and consumed by bots. There were only a few big name (human) writers, and also a very small cadre of readers of human-produced writing. Human writers and readers tended to cluster in global portal cities and university towns.

After three more critically acclaimed novels, Davidson retired from Thoth to accept the inaugural Professor of Literary Production at the University of Iowa. His appointment was celebrated by the faculty who, with only token opposition, welcome a first-of-its-kind prize-winning author as a way to revive Iowa's once-thriving creative writing Workshop. Now that there was a literary prize for prompting, a new generation of students came to university with a renewed interest in writing. The success of the literary start-up scene meant that there was a revival of the English major at many schools, albeit still limited to the Ivies, the select liberal arts colleges and the large state flagship schools. He taught generations of students how to prompt, how to coax great writing from a sophisticated Writer by composing the most evocative and inspiring prose.

Ever the innovator, Davidson used his academic position to promote musing—he had finally come to accept the term—as a new form of literary criticism: that considering the process of literary production was an effective way to read and interpret literature. He worked with apprentice writers to examine how books from the past were assembled, from creative idea, to early drafts, to sources of inspiration, to editing, to publication. He taught that understanding how a work of literature was produced was key to how we should read and interpret it.

After he had won the Pulitzer, Davidson's prompts were collected and published, first as an appendix to *The Deification of Adam and Eve*, later as a collection. To this day, critics continue to view Davidson's prompts almost like studies or sketches ahead of some great painting or sculpture, valuable to read and critique as any other piece of literature. Indeed, they still led some readers to wonder if the prompts were the real literature, that the Writer could not produce a work of great power and beauty without the human prompter providing so much of the text. Only the prompter, the muse possessed true creative imagination.

Key Futures Themes

- Human-AI Collaboration in Creativity
- Intellectual Property and Cultural Heritage
- Cultural Resistance
- Literary Futures

Bibliography

Caldwell, Mackenzie. 2023. What Is an "Author"?-Copyright Authorship of AI Art Through a Philosophical Lens. *Houston Law Review* 61:411. https://houstonlawreview.org/article/92132-what-is-an-author-copyright-authorship-of-ai-art-through-a-philosophical-lens.

Childress, Clayton. 2019. *Under the Cover: The Creation, Production, and Reception of a Novel.* Princeton: Princeton University Press.

du Sautoy, Marcus. 2019. *The Creativity Code: Art and Innovation in the Age of AI.* Cambridge: Belknap Press.

Miller, Arthur I. 2019. *The Artist in the Machine: The World of AI-Powered Creativity.* Cambridge: The MIT Press.

Oppenlaender, Jonas, Rhema Linder, and Johanna Silvennoinen. 2024. Prompting AI Art: An Investigation into the Creative Skill of Prompt Engineering. *International Journal of Human-Computer Interaction* 41 (16): 10207–10229. https://doi.org/10.1080/10447318.2024.2431761.

Swirski, Peter. 2013. *From Literature to Biterature: Lem, Turing, Darwin, and Explorations in Computer Literature, Philosophy of Mind, and Cultural Evolution.* Montreal/Kingston: McGill-Queen's University Press.

Chapter 10
Richard Blankenship: Unproductive

Richard Blankenship watched his father struggle and vowed never to end up like him. Richard Sr. was a coal miner in West Virginia, but like many blue collar jobs, automation made it difficult to find work. Richard Sr. had trained to get his operator's license and become a long-haul truck driver, although the family had to go into debt in order to pay for this training. The Blankenships were not atypical, making sacrifices in order to keep up with the automation economy. Despite his father's retraining, Richard Jr. watched his dad lose his job: once trucks were made pilotless, crisscrossing interstates, the "driver" operated 8–10 of these rigs from a centralized location. Rather than trying to do something else, his dad left the labor force, ending up on disability, the only option he felt was open to him. Economists began counting those who no longer participated in the labor force, although they did not have any theories to address the reasons, the causes for leaving the labor force. The causes were too individual, too unique to craft a policy solution. This meant little to Richard Sr.

Richard was determined not to suffer the same fate as his father. He attended a coding bootcamp, which he understood to be an "in demand" job that paid well. The $25,000 cost was easily enough handled (interest rates were low, and he had acquired a decent enough paying job that his loan was paid off in less than a year.) But upon gaining his first job, he discovered that his coding skills were being automated. Indeed, much of his job involved writing code that would itself write code. After writing the code that would make him unemployed more times than he cared to remember, it finally dawned on Richard that he was being hired for the sole purpose of making himself redundant.

At age 30 he trained for a new job: biocoding. This required attending community college, as biocoding was not yet "bootcamped." Some companies started paying tuition for these future employees, and Richard was able to take advantage of this opportunity—there would have been no other way to afford his training. Richard takes a job with a biotech company after graduation, but once again discovers he

D. Staley, *Anticipatory Biographies*, Anticipation Science 10, https://doi.org/10.1007/978-3-032-08912-0_10

was hired to make himself redundant. This becomes the *modus operandi* of the automation economy: (human) workers are hired to either write the code or otherwise train autonomous agents to do their tasks.

Those who do the automating are the ones who retain jobs in this economy. Companies are run by entrepreneurs who create "automation/redundancy" firms. Automation/redundancy becomes the new buzzword, which at one time would have been "disruption and innovation."

Having been drummed out of the biocoding field, Richard trained to become a teacher, but even this job was automated. He found that he had joined a race to find jobs that have yet to be automated. But this was a race that many were running and, like Richard, were losing. His father told him to "learn a trade," but even these jobs were being automated. He even considered working as a farm laborer, but when automated fruit picking and harvesting became widely used, seasonal migrant labor dried up.

Richard Jr. was reaching an age when he could not continue to train for a new job. Either he could not continue to pay for his own training (actually, his own redundancy) or, as he grew older with more responsibilities, he could not afford the time to retrain, or indeed to expend the energy. Like many workers, Richard went through the repeating cycle of training—hiring—redundancy—training—hiring—redundancy—training…

His wife Maddie was a nurse (an acceptable job for a woman, the care economy was dominated by women). She learned some medical skills in the military and apprenticed at a hospital. She worked for a medical center that catered to an upper-class clientele. Autonomous agents carried out the bulk of most health care: it was a sign of wealth and status to have a human serving you. Medi-robots were for the poor.

She tried to convince her husband to find work as a domestic servant. Women were expected to carry out most caring functions—so it was difficult for Richard to apprentice as a nurse—but there were positions for butlers and valets. Richard daydreamed about becoming a gardener—he would spend summers growing up attending to the family garden—but most of this work has been automated.

The winners of the automation/redundancy economy felt they needed new ways to demonstrate their wealth. A large home in a toney neighborhood, a good education for their children, expensive, well-engineered personal automobiles were no longer sufficient. Nor were simply hiring gardeners and maids and au pairs enough: this class revived the practice of surrounding themselves with household servants. The new class marker was the number and type of servant one had at their beck and call. In an economy where so many jobs had been automated, jobs taken out of human hands, having humans serve you in your own home—as opposed to a waiter at a restaurant or a flight attendant—was the new status symbol.

Maddie implored him to take a servant's position. He did not know if he had the right training—or temperament—to be able to do this. She learned from a patient of a service that vetted prospective candidates and placed them with wealthy families. Reluctantly, Richard interviewed with the firm and within two weeks was connected to a family in a gated community.

Kayden Browne was a founder of a company that automated the low end of the nursing home industry. The company developed a line of AI-infused robots—not human-like, wanting to avoid the challenges of the uncanny valley—that would attend to the needs of the elderly on a 24-hour basis. One of the chief problems with nursing homes, skilled nursing facilities and other such enterprises is that, while the patients required and benefitted from around-the-clock attention, these businesses were rarely staffed with enough workers who could muster the compassion and care patients desired. Browne's company would disrupt this industry: the robots, aided by sensors and other surveillance technologies, would constantly monitor patients, determining their needs at any given moment, whether that was food/nutrition, medicines, sleep or, most often, companionship. The robots—and here is where AI was most helpful—were excellent listeners and conversationalists. Browne claimed to have eliminated loneliness in his company's facilities, or at least had reduced it greatly. Richard would later wonder why these jobs couldn't be filled with humans, even if it involved cleaning bed pans and other unpleasant duties, which they were, of course. In high-end nursing facilities, human nurses, doctors and orderlies attended to their wealthy patrons, the kind of place Browne was destined for in a few decades. The irony of the mission of the company was, of course, lost on Browne: that the wealthy and privileged surround themselves with human servants, finding robots very much beneath them. For now, the founder would reap the benefits of automating yet another part of the care economy.

Before he was officially hired, Richard met with Browne mostly to confirm the placement agency's decision that they would be a good match, especially since Richard's job would be to serve as Browne's valet. The word had re-acquired its original meaning: Richard was to serve as Browne's personal attendant, making certain that his clothes were pressed and well-tailored. Richard was responsible for laundering his suits and jackets, which meant taking them to the dry cleaners. (Since cars now parked themselves, the valet as a parking lot attendant had largely disappeared.) On a day-to-day basis, this meant that Richard would prepare Browne's shower, making certain towels, shampoo, body wash were laid out. Some days he would shave Browne and even trimmed his hair. His only prior experience was shaving himself, and so Richard frantically scoured on-line tutorials for how to cut hair. Richard elaborated on his application that he knew how to perform such personal grooming services, and indeed the first time he shaved Browne there might have been a small nick.

Most days, Richard would accompany Browne to business meetings or other events, ostensibly to attend to whatever needs he might have, but in reality to serve as a living display of Browne's conspicuous consumption. Evenings were taken up with preparing his eveningware, keeping his tuxedo creased and free of lint. As a valet, Richard was expected to maintain himself: clean shaven, hair stylish. He was provided with a uniform of well-tailored sports coats and slacks, and was expected to carry himself in a quiet, dignified, supportive—if unobtrusive—manner. Browne invited Richard to converse with his business contacts and was expected to be a raconteur. He did not understand all the references his interlocutors used, but thankfully any such conversations were at the level of sophisticated small talk. He had to admit that in addition to dressing well, Richard learned a great deal in the three years he was employed.

Richard settled into this life, uncomfortably at first. To Richard, preparing a shower or laundering a shirt struck him as "women's work," or more precisely the job of a parent to a child, something unbefitting of a man—Richard often wondered what his father would think of his new occupation. By the end of his first year of employment, Richard had earned the trust of Browne—ten years his junior—such that the two would engage in easy conversation during their commutes to places. Perhaps the biggest disruption to Richard and Maddie's lives was the long trips Richard was required to take with his employer. Browne would usually not pack clothes on business trips; instead, Richard would, upon landing in a new city, shop for shirts, suits, undergarments, socks and shoes. Occasionally, this meant retaining the services of a tailor in whatever city they might be in. Richard intended to learn how to tailor but would never have the time to do so. Upon reflection, Richard found these trips to have been the most memorable of his time in Browne's employ: he would never have had the opportunity to travel the world. This schedule kept him away from Maddie and family for long stretches; Browne provided him with a small apartment at the family's compound, about 30 miles from Richard and Maddie's apartment. The strain on their marriage was offset by the steady and substantial paycheck Richard provided. Although she missed her husband, Maddie was delighted that Richard was finally contributing support to the family.

One evening when Maddie was working a night shift, Richard ordered a pizza for himself and his two sons, a rare treat that might help him reconnect with his family. The delivery app said 30 minutes, and that Richard could track its progress to their apartment on his device. Richard had had food delivered countless times, so it was only in hindsight that he noticed it on this occasion. He opened the door to stand face-to-face with the delivery drone. He had already paid, of course, and now only had to input his delivery code to unlock the compartment that held his pizza. As he stood motionless, the drone beckoned him to input the code, a simple procedure. The pleasant, if automated, voice woke him from his stupor, and he inputted the code. As the door released, something inside Richard snapped. After removing the pizza and before closing the door Richard grabbed the iron rod he kept by the door for security purposes and, mustering all his strength—or was it rage?—smashed the device out of the air. He had caught the rotors with enough force that he could down the drone, falling to the ground like a wounded bird. He proceeded to pummel the device, rendering it inoperative. He did not know, or care, if there were any other deliveries in the box that would now go undelivered. The entire incident lasted only about a minute and a half, but its consequences would linger for the rest of his life.

Although it was not uncommon for delivery drones to be tampered with, there were only a few instances of the kind of vandalism Richard had engaged in. Perhaps because of the damage to the property, Richard was fined $500 and spent 30 days in jail. House arrest was a more common punishment, but the judge wanted to make him an example. In those 30 days, Richard reconstructed what happened, something he could not explain to the magistrate at his hearing. Something snapped. The delivery drone came to symbolize his life, or the threats to his life. At one time, there was a human being who would have walked up to his door to deliver his food. Maybe he would have even struck up a conversation, talked about the game last night. Maybe he was a familiar face, a guy with a family like him. All that was gone now, of course, the pizza guy replaced by a machine. Just like him.

That pizza drone was a personification of automation and redundancy, that…thing he had been resisting his entire adult life. (His father succumbed as well, without resorting to violence.) Maybe, if he destroyed this one drone, he could bring a job back to just one human delivery driver. If there were no machines like the drone, maybe he would not have to be a servant. "That machine caused my servility," he reasoned from his jail cell. "That's why I can't look at my kids…"

His confinement afforded Richard the time to consider what his life had become. He was a valet, a "manservant." Right there in the name: he was a servant, he *served* someone. He had been taught that "service" was a noble calling, even an obligation from God. What he did was not service: this was servility, menial, subservient, demeaning, dehumanizing. "My God," he said aloud in his cell one afternoon, "I help a grown man who cannot wash or dress himself!" The last time he was in this position was when he would give his boys a bath or to help them tie a necktie before special occasions.

After he had served his 30-day sentence, Richard slinked home and retreated to his basement. He, of course, lost his job as a valet—no self-respecting family would have a criminal on their staff. In addition to losing his job and the jail sentence, Richard was mocked and ridiculed on the feeds. Surveillance-cam footage had captured his assault on the delivery drone, and Richard's rage against the machine became the stuff of comic memes. Most commentators laughed at the fury unleashed on an inanimate object. "Didn't get the order right?" snickered other commentators. As with all memes, Richard's attack was excised from its original context to be placed in new settings by clever content creators. Richard was now depicted attacking hated celebrities and influencers in one, the quarterback of a hapless team in another, a politician's opponent in yet another. Beyond his jail sentence, the humiliation of being a meme was probably enough for him to be unemployable.

Confining himself to the basement, at first he played video games, escaping into fantasy worlds. He found himself drawn to increasingly violent games, where he was playing the role of a terrorist. Without thinking about it too much, Richard found himself drawn to the "bad guys" in these games. He disconnects from his family, does not volunteer, and certainly does not attempt to find another job. Finally, after two months of this, Maddie wanted nothing to do with him and filed for divorce.

It is not clear exactly what happened next, whether Maddie kicked him out of the house or Richard snuck away, but in any case he found himself looking for a place to live. He bunked with a friend for a few months, but even he grew weary with Richard's sloth and indolence and inattentiveness. Richard found himself out on the street again. He tried panhandling, becoming one of the countless vagrants standing at intersections looking for a handout, food, money, a friendly smile. Cities were not equipped to deal with "the vagrancy problem," and there were few municipal services for people like Richard. In some cities, churches and other religious institutions provided a place to sleep, a hot meal, the occasional shower. For a time, in

Rockford, Richard volunteered to provide shaves and haircuts to vagrants, in exchange for a place to live. In a way, he was serving as a valet for the poorest of society. He might have stayed at the Faith Mission but eventually left because he could not abide their proselytizing. He did not particularly feel like a child of God, created in His likeness. Besides, the Mission had to end its services: too much need, too little resources.

His coding skills came in handy when he learned how to highjack autonomous vehicles, which allowed him to move from place to place. He stowed away on an autonomous truck that brought him across the country. He and others settled for a time in state parks—what few remain—squatting in cabins or otherwise camping in the woods. This was not the best way to live: hiding from park rangers and trying to avoid the wildlife, especially at night. These risks were offset by the opportunity to burgle campsites for food and other supplies. Richard already had a criminal record, so why not turn to crime, he reasoned. No robot or autonomous system had yet been devised to commit crimes—which wasn't exactly true, of course. AI systems for swindling the financial markets were common enough now. But Richard felt that perhaps crime was the only productive activity left for human beings.

Other squatters told him of job opportunities in New Mexico, water reclamation jobs that welcomed human laborers. He hitched a ride on an autonomous semi to Taos where he worked for three months at a dangerous and filthy job working underground to tap into aquifers, those that had yet to have been drained dry, of course. All the while, he was trying to determine why this job, of all the jobs in the world, wasn't being done by robots. He eventually learned that the company that hired him had calculated that the capital investment in a lost or irreparably damaged machine was significantly higher than the loss of a human life. Once he realized this, he quit on the spot. He eventually made his way to the West Coast, as far as Portland. He pondered a life at sea—if they still required human sailors—but contented himself with panhandling again. To an earlier generation, he would have been labeled a "hobo."

Richard had become a living example of a sociological phenomenon: the "productivity crisis." Pundits and commentators and trolls on the feeds identified Richard's condition as "his problem" because he didn't try hard enough or was too lazy or was too incompetent. Zachary Banks had been a professor of sociology at Harvard who studied the growing ranks of the "unproductive." Richard later thought he might have encountered him once doing field work at a flophouse he was staying at. Banks did not coin this term but appropriated it to identify the class of people who had been made redundant from automation/innovation and had simply given up trying or were too exhausted to continue to retrain for work that was destined to be automated. Banks redirected the meaning and connotations of "the unproductive" to be more sympathetic. He wrote a number of academic papers and gave conference presentations on his research but decided that the humans lost to automation were far more important than any academic accolades. Banks would write a modern version of *The Communist Manifesto*, and in fact he was identified as a new Karl Marx. The "unproductive" were victims of a society that had yet to figure out what to do when machines and autonomous agents were more productive than humans. A society that had bought into the automation/redundancy ideology had not thought through the implications of making an entire class of people perpetually redundant. (Richard lived during the time before federal universal basic income was established.)

Banks was convinced that this growing class of the "unproductive" were the vanguard of a new social revolution. He asked why haven't the homeless, the hobos, the vagrants ever organized into a social movement or revolutionary force? He concluded that they were too tired, too weary from trying to stay alive. They lacked access to weapons—if they had control of the "means of violence," they could affect real change. The unproductive lack trust in institutions and so were unlikely to band together under any kind of leadership. As more of the well-trained—people like Richard—descended into the ranks of the unproductive, Banks called on them to provide the energy and leadership to rise up, to re-assert the value and dignity of human labor. Banks published his manifesto knowing it would mean the end of his tenure at Harvard. His manifesto—more than Banks' leadership—catalyzed a neo-Luddite movement.

In keeping with his habit of playing "the bad guy" in video games, Richard was increasingly drawn to the saboteur, sneaking behind borders to wreak havoc on the unsuspecting. One evening while inhabiting the Saboteur video game at a flophouse in Portland, Richard was accosted by an avatar. He initially thought the avatar was a security agent seeking to halt his activities, but instead the avatar invited him to a heavily protected area of the game that required a password, one the avatar did not provide. The avatar said, cryptically, "Want to be a real saboteur?" Again, Richard thought this was simply a new level of the game. Although there was no password, Richard nevertheless figured out how to enter the portal—those coding skills came in handy after all—and within three hours of the initial invitation he found himself in a featureless space. Alone for what seemed hours, but was only about 15 minutes, Richard was joined by 11 avatars who circled around him.

The avatar who originally reached out to him greeted Richard. In these video games, of course, players were never identified by their actual names, and so Richard was startled to be called by his real name. Referring to the memes of Richard's attack on the delivery drone, the avatar said that the group did not view his actions as at all comical. Crude, perhaps, but with real intention and purpose. Smashing up the drone was an ancient act, reminiscent of the nineteenth-century Luddites who smashed up mechanical looms and other technologies of the first Industrial Revolution, technologies that threatened the jobs of craftsmen now made redundant. The eleven identified themselves as neo-Luddites.

Unbeknownst to Richard, this group of avatars had been using the surveillance footage as a recruiting tool for others who wanted to fight back against automated machines, indeed, the whole of the automation/redundancy economy. Had Richard only smashed a drone, the neo-Luddites would not have paid him much attention. But upon learning that Richard could easily hack into autonomous vehicles to commandeer them for his cross-country trips, the neo-Luddites had decided that Richard had both the anger and the skills to join their movement.

The neo-Luddites targeted autonomous systems, starting with the enablers of the servile economy. Each of the eleven, Richard soon learned, had been made redundant many times over by automation/innovation low-lifes. Richard thought of Kayden Browne here.

For the first time in years, Richard felt a sense of mission and purpose in his life. Whether engaging in sabotage would bring down the automation/redundancy economy or allow him to reconcile with his wife and sons, Richard finally felt like *doing something* again. "Creative destruction" they called it, repurposing the term used by the automation/redundancy entrepreneurs to justify their sociopathic behavior.

The neo-Luddites were almost all trained as coders and developers, and their targets were autonomous systems. Richard was adamant that he would not participate in any sabotage that resulted in injuries to innocents. He was thinking of the nursing home residents who might be harmed if the care-bots were tampered with in any fashion. The group were largely in agreement, although this after some debate that perhaps if calamities were to befall innocents, then this would spur action against the use of machines. One target of the group was autonomous vehicles, especially those used to taxi people around the city. The goal would not be to make them crash, which could jeopardize human lives, but to make the cars drive erratically, unpredictably, unreliably. Portland was a test case for their sabotage; within six months, the public taxi system had been rendered so unpopular with riders that human taxi services reemerged from dormancy, like sprouts on a dead rotting tree. After Portland, the group targeted other systems in other large cities. The large driverless semi-trucks that crossed the flat and straight interstate highways were another target. Richard was especially keen to work on this project, feeling as if he were exacting some revenge for his father.

The neo-Luddites were not seeking ransom and were not extorting the companies they attacked for money. They declared success when a formally automated sector began to re-hire human beings, or where humans were once again put in charge of managing or overseeing machines. The neo-Luddites turned their attention to the restaurant industry, sabotaging server-bots and food preparation devices. Initially, the devices were hacked to misprepare food to produce very low levels of food poisoning, enough to cause discomfort in patrons but not enough to make anyone violently sick. The server-bots were hacked to be insubordinate, clumsy, dropping items and spilling drinks on patrons. Slowly, and then suddenly some restaurants were closing down as patrons avoided places where the service was so unreliable. Some human-centered restaurants opened, luring customers with the promise of reliable, friendly human service and human-prepared food.

Some within the neo-Luddite movement felt these successes were still too inconsequential. One particularly vocal faction felt that real change would not occur until the group targeted consequential autonomous systems. This faction wanted to target the military. Is it really a triumph, this faction asked, if human jobs are confined to restaurant servers or cab drivers? Why not go after the care industry? If a few old people are inconvenienced, this is surely a small price to pay to realize higher objectives. Richard asked, innocently yet knowingly, *what are our objectives*? For Richard, there was no replacing the genie in the bottle. Even as the group were sabotaging some industries and having humans rehired, those same industries were fighting back: the neo-Luddites were nearly revealed by one company's efforts to block the hacking. Richard said that the goal should be to disable the autonomous/redundancy economy enough to then make a real demand: that the government care for, or otherwise provide for those made redundant, to finally care for the "unproductive."

The group had never had a leader or spokesman before, but it was decided that Richard would be the voice of the movement. He would remain anonymous, would not be revealed, and would take the *nom de guerre* Ned Ludd when addressing the world.

The nineteenth-century Luddites did not stop the spread of industrialization. Indeed, scholars have long contended that such acts of worker activism have never succeeded in stopping the march of technological progress or of restoring jobs. In this the neo-Luddites were no different, as the automation/redundancy economy continued apace. And while not the only or even the proximate cause, the actions of Ned Ludd and the neo-Luddites did help to usher in the care society, that moment when the "unproductive" had eventually triumphed.

Richard would not live to enjoy this moment. Eventually, the cell was nabbed by the authorities. Justice was unforgivingly swift in this case, a jury rendering their guilty verdicts in a matter of three and a half hours. Richard was not given jail time but would be required to wear a perpetual ankle monitor. His movements would be free but his actions would be surveilled. In theory, Richard could go about the rest of his life in peace. But the very visible monitor was a signal to employers to avoid the trouble. Richard returned to panhandling and would die of heat stroke on the streets of Oklahoma City. In his delirium, he believed that he was no one's servant.

Key Futures Themes

- Automation
- Rise of the "Unproductive" Class
- The Service Economy
- Breakdown of Social Mobility
- Dignity in Work
- Neo-Luddite Resistance
- Criminal Justice
- Environmental and Resource Constraints
- The Care Economy

Bibliography

Armstrong, Ben. 2020. Automation, Training and the Future of Work. *Watson Institute*. https://watson.brown.edu/taubman/files/taubman/imce/AUTOMATION%2C%20TRAINING%2C%20AND%20THE%20FUTURE%20OF%20WORK%20-%20Ben%20Armstrong%20Policy%20Brief%20-%202.4.20.pdf.

Armstrong, Ben, et al. 2024. Automation from the Worker's Perspective: How Can New Technologies Make Jobs Better? https://ipc.mit.edu/wp-content/uploads/2024/09/workers_and_automation_r04M.pdf.

Brynjolfsson, Erik, and Andrew McAfee. 2014. *The Second Machine Age: Work, Progress, and Prosperity in a Time of Brilliant Technologies*. New York: W.W. Norton & Co.

Coleman, Gabriella. 2015. *Hacker, Hoaxer, Whistleblower, Spy: The Many Faces of Anonymous*. London: Verso.

Harari, Yuval Noah. 2018. *21 Lessons for the 21st Century*. New York: Random House.

Hilsenrath, Jon. 2024. The Manicure Economy. *Financial Times*, 20 May 2024. https://www.ft.com/content/f3cc3767-b0c3-4dd1-983a-6f158799b6c4.

Jacobs, Julian. 2025. AI Labor Displacement and the Limits of Worker Retraining. *Brookings Institution*, 16 May 2025. https://www.brookings.edu/articles/ai-labor-displacement-and-the-limits-of-worker-retraining/.

Chapter 11
Jayden Meyrick: Climate Immigrant

His great grandparents had moved to the Valley of the Sun from Pittsburgh in the 1970s. Like many others, they were lured by the plentiful jobs, the ballooning economy, the sunshine. The Sun Belt beckoned Americans from the dreary, inert, rusting Northeast and Midwest. His great grandfather was a manager at a steel factory and lost his job when it shuttered in 1978. At a loss for what to do next, Joseph and Joan Meyrick did not even consider moving, let alone to Phoenix, until it was clear there were few opportunities for them in Pittsburgh. Higher education and healthcare were the burgeoning industries there and Joseph felt unqualified to easily find work. Phoenix held the promise of high-tech industries, which were always searching for skilled technicians. Although he worked in the steel industry, Joseph was a Republican and was anti-union and Phoenix offered a welcoming atmosphere. And so, Joseph and Joan Meyrick bid farewell to the cold and the smokestacks for the sun and clean tech office parks of Tempe.

Being an American had always been defined by a set of inalienable rights. Some were codified in foundational documents, others were claimed and demanded even if the law was not so explicit. The right to free speech, the right to worship freely, the right to assemble. For many Americans, the right to travel, the right to move freely about the country, was as hallowed as any enshrined in the Bill of Rights. Americans allowed themselves to enjoy absolute freedom of movement. One needn't be a Beat poet or a hippie to recognize themselves in Kerouac's *On the Road*, or *Easy Rider*. These American songlines were like their Aboriginal counterparts, both a map and an archive of cultural knowledge. Joseph and Joan enacted the American songline when they and tens of thousands of others found opportunity by moving. Young Americans always sought to "find themselves" by picking up stakes and moving, young men ever going westward. The myth of the frontier, even after the Census Bureau declared it closed in 1890, continued to mesmerize the American imagination. Like the Okies memorialized by Steinbeck and forced by circumstances to move, Americans long believed that opportunity was always to be found by migrating.

D. Staley, *Anticipatory Biographies*, Anticipation Science 10,
https://doi.org/10.1007/978-3-032-08912-0_11

Jayden Meyrick had never read Steinbeck or Kerouac nor had he ever seen *Easy Rider*, but he certainly possessed his great-grandparents' sense of wanderlust. As a young man, Jayden productively wasted many months riding his e-cycle across the country. He never had a destination in mind. He would pack lightly, pick a direction, not even consulting his GPS, hop on his bike and ride for days, weeks, until he felt like turning back. Then he would wind his way home to Buckeye, a suburb of Phoenix. Those summer adventures took him to Texas and Tennessee and Oregon and Montana. He was not the introspective sort, and so never kept a journal or otherwise recorded his thoughts while traveling, although a few photos have survived, upon which he would look wistfully in his old age.

Jayden's wandering estranged him from his parents. His father, Owen, wanted his son to work when he wasn't attending to his learning chores. Katy, his mother, oversaw his education and formed more of an emotional bond than he ever could with his father. His mother understood Jayden's e-cycle treks. She asked him to describe what he learned from his travel—she conceived these as part of his education—but nevertheless worried about him alone on the road.

But being left alone is exactly what he wanted to be. Much of his childhood was spent alone owing to being homeschooled, perhaps, but was not at all characterized by loneliness. Indeed, on his travels, he met many fellow travelers at the rest stops he gravitated toward, at coffee shops, at campsites. One April, while when riding through the Rockies, he met Ashe who was riding her bike from Brooklyn to San Francisco. Although he fantasized about a sexual relationship, she was even more introverted and rootless than he was, and she seemed to be riding to escape from someone or something, although she never said so. Freedom of movement often meant the freedom or necessity to flee.

Owen Meyrick was a waterman, a water carrier. He boasted that it was a job not yet automated, but Jayden was uncertain how long that would last. It was also a dangerous job. It took two armed men to carry this task out. Owen wanted him to join the family business, but Jayden rebelled. Watermen were often attacked, and Jayden grumbled that being a water pirate was probably a more stable and secure line of work. Jayden always assumed the reason they still used humans was to make them easier targets, a lightning rod for customer's anger. People could unleash their wrath at a person rather than a robot or faceless corporation that was gouging them for water.

The watermen delivered a weekly allotment of water to each residence. Most homes included a large barrel, usually in a basement or sometimes in an interior room. A spigot on the outside connected to this barrel, and it was here that water was delivered each week, not unlike a milkman in bygone days. At first, these barrels were located in backyards. Many were repurposed rain barrels, but it was quickly discovered that water thefts were too common, necessitating the architectural redesign of dwellings. A standard tank held about 50 gallons of water, and most people on Owen Meyrick's route paid to have the tank filled each week. When Jayden was young, water sold for about $10 a gallon. As the price continued to rise, more and more families paid for only half a tank or less. By the time Jayden had married and started having children, the cost of water consumed nearly 45% of his family budget.

The job required armed protection, since theft was an omnipresent threat. Water pirates came in many forms. Some were ordinary families unable to afford the high price of water and stole out of desperation. Organized gangs also formed to control the supply of water and extort even higher prices. Owen frequently had to fend off pirates at least once a week. He sometimes mused that his job was like a Wells Fargo stagecoach driver from the nineteenth century, or an armored car driver from the 20th. And why not? All involved transporting a valuable commodity.

Instead of being a waterman, Jaden spent his entire working life installing and maintaining artificial trees. These were tall, cylindrical objects that slurped carbon dioxide out of the atmosphere. Study after study conclusively demonstrated that they were more efficient at removing CO_2 than natural trees, and these now forested the Valley of the Sun. His job was to ensure that the mechanisms were functioning properly, repair them when they weren't, and emptying the devices of the captured CO_2. His was not the most glamorous or stimulating job in the world, but it was a good job, one that paid just enough to support his family, and most significantly, showed little sign of being automated. It was certainly safer than underground water mining or delivering water. Artificial trees were welcome and necessary if the Valley of the Sun was going to remain habitable, long bereft of trees and forests. What few trees that did grow in the region had long since dried up. Persistent drought had decimated the growth of forests, and those that did exist were small and meager and impotent at CO_2 removal. Cities like Tucson had instituted tree planting programs, especially for cooling the heat dome that enveloped western cities. But these trees wilted in the heat and were thirsty for water. Artificial trees were an acceptable substitute, although they did little to cool urban areas. Eventually, solar panel "leaves" were included in the design of the trees. Early in his career, Jayden retrofitted artificial trees with solar leaves. These leaves helped to power the tree and also generated a not inconsequential amount of electricity. They were also intended to simulate the shade natural trees provided. While not as awe-inspiring to look at, artificial trees nevertheless provided a vital service to the region.

Getting a job meant that Jayden could no longer up and leave and cycle across the country on a whim, when his wanderlust demanded. He liked the job but chafed at how it confined him to one place. While he maintained artificial trees across Arizona and parts of New Mexico, that was the extent of his travel in any given year. Those weekends he had off were for riding, but his range was limited, as he had to be back to work on Monday. And so over time, he stopped riding as much and just stayed indoors, usually experiencing video games. He did have vacation time, two weeks a year, that did afford him time to wander, the impulse to move still very much present.

Because he was more sedentary, Jayden found himself socializing more, which came as a surprise to this introvert, to this man who preferred solitude. Her name was Britley, and he met her at a concert. She was a home health care aide, mostly serving upscale residents at a retirement community. Britley was also fiercely devoted to her family, emotionally bonded, not only to her parents, but to her brothers and sisters and cousins and aunts and uncles, a family dynamic wholly alien to Jayden. But he was attracted to her, and he eventually fell in love with her, and they were married after an eight-month courtship. They would ride together on his e-cycle, and while Britley loved clinging to Jayden as they rode through the arid landscape, she preferred nightclubs and concerts and other diversions that didn't require a three-hour bike ride. Because of her devotion to family, she was also wedded to the Valley of the Sun. She could not even conceive of leaving the area. Jayden didn't have the attachment to family in place that Britley did. He eventually assented to her wishes to remain in Arizona, although she did agree to yearly vacations elsewhere. The birth of their two sons and a daughter further cemented Jayden in place.

As he got older, Jayden started thinking more and more about moving from Buckeye. His job was stable and lucrative enough that he was unlikely to find something comparable elsewhere in the country. But the summertime heat was becoming intolerable, even for a native like him, and the price of water was eating up more and more of his family's budget. The availability of water, or rather, the lack of available water, had long defined this region. If Jayden thought about it at all, he marveled that anyone would have settled here, let alone the millions who continued to sprawl throughout the Valley. What on earth were his great-grandparents thinking? Why hadn't his parents moved? The Colorado River had dried to a trickle, not too long after the Great Salt Lake evaporated. Western governors had, for decades, attempted to negotiate and then pleaded with governors from the Great Lakes region to build a pipeline to provide water, pleas that were always politely, then angrily, ignored. The water that Jayden and his family used was shipped in from a California-based desalinization plant. The process was just as costly as it had always been, which made the price of water one of the largest expenditures of a typical family budget, more than food and almost as expensive as rent. Jayden's children had never taken a bath or shower. Like many families, daily bathing was accomplished with a Miracle Towel. This was an engineered loofah that one dipped in a very small amount of water and then applied to one's body. Although she has been using one all her life, Britley never really accustomed herself to this method of personal hygiene, although her children knew no different. Most new homes and apartments in Arizona were no longer built with showers or bathtubs, some even without sinks or basins. Instead, there would be a kind of platform one would stand on, closing a door to provide some privacy. Older homes were retrofitted with flushless toilets. Some even returned to outdoor latrines.

One summer, Jayden Meyrick took his family on an RV vacation to the Oregon coast. It was the first time his children had seen greenery in such abundance, to say nothing of the Pacific Ocean. They could not even imagine that much water and naturally asked if they could drink it. Meyrick had to explain about the salt content of seawater but also explained that the water delivered to their house came from this ocean, after all the salt had been removed. His kids enjoyed splashing in the water and the relatively cooler temperatures of Oregon. They had set up their RV at a site 40 miles south of Portland. It was here that Meyrick felt the first indications of a culture change that would curtail freedom of movement in the United States.

One evening, after returning from a family hike, Meyrick had discovered that someone had spray painted on the side of his RV. "Go back to where you belong!" Meyrick stood in stunned silence for a few minutes before raging at his wife, "Who did this? What does it mean: 'back to where you belong?' I am an American, for God's sake, I'm not an alien!" The word *alien* was once whispered as a racist dog whistle to refer to any immigrant or refugee to the United States. Now it was back in fashion and sneered aloud and unashamedly in public by almost everyone. "They think I'm an alien!" Meyrick was dumbfounded. His license plate clearly indicated he was from Arizona, and he and his family all wore their badges. Why did they have to prove their citizenship?

All American citizens were required to wear and prominently display a digital badge that indicated they were a citizen of the United States. These were made mandatory when Jayden was a child. At first, they were made from a hard-to-fabricate polymer, the purpose of which was to publicly announce one's citizenship. Anyone in the country illegally was therefore, in theory, easily recognizable. Anyone without a badge was immediately detained, and if determined to be in the country illegally were summarily deported. There were occasions where citizens forgot their badges, the way someone might leave home without their wallet. In these cases, the authorities would detain the offender but rarely take them into custody. Jayden recalled one day his mother was driving with him to the store, and when they arrived, she realized that neither of them were wearing their badges. He recalled that a police officer noticed the two of them and briefly stopped them. Obviously, they were Americans, Katy Meyrick stammered, and the officer agreed, letting them off with a warning. Jayden also recalled that black and brown people were frequently detained, even if they were wearing badges. Counterfeit badges were a lucrative business, but the badges had a specially designed chip that could not be so easily faked. Just looking at a counterfeit badge would not necessarily reveal the deception. Officers carried with them a device that would validate the badge. This did not prevent many people being unnecessarily and embarrassingly retained while the police verified the badge.

But politicians maintained that the system worked. Immigration from Central and South America to the United States did indeed drop sharply in the two years after the introduction of the citizenship badges. It was the southern border states of Texas and Arizona and New Mexico who first legislated the badges. But soon enough, other states adopted the practice, such that it became a de facto national law. "Rebel cities" sometimes flaunted the badge law or looked the other way at those not wearing them. But for many, the risks of moving around the United States without a badge—this inverse of a scarlet letter—were simply too great.

Jayden Meyrick called the police to report the vandalism on his RV. He explained to the impassive officer that he was from Arizona and that he had dutifully worn his badge and that no one could possibly accuse him of being an alien. The officer took his statement and said that he would investigate, but that the vandals would be difficult to apprehend. Meyrick was incredulous. "Well start by interviewing everyone at this park!" It was clear the officer was nonplussed by the vandalism, explaining that it was precisely because he was from Arizona that Meyrick was being told to leave. "They see you are from Arizona and assume you are here to take water with you back home," the officer explained. It was true that there were many people who traveled to places in the United States with more abundant water supplies and attempted to smuggle water back home, the expense of traveling not nearly as great as the cost of water. "People see your RV and assume you're here to steal water." It hadn't even occurred to Meyrick to do this, although, after he heard the officer's explanation, he wondered if he shouldn't steal some water. What Meyrick did not pick up on was that the officer tacitly agreed with the vandals. He counseled Meyrick that he should probably just pack up and leave and return to Arizona. Bewildered, Meyrick and his family did indeed leave Oregon, two days earlier than planned. His anger gradually subsided, but what Jayden Meyrick did not yet fathom was that this episode would be repeated with increasing frequency across the country, such that this prejudice against people from Arizona and the American Southwest would eventually become enshrined in many state laws.

The Meyrick family continued to travel for vacations, but their destinations grew closer to home, and by the time the kids were teenagers, they stopped traveling for vacation altogether. Jaden and Britley would sometimes vacation together or meet with other couples to travel to Taos or even as far as Houston. As he grew older, Jaden Myrick lost some of his zeal for travel. Some of that may have to do with the logistical challenges of traveling across the United States.

One summer, when Meyrick was on the cusp of retirement, he and Britley planned an elaborate family vacation to a water park on Lake Erie. The couple had saved over the course of seven years for this trip, one that will allow them to spend time with their grandkids. The parents would not be accompanying them on this trip, both because of work obligations and also because of the visa requirements.

The trip took two weeks of planning, mostly to receive the necessary vacation visa from the state of Ohio. Over the course of the last two decades, there had been a slow but steady stream of people moving from the southwest to the Midwest and Northeast, a reversal of the population movement of the 1970s that brought the Meyricks to Arizona in the first place. At first, states like Ohio welcomed the internal immigrants, which helped reverse the population decline. States like Ohio had been suffering, but now Ohio and other states wanted to control who was moving to their state. The first visa controls were aimed at keeping illegal aliens out of the state, but they were later expanded to keep out other undesirables. Young workers were almost always granted admission to the state, especially if they brought with them lots of young children or at least held the promise of producing young children.

Once the southern border of the United States had been "secured," owing to the adoption of the citizenship badge, Americans started seeing borders everywhere else, and now borders crisscrossed the United States, delineating states, cities, social classes, identities. These borders were enforced with a ferocity once reserved for illegal immigrants. Indeed, after the southern border was closed, Americans transferred their distrust of outsiders to other Americans. This made travel across the United States a slow and cumbersome process.

Britley corresponded with the travel office in Ohio to have their citizenship badges updated to include a tourist visa. Ohio was very welcoming to tourists like the Meyricks and made it relatively easy to obtain the necessary clearances to spend time at the water park. Tourists could spend up to one week in the state. They could apply for longer without much difficulty, although there were more hoops to jump through if a tourist wished to spend a month in the state. If out-of-staters were visiting family, they could apply for lengthier visas, but these involved background checks and other intrusions not found with the tourist visas. The Meyricks had budgeted for a five-day stay on Lake Erie and were granted their visa happily and without delay.

Ohio was one of a growing number of states who redeployed the citizenship badge as a mechanism of residential registration, like the old *hukou* system China used. The state could more easily identify permanent residents and simultaneously control who was residing in the state. The "undesirables" the government wished to keep out were the "unproductive"—those people who did not hold jobs, having given up on finding work in an automated economy—those who would be a burden on social services or who might otherwise crowd cities panhandling or being a nuisance. But "undesirables" also included older Americans, and retirees specifically. Ohio was already top heavy with people over the age of 65. Its population over 80 was nearly 25% of the state's total, one of the largest in the country. For the past decade, Ohio had emerged as an attractive retirement spot, but the state did not want the burden of caring for so many elderly Americans. When applying for their tourist visas, Britley found that the process took slightly longer than she had anticipated. It turned out that the ages of Jayden and Britley were at issue. Ohio wanted to make certain the 60-something Meyricks were not using the tourist visa as a way to sneak into the state to become permanent residents.

Instead of traveling to Ohio by RV, the Meyricks used the rail, which was a faster mode of travel than driving, but only slightly so. Traveling across the western states was not complicated, but once the train reached the Kansas state line, the train halted at a station. All the passengers had to have their citizenship badges scanned by the conductor, chiefly to monitor who was entering the state and to determine their legal status. A scan of the Meyrick family revealed that they were traveling under a tourist visa. The process took about a half an hour to scan all passengers, then the train continued, only to stop again at the Missouri border and at the Indiana and at the Ohio borders. At the Indiana stop, there was some confusion about the status of Britley, a mix up that was quickly resolved—why hadn't there been any problem at the other checkpoints?—and the family could continue on to Lake Erie. But the entire enterprise of traveling across the country irritated Meyrick, who remembered riding directionless, without a plan and certainly without receiving permission and official approval to travel. All his life, Meyrick had approved of efforts to secure the Southern border but now found himself frustrated and angered that those border protection measures aimed at American citizens like him.

Once they finally arrived on the shores of Lake Erie, his grandkids were stunned. No amount of preparation could have readied them for the spectacle they encountered at the water park. In addition to playing in water, to having hundreds of gallons of it dropped on their heads and in taking raft rides down artificial rivers, the grandkids experienced their first ever baths in an actual bathtub, something even Merick's children had yet to experience. When they decamped in their hotel room, Britley luxuriated in her first shower in years. At the hotel restaurant, the servers brought them all tall, icy cold glasses of water without even asking for it and without having to pay extra. Whatever challenges the state might have been dealing with, Ohio and much of the Midwest had plenty of water, to drink, to bathe in, to water agricultural fields, even to play around in (watering lawns was not permitted). While it was not the principal reason, the availability of water was part of what made the Midwest an attractive vacation destination. It was not as hot as Arizona, but it certainly was more humid. Meyrick must have surely reflected on the opulence and luxury of playing in water—this trip to Ohio was not his choice, he wanted to take the kids to the Great Smoky Mountains. But the trip to Ohio nevertheless provided a respite from the oppressive and arid heat of Arizona.

Despite the travel hassles, the vacation with his grandkids delighted Meyrick, and he returned to Arizona in an effervescent mood. As he gave it some thought, Meyrick concluded that life in Ohio was infinitely better than in Arizona. If nothing else, the cost of living seemed to be lower in Ohio. It was not as hot as Arizona, had more outdoor recreation and was welcoming of people like him. Jayden and Britley talked it over and decided there they would be retiring to Ohio. They had settled upon a small house on Buckeye Lake just outside Columbus. Living on a lake would be a new experience for both of them. Boating, fishing: these were pursuits Meyrick had no experience with, having never had the opportunity growing up. The Meyricks began the process of moving to Ohio, which turned out to be more challenging than arranging a vacation.

The state had to first grant the Meyricks permanent resident status, and this proved impossible for them to obtain. Without it, they would not be able to rent, let alone purchase, a place to live. Meyrick's age and income level were the main reason they were denied permanent resident status. There was little market for artificial trees in Ohio, and so it was not evident what job he might take. If the couple were there to retire, this was even more problematic, for the state was already strained—in the State's estimate—under the weight of too many old people. Unless the Meyricks could demonstrate they would not be a burden to the state, their application was denied.

Meyrick was furious and thought about suing the state for age discrimination. He was assured by a lawyer he consulted that Ohio's restrictions were perfectly legal and had withstood previous lawsuits. The Meyricks then considered Michigan as a retirement location, which had even more lakes and was more temperate than even Ohio, although the cost of living was substantially higher. But here too, they could not obtain legal residency clearance.

Meyrick faced the prospect of living out his days in the parched and increasingly inhospitable Arizona desert, which is why, unbeknownst to Britley, he decided to enlist the services of a coyote. Like their predecessors, who trafficked people across the Southern border, today's coyotes also illegally smuggled people across borders. Specifically, a coyote was a hacker who manipulated the citizenship badge to make it appear that the wearer held permanent residency. In Meyrick's case, the coyote had to fabricate a backstory of Jayden being a lifelong resident of Ohio and that he was simply moving within the state. This fake identity would cost Meyrick $20,000 but came with assurances from the coyote—whose name Meyrick never learned—that he would be able to move to Ohio without difficulty.

Myrick explained to Britley that there had been a change of heart by the state, and that they would be able to settle on Buckeye Lake, and that he was traveling to Columbus to see to the arrangements. The coyote advised Myrick to conduct this business in Columbus, specifically. The city had not yet declared its independence from Ohio but was very much one of the "rebel cities." Residents there largely ignored the citizenship badges or looked the other way at fraudulent or counterfeit badges. Columbus residents favored free travel in the United States and so—as with many other issues—were at odds with lawmakers at the Statehouse. Working with a realtor in Columbus would be safer than any other part of the state.

He was stopped at the checkpoints on the train ride, and this time, had to answer more pointed questions. If he was from Ohio, as his badge indicated, what was he doing on the train traveling there? He lied that he had business in New Mexico from where he was traveling. Even though this was not noted in the scan of his badge, conductors nevertheless allowed him to continue on. But Meyrick was unaware that the train authorities were already alerting the state of Ohio of his arrival. When he arrived at the realtors to discuss purchase options, he was met by State Police. Myrick was briefly detained, brought before a judge, and found guilty of falsifying his residency status.

Owing, perhaps, to his advanced age, the judge did not imprison Jayden Meyrick, but instead, extradited him to Arizona, sending him back where he belonged.

Key Futures Themes

- Internal Climate Migration and Erosion of Freedom of Movement
- Environmental Infrastructure Collapse and Replacement of Natural Ecosystems
- Economic Stratification
- Transformation of Residential Architecture
- Surveillance and Control
- Collapse of National Unity and Regional Xenophobia

Bibliography

Braun, Marius. 2021. Spatial Dependence in the Relationship Between Climate Change and Internal Migration: Evidence from the United States. *SSRN*, December 2021. https://papers.ssrn.com/sol3/papers.cfm?abstract_id=3906643.

Carbon Collect. https://carboncollect.com/.

Craig, David J. 2024. America's Great Climate Migration Has Begun. Here's What You Need to Know. *Columbia Magazine*, Fall 2024. https://magazine.columbia.edu/article/americas-great-climate-migration-has-begun-heres-what-you-need-know.

Faller, Mary Beth. 2022. The Future of Water in Arizona. *ASU News*, 15 November 2022. https://news.asu.edu/20221115-arizona-impact-future-water-arizona.

Fan, Qin, Karen Fisher-Vanden, and H. Allen Klaiber. 2018. Climate Change, Migration, and Regional Economic Impacts in the United States. *Journal of the Association of Environmental and Resource Economists* 5 (3): 643–671. https://doi.org/10.1086/697168.

Graziano, Manlio. 2018. *What is a Border?* Stanford: Stanford Briefs.

Jaramillo, Eduardo. 2022. China's Hukou Reform in 2022: Do They Mean it this Time? *Center for Strategic and International Studies*, 20 April 2022. https://www.csis.org/blogs/new-perspectives-asia/chinas-hukou-reform-2022-do-they-mean-it-time-0.

Kelley, Mikayla. 2022. Future Forests Will Have Smaller Trees and Soak Up Less Carbon, Study Suggests. *University of Arizona News*, 26 January 2022. https://news.arizona.edu/news/future-forests-will-have-smaller-trees-and-soak-less-carbon-study-suggests.

Robbins, Jim. 2019. In Era of Drought, Phoenix Prepares for a Future Without Colorado River Water. *Yale Environment* 360, 7 February 2019. https://e360.yale.edu/features/how-phoenix-is-preparing-for-a-future-without-colorado-river-water.

Rossi, Marcello. 2024. Planting Trees and Equity in the Arizona Desert. *Reasons to be Cheerful*, 3 May 2024. https://reasonstobecheerful.world/tucson-million-trees-equity/.

Chapter 12
Zheng Jiehong: President

He might not have been the first, but Zheng Jiehong has been widely acknowledged to be the most ruthless eco-dictator in modern history. After Xi Jinping's long reign, the Party reinstituted what amounted to term limits for the Party Secretary and President. The Party wanted to ensure that the next president harbored no illusions that he was ruling for life. Zheng was still too young to have aspired to the post. He had only recently been selected as Environmental Minister after having served as governor of a major province. Besides no one wanted to be the leader to succeed Xi: any achievements this person might realize would be lost to history, subsumed by the accomplishments of The Great State Chairman. Zheng would bide his time, build relationships, avoid generating enemies, until he finally achieved his goal.

He was born in Changsha, where his father was a local party official. From a young age, Zheng was impressed with the ability of the Party to direct change. Whatever goals the Party set were achieved through a combination of persuasion and rhetoric, and naked force if necessary. He learned about the power of rhetoric from his father, who would often have occasion to speak to the local population angered by some transgression or inconvenience. From his father, he learned how words could enforce obedience, although in private, his father often resorted to physical violence against both Jiehong and his mother to impose his will. Filial piety, rather than love or admiration, governed Jiehong's relationship with his father.

Zheng attended Tsinghua University initially with the intention of studying chemical engineering, as Xi had done. But while at university, he was introduced to the work of the Japanese Marxist Kohei Saito, who made a clear and persuasive case for degrowth as the only solution to the world's climate crisis. Balance, harmony, maintaining an economic steady-state should guide our economic actions rather than unsustainable, physically-impossible growth. Zheng huddled with a small cadre of student radicals to absorb Saito's work and philosophy. This was an act of subversion, for imbibing the work of a Japanese intellectual was still a disobedient

D. Staley, *Anticipatory Biographies*, Anticipation Science 10,
https://doi.org/10.1007/978-3-032-08912-0_12

act in China, where the Japanese still regarded with suspicion by the Party. But Saito was a Marxist and—in theory, at least—the Party still adhered to the spirit of Marx. In any event, this radical clique, who dubbed themselves the Green Chinese, translated Saito's ideas into a Chinese idiom. Balance, harmony between human civilization and nature, was rooted as much in Chinese philosophy and culture as it was in Japan's, they argued, and besides the idea of balance and harmony contrasted sharply with Western philosophy. The Green Chinese cadre danced on the edge of rebellion, which might have proven problematic to an aspiring Party member like Zheng.

Reading Saito, joining the Green China cadre, led Zheng away from chemical engineering and toward environmental engineering. Ideas around the circular economy—confined to white papers and theoretical treatises in western universities—were more common at Tsinghua University, represented by a school of circular economic thinkers. Again, the Party tolerated what might have otherwise been construed as heterodox thinking, largely because its professors drew a contrast between circular economics and what was being taught in Western universities. Circular principles held that industrial processes—indeed the entire production/consumption cycle as it had been practiced—was linear. Resources were extracted from nature, converted into products with limited use—with pollution being one byproduct—which were then discarded when no longer deemed useful. The ultimate product of the industrial economy is waste.

Circular economic principles bent this line into a circle. After their use had ended, products would be reused or recycled, so that there would be no need to extract again from nature. Circular economists taught that natural systems did not produce waste, for anything produced by nature can serve as food for something else, input back into the system. A dead fallen tree is consumed by fungi, the tree dissolving into the soil to become nutrients for new plant growth. Even the waste products of urine and feces provide food or nourishment. Zheng absorbed the truism that there is no waste in nature.

Zheng learned that industrial systems should mimic nature, that all that is produced must continually cycle through the system. Zheng's professors said that the goal of environmental engineering was nothing less than the redesign, the rebuilding of industrial society, the economy reimagined as a natural system. As President, Zheng would declare that "the West is linear, China is circular." The failures of the past, the degradation of the planet, were the result of Western linear thinking. China would lead a new Circular era.

There was little doubt he would follow in his father's footsteps and become a Party official. After a short time functioning in a small rural area, he was elevated to the position of environmental minister in the populous province of Guangdong. He would serve for 5 years before becoming provincial governor. Given its size and economic influence—and its geographic distance—governors from Guangdong had long been held in suspicion by Beijing. Governors tended to act on their own and Zheng was no different, using this post to introduce environmental policies that gave a foretaste of how he would rule as President.

Travel bans and the restriction of movement had long been practiced in China, but Zheng would reconfigure these around environmental principles. Starting first with movement within the province, and then extending to anyone arriving in the province, travelers could only employ carbon-free means of travel. Within cities, he held walking up as the purest form of movement, and Zheng instituted a campaign to hail walking as character building, the very definition of "socialist travel." Restricting movement in this fashion was a relatively simple measure to institute. China had already established itself as the world leader in both in the production and consumption of electric vehicles. Much of the travel in Guangdong was already carbon-free, although some areas outside the cities, in the rural places, were most affected since EVs were not yet standard transportation.

Zheng instituted these travel restrictions mostly to signal that provincial government policy would be driven by environmental concerns. He began an anti-waste campaign, praising the Chinese for adopting zero carbon travel. At the same time, he lectured them on their consumption habits. City-dwellers were enthralled by Western ideas of consumption, with landfills growing larger by the day and Chinese trash littering the oceans. Cities were electrified by coal burning plants. He drew special contempt for Hong Kong which, although fully Chinese, retained too many Western habits, waste chief among them. Whether Hong Kong was actually producing more waste than any other city in China was disputed by the most reliable data. But that was not Zheng 's point: turning his anti-waste campaign on Hong Kong was his way to bring the city state to heel. Beijing approved of his tactics.

Zheng understood that the redesign of society could not be accomplished by technocratic means alone, that he would have to reshape people's behavior. One way he did this was by recalibrating the Chinese social credit system to include environmentalism. Having long evolved from an app that tracked a user's credit scores—not unlike a Western FICO score—Chinese apps had progressed to measure "social trustworthiness." Developers touted this as the first reliable measure of social capital, a concept growing in popularity in the West. The app depicted friendship networks, especially noting the quality of the friends in one's network. If one's friends engaged in socially beneficial behaviors, then the quality of one's friend network was judged superior. Antisocial behavior among one's friends lowered one's score and ended many friendships. This was not just an amusing entertainment. One's social capital score affected everything from job opportunities to places at university to marriage proposals. The app was not state owned, but the Party worked closely with many of the developers such that it was a de facto Party asset.

Bringing about his vision of a circular economy for China would involve changing behavior, and the social capital app would prove a very effective instrument of social engineering. Zheng worked with the lead developer to redesign the algorithm to identify and reward environmentally-positive behaviors. Refraining from the use of plastics, repairing objects rather than discarding them, practicing vegetarianism improved one's score. In his speeches, Zheng started using a term he coined: environmental capital. As with previous iterations of the social trustworthiness app, becoming friends with those who also engaged in these approved practices enhanced one social capital score. Rhetoric, persuasion—rather than overt force—was the most successful means of changing behavior, of convincing others to act in ways that the Party demanded. Zheng had learned this from his father; he would have no doubt approved of Zheng's technological persuasion.

For those who had low levels of environmental capital, Zheng instituted eco-reeducation facilities, demonstrating that he was not above using overt force when persuasion failed. Officially, they were called "environmental training centers." Subjects whose environmental capital scores fell below a certain level were required to report to the centers. Transgressors were not arrested as such, nor were they imprisoned, but they were required to attend daily classes at the center and pass a stringent exam. Failing the exam meant they would have to retake the entire course. Having to serve time at one of the centers meant a disruption in the individual's life, time away from work, from family. Some people lost employment because they repeatedly failed the exit test and were perpetually having to be reeducated. Violators were not confined to the training centers. This punishment was more like a community service sentence in some Western countries or like taking a test after a traffic violation. That is, these began as low stakes reeducation centers. When Zheng became president, he would establish these nationwide and would convert them into fully functioning internment camps, targeting not ethnic minorities or political activists, but environmental transgressors.

After ten years as governor, he would be named to the Politburo Standing Committee, and eventually Environmental Minister. He was relatively young when he became president at age 55. Zheng was driven by ambition of course, but an ambition born of his conviction that China could not remain a Great Power on a despoiled planet. Ruling China was only the penultimate step; he would only be satisfied if China exerted a globe-spanning power to restore the health of the planet. Like Xi, he was named general secretary of the Chinese Communist Party (CCP) and chairman of the Central Military Commission (CMC). He would eventually take the title *Tiānzǐ*, "son of Heaven," a title once reserved for Emperors (he would never go so far as to call himself Emperor.) Zheng vowed to remake the Chinese economy along circular principles. He would not tolerate dissent, his vision could only come about by changing and enforcing new behaviors.

At his inauguration, Zheng first announced the idea that "there is great disorder under heaven," meaning the condition of the planet. Without mentioning China's culpability in the crisis—especially its continued use of coal burning plants to produce electricity—Zheng said that it was time for China to lead. It had been a complaint for decades: as China's economic and military power grew, it provided proportionally less leadership on the world stage. China had no desire to become the world's policeman—Zheng said this publicly, at least—but some power would need to emerge to fill the vacuum left by America's slow withdrawal.

Evoking the ancient idea of *tian*, Zheng said that a goal for China would be to restore global ecological and environmental harmony. China would model this good behavior, and its example would provide a model and inspiration for the rest of the world. The speech was carefully calibrated to cast China's leadership as one of soft power: foreign adventures were of little interest to Zheng.

In his address, Zheng castigated Western governments who, under the cover of international conferences such as COP and ineffective bodies like the United Nations, failed to institute any real action on the climate crisis, aside from unenforceable goals and targets. Zheng 's critics in the West blasted him for these remarks. China had been an unrepentant carbon emitter and continually failed to lead. Lecturing Western governments about their failures struck many as hypocritical at the very least: Chinese leaders were as adept at climate avoidance as any other.

Zheng would offer a similar speech at the World Economic Forum and the United Nations, where he again signaled that China would be taking the lead in climate mitigation, striking a conciliatory tone, inviting other governments and global corporations to follow China's lead. Outside of Davos and New York City, Zheng spoke more bluntly about the current state of affairs. For decades, the assumption among climate activists, government leaders and their envoys was that it would be the liberal Western democracies that would successfully address climate change. But Zheng would constantly say—in private at first and then gradually and more assertively in public—that democracy had produced the crisis in the first place, again, sidestepping Chinese culpability. To expect democracies—with their chaotic, imprecise and unpredictable decision-making processes—to solve this global problem was a fool's errand. Only authoritarianism, only the wise guiding hand of the Party could bring about the necessary changes in behavior required to heal the planet.

Although he would never admit it, Zheng's refashioning of the Chinese economy around circular principles could never have been achieved without the operationalization of fusion power generators. Having long been theoretically predicted, scientific labs around the world had been working on fusion generation for decades. There had been many successes in producing fusion reactions of a few seconds, and 10 years before Zheng 's ascending to power European scientists in Heidelberg had produced a sustained fusion reaction, in effect creating a "microsun" in their labs. It turned out that creating the reaction and sustaining it was the relatively easy part. Given the enormous heat produced, building a container to house the reaction was an engineering wicked problem. Engineers had settled on containing the reaction within a plasma field as the best solution and eventually a number of labs, including one at Tsinghua University, had created fusion generators that could produce electricity to operate a multi-story building.

China's great triumph was solving the scaling problem. A small reaction in a lab was an impressive achievement. Maintaining a reaction at a scale capable of powering a city was quite another. Chinese engineers, under the guiding hand of the Party, succeeded in creating an industrial-sized "fusion dynamo" that could power a small city of two million. While not yet "too cheap to meter," China's fusion dynamos were soon powering many large cities, and the country could finally start to wean itself off of coal power plants. Zheng's predecessor had overseen this technological triumph, but Zheng would reap the benefits. Had this technology been perfected in the West, the patent would have been fought over by competing interests, the intellectual property commercialized in the form of a startup profit-seeking entity. Zheng 's predecessor had taken steps to ensure that the fusion dynamo technology was the monopoly of a Party-owned or at least Party-controlled entity. Zheng 's predecessor had left office just as fusion dynamos were going online. Under Zheng 's leadership, the dynamos demonstrated their effectiveness.

It was up to Zheng to decide how or whether the technology would be shared with others. Zheng weighed his options carefully. On the one hand, other countries might independently solve the scaling problem and would have no need for Chinese technology. But Zheng did not necessarily want to give the technology away on altruistic grounds either. However, doing so would burnish Chinese credentials as the global leader in addressing planetary climate challenges, and so Zheng decided to sell the technology and the patents to any country willing to pay a nominal price. Like the earlier Belt and Road Initiative, Zheng wanted to present fusion dynamos as a gift to the world, not neocolonialism.

But beyond the gaudy ribbon cutting ceremonies, China would extract payment for the technology, scheduled in such a way as to hide the true cost and impact on the countries who dealt with China. In Zheng 's mind, this was similar to the way the world's kingdoms once paid tribute to the Chinese emperor. China would lead not by venturing out into the world; instead, the world would come to China, the Mandate of Heaven. Many cities across Greater Asia as far as Lebanon were offered fusion dynamos. Laos, Cambodia, Vietnam were eager to participate. Even Australia considered striking a deal. Technical training was a small-print feature of such agreements, and a diaspora of Chinese engineers encircled the globe. Zheng would deploy Chinese investment and expertise to encourage environmental authoritarianism around the world.

Europeans debated their participation in the scheme, with most cities gambling that their own researchers would solve the scaling problem. But it was clear the West lagged significantly behind in scaling fusion energy. The American government refused the technology as did most of its state governments, although the mayor of San Francisco controversially travelled to Beijing to secure a dynamo for his city. He posed for a picture with Zheng, the Chinese President smirking at this diplomatic humiliation of the Americans. Given the "success" China enjoyed under Zheng's leadership, Western climate activists found themselves in a philosophical quandary. Many believed in democracy, even anarchism. Generations had argued that global cooperation between the world's governments was the only path to reach climate goals. When China began to act on these programs and appeared to be meeting climate targets, climate activists—like the mayor of San Francisco—suddenly found themselves in the uncomfortable position of having to defend the actions of an authoritarian.

Zheng would expand the range of existing Marine Protected Areas (MPA) to cover regions far beyond China's territorial claims. Under Zheng, China assumed a greater leadership role of the Marine Protected Area Agency Partnership and pushed for a more aggressive set of policies. To take one case, Zheng forbade cruise ships from traversing Chinese MPA protected waters, claiming that these tourist vehicles were "floating environmental catastrophes." Under cover of MPA regulations, China would expand its projection of power. Critics argued that China was trying to police or lay claim over the South China Sea and areas even further afield, all in the name of preserving the planet. It seems absurdly simple in hindsight, decades of saber-rattling over the status of Taiwan were ended when Beijing and Taipei agreed to an MPA that would include the "renegade" island. Beijing would encircle Taiwan with environmental laws. Working closely with the government, Beijing laid no claim over the island itself. And legally the waters around Taiwan did not belong to China, although it was a kind of de facto protectorate. International lawyers debated for years the legal status of these claims. Leaders in Taipei were seeking detente with Beijing, still harboring no desire to be annexed. As US global commitments waned, Zheng saw an opportunity to address the "one country, two systems" solution via environmental means.

Protecting the oceans around its regional neighbors was a projection of soft power. Complaints from Vietnam, the Philippines and others were met with invectives from Zheng, who labeled these countries Western lackeys, and chastised their profligate ways. To resist the extension of Chinese MPAs was to perpetuate the degradation of the planet. The seas were traversed not by Chinese warships, but by eco-friendly research vessels, measuring ocean temperature and acidity and ticketing any ship deemed damaging to the ocean ecology. By the end of Zheng 's reign, China had extended MPAs as far as Papua New Guinea, Indonesia and Sri Lanka, although New Delhi would halt the spread of Chinese influence, laying claim to the entirety of the Indian Ocean as its own MPA. South Korea and Japan similarly established its own joint MPA, the Yellow Sea and the East China Sea emerging as ecopolitical flashpoints.

It was difficult to argue that China was acting imperialistically—who wanted to argue against protecting the oceans?—and the fact that Zheng seemingly demilitarized this initiative made it more palatable. But Zheng was unmoved by claims that Chinese protection was too harsh, too draconian, another example of Zheng 's environmental authoritarianism.

The redesign of society around circular principles required the creation of new jobs, and the Party had decades of experience and an elaborate infrastructure for inventing jobs. The more difficult task would be in forcing young, university-educated Chinese to take up these jobs, many of which were dangerous and unpleasant. But Zheng droned on and on about their importance to the new Green China. The new jobs included laundering environmentally polluted areas, retrofitting old factories, rebuilding offices to meet rigid environmental standards. Zheng created an entirely new sector devoted to recycling, which required human laborers—robots were still not precise enough in their diagnoses—to comb through trash, separating waste products into separate bins, to be remade into new products. Adjacent to the recycling centers was an environmental police force who would examine the trash produced by businesses and apartment blocks, to ferret out those still consuming and discarding non-recyclable objects. At first, the police force would ticket customers, but Zheng would extend their jurisdiction to imprison the producers of circularly unsound products in reeducation camps.

These measures obviously affected trade relations with the rest of the world. Nothing would be imported into China that did not meet stringent environmental standards. Trade with the United States slowed to a trickle, as most US products were so badly made that they could not be reintegrated back into the Chinese circular economy. State-owned industries benefited from the trade restrictions, but only in as much as they adhered to the environmental standards. Zheng encouraged enterprising Chinese to set up environmental cleanup businesses, and a new generation of entrepreneurs established recycling businesses, which Zheng lavished with state capital. Material science—engineering recycled and reusable materials and integrating these back into the consumer society—became the top major at Tsinghua University, followed by environmental engineering. Party elites had always been drawn from the ranks of engineers. Under Zheng 's presidency, environmental engineers became the personification of the new Green China.

The thriving middle class that had emerged in China decades earlier had given way to what Western critics called a "new pauperism." Zheng demanded that social media influencers wear simple, handmade, circular fashions; for his part, Zheng was always seen in public wearing a suit made from hemp and recycled biopolymers. He had hoped that loyal Chinese subjects would emulate his style. When party bosses in the provinces were videoed riding around in expensive automobiles—they were EVs, at least—he instituted a purge of these lower-level functionaries. Many governments around the world had instituted carbon taxes, levied on energy producers and global corporations, all in an effort to change business practices toward ecological sustainability. The results were decidedly mixed, as corporations often bought carbon offsets that allowed them to skirt the rules. Zheng never had faith in carbon taxation but was persuaded by a trusted advisor to levy an individual carbon tax on his subjects. Each person was taxed based on their individual carbon emissions, determined by the products they consumed and their means of transportation and their energy use in their dwellings. Economists had long argued that such a tax was impractical to implement, as a state could never hope to measure every individual's carbon footprint. But Zheng reoriented China's pervasive surveillance infrastructure to home in on individual environmental choices. Local Party officials were expected to monitor people's habits. Many ordinary Chinese balked at the new restrictions, and protests erupted in many cities.

Harking back to his university days, Zheng insisted that the Ministry of Finance stop tracking economic growth, which would no longer be the metric that would define the health of the economy. Zheng began speaking about "Enough." That one-word slogan became China's new economic target, and Zheng announced the first five-year plan to achieve "that which satisfies, that which is required, and nothing more."

The Chinese government had never allowed technological unemployment to spread. Leaders understood the disruptive effects of automation in the United States especially, and were wary about producing too large a class of so called "unproductives." Zhang couched Enough in these terms: the Party would assure every Chinese subject that they would have shelter, food, access to medical care—the lower part of Maslow's hierarchy—but nothing more, because nothing more was necessary. The Party would create new jobs to replace any that had been automated. Zhang wanted to mitigate extreme poverty, and announced that no Chinese subject would be poor or homeless or without work. Zhang wanted all Chinese to aspire to Enough.

Zheng had not yet reached the stage where his every utterance became "Zheng Thought," and thus the Chinese resisted the Enough campaign. Zheng had little patience for this resistance; those who were determined to have more than enough—more possessions, more food, more money—were assigned to eco-reeducation camps, which had spread under his presidency and had grown to become full-fledged internment camps. At their height, two million Chinese were imprisoned, to serve as examples to the rest of the population of what an "environmental degenerate" looked like. Zhang promised to deport anyone to the "linear West" who resisted Enough. A growing dissident movement emerged from these internment camps, which would stalk Zheng until the end of his reign.

Zheng had what can only be described as a conflicted relationship with China's cities. Decades of research by advocates of the circular economy had concluded that cities, on the whole, were better for the ecological health of the planet. And yet, Zheng argued, cities generated most of the solid waste, most of the greenhouse gases, most of the air pollution. Cities vacuumed up resources from their surrounding hinterlands and were responsible for the loss of biodiversity. While population density might have positive ecological benefits, cities were also the source of the political unrest that had dogged his reign. With more fusion-based dynamos going online, coal fired plants were being shuttered, reducing the resources required to power China's cities, and significantly less pollution was being generated. Cities were also the sites of a thriving sharing economy, where urban dwellers split the use of appliances like mixers or vacuum cleaners or automated dusters, meaning fewer of these household items were being manufactured and used. Many Chinese companies converted their businesses into product-as-services firms where the object cost a consumer little to nothing to buy, while the maintenance and service and repair of the object was where the money was made. Rather than discarding objects, consumers had them repaired, extending the lifespan of many consumer items four to five times longer than usual. While far from perfect, Chinese cities were among the most environmentally sustainable on Earth.

None of this satisfied Zheng. Environmental capital scores remain distressingly low for him, although a more objective assessment would have revealed that the Chinese were among the most ecologically conscious in the world. At a Party congress, Zheng announced what became known as the "Down to the City" campaign. This was to be the inverse of Mao's "Down to the Countryside" in the 1960s and 70s, where disobedient pseudo-bourgeois youths were exiled to the countryside, there to learn from the peasants and rural dwellers. Zheng had no intention of returning people to the countryside. Instead, he instituted a massive urban agriculture program. Every city in China above 10 million inhabitants was required to become agriculturally self-sufficient. This entailed refitting buildings to hydroponically produce crops. The exterior and roofs of buildings became fields to grow rice, wheat, potatoes, tomatoes, sorghum, peanuts, tea, millet, barley, cotton, oilseed, corn and soybeans. Former office towers became stables and pens and sites for animal husbandry.

And most controversial of all, young urbanites who had established careers in marketing, finance and other knowledge industries were forcibly retrained to be farm workers. There was no need to relocate them to the countryside, as in Mao's time. These newly made farmers could keep on living in their flats, only now they reported to the soybean manufacturer or chicken processing facility a block or two away. There was the predictable resistance to this social engineering project, and new unrest erupted in many cities, which Zheng violently suppressed. The agitators were adherents of a discredited economic ideology that had led to the climate crisis, he bellowed. Their resistance served no other reason than to prop up their personal aggrandizement. Suppression, arrests, internment, these measures dampened the resistance to Zheng's reforms but did not extinguish them.

After the long reign of Xi Jinping, the National People's Congress returned to its regular practice of selecting presidents to serve five-year terms. Zheng's predecessor served 8 years; he was granted a second five-year term, but midway through was removed by a faction aligned against him. Zheng was not a member of this faction, but their actions gave him the opportunity he was seeking. Zheng came to power with no intention of being term limited. Term-limits were a product of short-term Western thinking, he said. For a polity that traces its lineage over five millennia, "clipping a leader's time" would be like recklessly pruning the tree. The NPC granted him a second term and as the end of that term approached, Zheng maneuvered to be awarded a third term. Because he ascended to power at a relatively young age, Zheng remained a vigorous leader and saw no reason why he should be retired. After much wrangling, the Congress granted Zheng a third term, but they were clear that it would be his last. The changes he wrought—even if they had the effect of making China the leader in climate mitigation—provoked too much backlash. The National People's Congress determined that in achieving ecological balance and harmony, Zheng had created far too much disorder under Heaven.

Key Futures Themes

- Environmental authoritarianism
- Circular Economy
- Social Credit Systems
- Eco-Reeducation
- Environmental Imperialism
- State-imposed Degrowth
- Urban Agricultural
- Environmental Surveillance
- Elimination of Technological Unemployment
- Government Suppression of Consumerism
- Individual Carbon Taxation

Bibliography

Enninga, Justus. 2023. Environmentalism, a Flirt with Eco-authoritarianism and the Robustness of Ordoliberalism. *Constitutional Political Economy*. https://doi.org/10.1007/s10602-023-09406-z.

Four Plausible Futures: 2050 Scenarios. 2019. ARUP, December 2019.

Hou, Rui, and Diana Fu. 2024. Sorting Citizens: Governing via China's Social Credit System. *Governance: An International Journal of Policy, Administrations and Institutions* 37 (1): 59–78. https://onlinelibrary.wiley.com/doi/10.1111/gove.12751.

Lo, Kevin. 2021. Authoritarian Environmentalism, Just Transition, and the Tension Between Environmental Protection and Social Justice in China's Forestry Reform. *Forest Policy and Economics* 131:102574. https://doi.org/10.1016/j.forpol.2021.102574.

Ma, Wenting, Thomas Hoppe, and Martin de Jong. 2022. Policy Accumulation in China: A Longitudinal Analysis of Circular Economy Initiatives. *Sustainable Production and Consumption* 34:490–504. https://doi.org/10.1016/j.spc.2022.10.010.

Marine Protected Area Agency Partnership (MPAAP). n.d. IUCN (International Union for Conservation of Nature). https://iucn.org/our-work/topic/marine-ecosystems/marine-protected-area-agency-partnership-mpaap.

Tripathi, Aman. n.d. US Plasma Effect Breakthrough Could Boost Nuclear Fusion Reactor Efficiency, Lifespan. MSN. https://www.msn.com/en-us/money/markets/us-plasma-effect-breakthrough-could-boost-nuclear-fusion-reactor-efficiency-lifespan/ar-AA1Eyv5Y?ocid=finance-verthp-feeds.

What is a Circular Economy? Ellen Macarthur Foundation. n.d. https://www.ellenmacarthurfoundation.org/topics/circular-economy-introduction/overview.

Chapter 13
Amar Chaudhri: Storm Chaser

Like hundreds of thousands of others, Amar Chaudhri's parents, Kumar and Jothi, were forced to leave Delhi. As the temperatures made the city largely uninhabitable, the annual deaths from extreme heat regularly numbered in the tens of thousands. They were part of the first wave of the Bharatiye diaspora throughout the Indo-Pacific. Initially, professional couples like the Chaudhris were relatively safe in Delhi, as they had access to temperature-controlled shelter that offered some relief. As the city continued to warm, professionals left the city, at first for "summer homes." Others began to look for more hospitable climes outside of Bharat to resettle. Kumar and Jothi moved to Perth, which was relatively cooler compared to Delhi, although not by much.

At first, they moved to Visakhapatnam on the Bay of Bengal, which provided some relief from the soaring temperatures. But their home was struck by two major cyclones just 3 years apart. Coastal flooding and erosion were already major problems. Now more frequent, more intense storms made even Visakhapatnam unlivable. Like people almost everywhere else in the world, Kumar and Jothi became part of the great climate migration, that vast movement of people.

Moving to another country was quite difficult. Many states erected legal and physical walls to prevent people from entering "climate oases." But Kumar and Jothi were able to emigrate to Australia as they fit the profile set by the Australian government. Australia welcomed immigrants if they met two criteria: immigrants had to be professionals, those deemed productive and unlikely to depend on public welfare. This meant almost all the world's "unproductives," those made redundant by automation, were excluded. Second, immigrants would need to arrive in families with children already, or with the expectation that they would produce children. Like many nations, Australia looked to reverse decades of population decline by encouraging targeted immigration. Kumar was an environmental engineer, and Jothi was a synthetic biology technician. Further, Jothi was pregnant with Amar when they were admitted into Perth. It turned out that because they were Bharatiye,

D. Staley, *Anticipatory Biographies*, Anticipation Science 10,
https://doi.org/10.1007/978-3-032-08912-0_13

they had another advantage that other climate migrants to Australia lacked. Both belonged to the Kshatriya caste, although neither ever gave much notice to this designation. The Australian authorities used caste designation as an unstated factor in whether to admit migrants from Bharat. Long assumed to be a vestige of Bharat's past, caste inexplicably turned out to be a key determinant in how Bharatiye immigrants were received by their new countries.

As a boy, Amar understood very little of his parents' history. He was Australian through and through. His friends called him Marty, and he was a rabid supporter of the West Coast Eagles. His parents never grasped the appeal of Australian rules football, but Amar had an aptitude as a half-forward, and the sport made him lifelong friends. Amar looked different, of course, and he occasionally had to endure racist barbs. Living in a relatively wealthy suburb of Perth, his parents connected with an Bharatiye expatriate community. Amar, for his part, distanced himself from his parents, their friends and their rituals. His was a typical story often repeated: of the child of immigrants who was not of his parents' country, but not entirely of his host country, either. Like many second-generation immigrants, Amar identified principally with his new home, which was never "new" to him. Perth had always been home. His assimilation was complete—and a small rift opened with his father—when Amar supported Australia in the Test match against Bharat in Melbourne.

Amar was a good student and earned his Senior Secondary Certificate with a particular interest in maths. Like many ambitious young Australians, Amar was interested in climate change mitigation: living with and adapting to global warming and its consequent effects. Unlike the Americans, who continued to ignore the challenge, or the Chinese with their eco-authoritarianism, Australians set about the task of adapting to the new reality. They continued to reduce their carbon emissions and transitioned to a nuclear-based energy grid, but Australians also realized that the opportunity to return the Earth to its climate status of 150 years ago had long been squandered. Government policy was aimed at learning to live in the new reality, in managing the effects of climate change. Enterprising Australians turned their imaginations toward "acclimatization tech." In those parts of Australia that saw regular summer temperatures in the 50 °C range, one Australian startup developed a slender body suit that cooled its wearer such that they could easily withstand the oppressive heat. (Amar's parents wondered if they might have stayed in Bharat had they owned such suits.) It should also be said that most residents of Darwin stayed indoors in the summer, but the suits made it easier for the city to provide services. Anyone who had to be out of doors in the summer was afforded at least some protection. The suits became worldwide bestsellers. Some observers predicted that wider distribution of the suits would certainly curb the pressures of climate migration.

Amar had a particular interest in meteorology. "Weather tech" was another high-growth sector and, again, Australians were the world leaders here. His interest in meteorology was driven in part by the prestige the field enjoyed in Australia, but it was also the result of learning more about his parents' journey. Before leaving for university, Amar sat with his parents at the dinner table one evening and asked them to tell him about why they moved to Australia. This interest began as curiosity about his own origins, about why he was called Amar, about their attachment to Bharat. In learning more about their lives, he was learning more about himself. But even as a teenager, Amar was not blind to the global climate migration phenomenon. As he matured, as he learned more about the world, it was clear to him that his identity was wrapped up with climate migration. Although he never publicly admitted it, becoming a meteorologist was the result of the choice his parents were once forced to make.

Chaudhri attended the University of Melbourne and earned a fellowship at the Flannery Institute of Climate Research. His graduate research was in paleotempestology, the study of historical data on storms, cyclones, hurricanes, all with the goal of identifying patterns to learn more about how severe storms are born and nurtured. The ultimate prize of this research was developing a model that could predict when, where and how storms would form, and also the path those storms might follow.

Prediction had long been a challenge, but in the first quarter of the century, meteorologists were improving their methods such that many scientists were promising near complete accuracy in storm forecasting. This work applied not only to cyclones and hurricanes, but to American tornadoes as well. (Ironically, the Australians had more interest in tornadoes than American scientists did.) But these rosy visions of the future were dashed as climate change accelerated. Models that worked in retrodicting storms were no longer valid as storms began exhibiting hitherto unseen behaviors. Chaudhri's research involved taking a *longue durée* approach to understanding Indian Ocean cyclones. He assembled data on storms dating back decades and used this temporal context to better understand contemporary storm formation. In some ways. Chaudhri thought himself as much an historian as a meteorologist. His PhD marked him as a rising star and after graduation he began fielding offers to join a number of weather tech companies.

Chaudhri met Laurel Antoniou at university, and they dated steadily even after he joined the Flannery Institute and she joined the Seven Network as a content producer. Antoniou read creativity and imagination at university—one of the "right brainers"—and at first, they seemed an unlikely pair. They were labeled "the scientist and the dreamer." Antoniou was one of a growing cohort of "humanities" scholars. These were not the traditional disciplines like history or philosophy, the "new humanities" were those practices that studied and sought to enhance human attributes. At a time when artificially intelligent systems performed many of the skills previous generations of students sought to develop at university, the new humanities identified uniquely human attributes such as the capacity for wonder and awe, storytelling, creativity, and empathy, attributes no AI had yet demonstrated. Antoniou studied the neurobiological basis of creativity, was an accomplished poet and conceptual artist, and practiced speculative journalism.

Chaudhri could not care less that his parents did not fully approve of the couple. His parents did not believe in or practice arranged marriages, but they would have preferred their son date a Bharatiya. It was Antoniou who introduced Chaudhri to Hindu texts like the Bhagavad Gita, and the Sanskrit Rig Vedas. As a boy, Chaudhri had demonstrated little interest in Bharatiye history or culture, and his parents were more than a little miffed that it was this girl from the Gold Coast that connected Chaudhri to his heritage. It should be said that in addition to these ancient texts, Antoniou introduced Chaudhri to the Epic of Gilgamesh and the Iliad and the Odyssey, expanding his education to include some of the root metaphors of human culture. Learning from Antoniou was one way in which Chaudhri saw himself moving beyond science, or that science alone was insufficient to understand the world.

He was invited to join the Australian Bureau of Meteorology, which was even more prestigious than any of the companies offering him an executive position. After working for a year as a storm modeler, he was selected to join the FitzRoys, a skunk works in the ABM. The ABM drew from their most innovative researchers, but also chemists, environmental and atmospheric scientists from academia and the private sector. Where an earlier generation of young Australians might have aspired to become the founder of a tech startup, some of Australia's best and brightest were assembled together as the FitzRoys.

The actual name of the group was the Advanced Projects Institute, but they were informally named after Admiral Robert FitzRoy, founder of England's Meteorological Office and generally considered to be the inventor of weather forecasting. The FitzRoys were given the freedom to devise new prediction methods with the specific goal of anticipating hurricanes, typhoons and cyclones. That their offices were located in the Melbourne suburb of Fitzroy was a coincidence.

Prediction methods had improved such that meteorologists could anticipate the number of storms that might form in a given season. But these methods had not yet been perfected to determine precisely when and where these storms might form. The FitzRoys worked exclusively in the Indian Ocean, and much of their work involved theorizing the placement of sensors to capture real time data about atmospheric conditions and, crucially, ocean temperatures. The group relied on Chaudhri's work with historical storms in developing a model that could predict the formation of storms. Early detection of the possibility of a storm led to advanced warnings, which were always valuable in preparing populations, but the FitzRoys were working on an even grander project. Beyond predicting storms, the group were developing methods to prevent storms from forming in the first place.

Chaudhri became the resident expert on the personality of storms. As part of the learning journey attempting to predict and control storms, the team thought it important to classify the different kinds of behaviors storms might exhibit. And storms were becoming more and more erratic. Chaudhri mused in his journals—but never made this argument in public—that he was becoming something of a storm psychologist.

At one time, tropical cyclones would form, grow, move through the ocean, wreak havoc on coastal populations, then dissipate. This pattern usually lasted a week to 10 days and, even if its genesis was not yet predictable, the trajectory of the storm was more or less predictable. Then another cyclone or two would pop up throughout the season and the cycle would repeat.

Or at least that was the case until a few decades ago. The reality of the moment was that storms in the Indian Ocean—and the Atlantic and Pacific—were lasting much longer, some swirling on for 3 or 4 weeks. The storm that finally forced

Chaudhri's parents from Visakhapatnam had formed 31 days earlier before slamming into the coast. Because the storms lasted longer, they could be studied in greater detail than was possible before, a small consolation.

Chaudhri's team created a new classification scheme for Indian Ocean cyclones. Rather than basing it on wind speed, the new classification system was based on the behaviors of the storm. Wind speed remained one factor, of course, distinguishing the cyclone from a depression. But some cyclones clung to older, more predictable behaviors. These storms took days to gestate, the gestation period itself adhering to predictable lengths of time. They would gradually rise in size and intensity before slowly weakening. These storms tended to follow predictable paths through the Indian Ocean such that a "cyclone highway" could be theorized by meteorologists. These storms were labeled "legacies."

Chaudhri's team classified and characterized the new kinds of storm behavior that had been made manifest over the last two decades. One category was labeled "exponential." These storms started small, and by all appearances, looked as if they would remain tropical depressions. After swirling for a week, the storm would suddenly and violently burst in size and intensity. Other storms were "stochastic," although younger members of Chaudhri's team called these the "drunkards walk." These storms eschewed the cyclone highway, blazing new trails through the Indian Ocean, or they might begin down a well-worn path, only to suddenly veer off the trail like a disobedient hiker. These storms, in particular, gave meteorologists fits, almost mocking these atmospheric scientists' belief that storms could be predicted. Some storms were called "lingerers." They would form and move even in predictable ways, but then stop suddenly and loiter and dawdle in one locale for days at a time, Cyclone Albine once lingered several hundred kilometers from Madagascar for nearly a fortnight. The residents of the island braced for a siege that was delayed again and again. Some residents felt that the warnings were a government plot to prepare for the imposition of martial law and let down their guard. Then, after lulling people, the storm suddenly began to move, devastating the island. Much of the damage and loss of life came to those areas that had abandoned their storm protection measure. Albine was the most extreme example of a "lingerer," but many other storms exhibited this "hide and seek" kind of behavior. Chaudhri started using the term *psychology* to describe storm behavior, but only in internal presentations at the Fitzroy. This was met with some fearsome pushback, especially from older colleagues who accused Chaudhri of anthropomorphizing storms. "It's bad enough we must assign names to these storms. Let's not go and assign human characteristics to them," this cohort exclaimed.

Cloud seeding was the long-established practice of dropping dry ice or silver iodide into the atmosphere to induce precipitation. The FitzRoys were working on an analogous kind of weather modification. Cooling the entirety of the Indian Ocean was now an impossible task, the tipping point in ocean temperatures having been passed some time ago. But the FitzRoys theorized that by first identifying the location of a latent storm, they could locally cool the ocean surface temperature to deny the storm the energy it required to grow. This process would be the mirror opposite of cloud seeding, or rather, would involve seeding to prevent precipitation. Chaudhri suggested reviving an idea developed by researchers decades earlier: to spread an oil slick over the surface to prevent the ocean water evaporation that gives the storm its energy. For 2 years, the skunkworkers experimented with different substances that could either cool the ocean or prevent evaporation, which was challenging work because of the need to determine the chemical composition of such a substance that was effective, that would easily dissolve after a while, with no environmental consequences, and that could be easily and quickly applied. It was that logistical problem that proved most intractable. The Indian Ocean covered over 27 million square miles. They theorized that a network of tens of thousands of floating drones could be arrayed over the vast surface. The drones had the further benefit of containing the sensors needed to monitor ocean temperatures, badly needed data if their predictive model was to be successful.

When the scheme was presented to them, the leaders of the ABM howled that the cost of deploying such a flotilla of drones was enormous. The FitzRoys countered that the cost of storm damage from the longer-lasting and more intense storms was far greater than the drone array, and so worth the investment. The FitzRoys were scientists, not diplomats, and so were not considering who might foot the bill for the Indian Ocean drone network. The Australian government alone would not pay for it, and neither would any single country that ringed the Indian Ocean. It would take a coordinated regional organization of countries to first agree to the plan, then to finance and maintain the system. The scheme was also based on the assumption that the FitzRoys could predict the appearance of storms. Indeed, the group could never develop a fail-safe predictive model. Despite 5 years of work, the model did produce some successful guesses, but when a major cyclone was missed by the group—a cyclone that caused significant and costly damage to Sri Lanka—it was clear that the model was no better than current ones. The group insisted that with the right amount of real time data, the model would work every time. But to get the data they needed would mean installing the drone monitoring system, a system that was predicated on having a foolproof predictive model. Again, the FitzRoys were scientists, not politicians. Their task was to imagine new solutions, however outlandish or outside-the-box they might seem. Their task was not to finance their ideas. After a decade of research, the FitzRoys were disbanded, their plans viewed as hopelessly quixotic, both because of the complex dynamics involved but also because there were just many more intense storms throughout the world.

Within 4 months of being reintegrated back into the ABM, Chaudhri was assigned tropical depression TD04. Part of the difficulty in predicting where storms would develop and grow was the shifting environmental factors. For a depression to form, sea temperatures would need to be 27 degrees. In the past, this meant a relatively select area of the Indian Ocean would serve as the "cradle of storms." But since ocean temperatures had been rising, the location of storm formation could now be almost anywhere. As with any new storm, Chaudhri would monitor it by noting sensor readings. This was largely an automated process, his task was only to check in on the data on a semi-regular basis. Indeed, he had other storms to monitor, to say nothing of his ongoing theoretical work.

TD04 began its life as any other tropical depression. An early indication suggested it could grow into a tropical storm, Chaudhri estimated within 5 days. This one was formed in the middle of the Pacific Ocean and moved into the Indian Ocean through the Timor Sea. The northern coast of Australia suffered damages. As it grew in size, TD04 moved slowly westward, then picked up speed as it headed toward the east coast of Africa. A week after it had been identified as a tropical depression, Chaudhri upgraded it to a tropical storm, as it now had winds of 70 mph. Two days later, it was a cyclone, advancing westward across the Indian Ocean.

Then without warning, when it looked all but certain to strike the coast of Kenya, the storm veered southward. Now named Tej, the cyclone clipped Madagascar, causing significant damage. In many cases, a storm making landfall would dissipate as it loses energy from the seawater. But Tej was of sufficient size that, although temporarily diminished, it gained more energy and momentum at some point along this journey. Chaudhri gave over his full attention to studying the storm.

Usually in such circumstances, when a storm became a cyclone, Chaudhri would devote most of his attention to collating and analyzing the telemetry from the sensors. From the start, Chaudhri realized this was no ordinary storm. When they pass over land, cyclones exhibit common behaviors, losing their energy at fairly predictable rates. Tej did not lose as much energy as the models would have indicated. That was not atypical: several recent cyclones had confounded the predictions, but Chaudhri noted it nevertheless. The storm glided eastward, growing in size and strength and appeared to be heading back toward Western Australia. Chaudhri hesitated to call for a warning, and this decision proved prescient. Unexpectedly, the storm essentially stopped 6000 km from Australia. It remained relatively stationary for 3 days, and then slowly made its way northward. As it did so, the storm was reduced in size such that Chaudhry gave it a Category One rating. Everyone assumed the storm would dissipate by the time it reached the equator.

Although it was theoretically possible, a cyclone could not pass over the equator, the shift in Coriolis forces when crossing into the northern hemisphere tearing the storm apart. Chaudhri watched as the storm danced right up to the line, losing some energy, but still a tremendous force. He began calculating the possibility of the storm crossing the equator and carrying on, possibly toward Bharat. Instead, after 4 days Tej doubled back, heading toward Africa again. Chaudhri would have expected the storm to continue more westward but was surprised at this doubling back behavior.

Chaudhri was now obsessed. Like Captain Ahab, he chased Tej around the Indian Ocean. Sometimes Tej would sit quietly, as a Category 1, languishing near the Southern Ocean. Then, suddenly, it would spring to life as a Category 3 and streak across the Indian Ocean, slamming into land, then retreat back to the sea, where it would saunter eastward. At first, Chaudhri observed Tej via satellite images and telemetry, but he felt he had to get inside the storm. Specially fitted drones were the tool of choice when flying into the eye of a cyclone. Chaudhri had once been in a plane that flew into Cyclone Asani 5 years earlier. He understood the safety concerns as the reason for using aerial drones, but nevertheless longed to see inside this bedeviling storm.

The eye of Tej exhibited unusual properties. Winds are usually calm at the center of a cyclone, and Tej certainly was calm, at least part of the time. The drone picked up eddies and swirls at the center, brief encounters, but still wholly novel. The eye of the storm fluctuated in unpredictable ways as it progressed on its journey across the Indian Ocean. As the storm edged southward, it once again lingered in the middle of the ocean before heading eastward again toward Australia. This time, the storm made landfall, missing a direct hit on Perth by only 20 km. Tej ravaged the coast for 2 days before heading back out to sea. It was showing no sign of diminishing. Indeed, it seemed to grow stronger with each encounter with land.

By this point, the storm had persisted for almost 2 months. After making landfall in Perth, the storm refused to dissipate, moving back out to sea and regaining strength. It slowly skittered across the vast reaches of the Indian Ocean, coming near Madagascar, but not enough to trigger warnings. It then swung back toward the east again and by the end of its third month—now unprecedented—it had once again reached Category Five strength.

Through Papua New Guinea a new storm had developed. As it entered the Indian Ocean, it quickly grew in strength to Category Two. It looked as though it would skim Northern Australia without consequence. The storm had been assigned to another meteorologist, but it was becoming uncomfortably clear that Manu, as it was called, and Tej were headed toward each other.

Very typically, storms trailed each other in a single file, all leading in the same direction. Tej was no ordinary storm, of course. The possibility of an extremely rare Fujiwhara effect was becoming evident by the minute, and Chaudhri was reassigned to monitor both Manu and Tej. For six harrowing days, a large-scale sumo wrestling event played out in the middle of the Indian Ocean. Both cyclones encircled each other, the two eyes rotating like binary stars with a kind of super eye forming in the midst of their encounter. Anything was possible here: the two storms might dance together, then fling each other to go their separate ways. Or one might consume the other. He made a request to take a plane to the site to observe firsthand, but was denied, forced to watch on a screen. Everything that was known about the behavior of storms had been rendered meaningless by Tej, the longest major storm on record. Tej was more powerful than Manu, and eventually the larger storm swallowed the smaller, becoming even larger, even more powerful. "The Storm Eater," the feeds described Tej, which was moving into the status of worldwide legend.

What would the storm do now? Chaudhri was beginning to wonder if the storm would ever lessen. As long as the warm ocean waters were feeding it, he postulated that the storm might last even longer than the one that lasted 88 days, the previous record. Theoretically, a storm need never dissipate, so long as certain highly improbable events converge. He began making calculations as to the likelihood of this scenario. Meanwhile, Tej continued to pinball through the Indian Ocean, exhibiting every one of the storm behaviors Chaudhri developed for the FitzRoys. Tej would linger for days, dancing on the border between the warm Indian Ocean and the relatively colder Southern Ocean. Chaudhri wondered—hoped, really—that the storm would travel southward, reaching the cooler waters around Antarctica, and thus run out of energy. But it never did, always teetering near the Southern Ocean. He began to feel as if the storm were taunting him, laughing at him.

By this stage, Chaudhri had become a regular feature on the Australian networks, providing updates on the status of the cyclone and its possible next steps. Like the audiences who tuned in each day and various government ministers, Chaudhri was becoming increasingly frustrated at his inability to predict the future behavior of the storm, or even to venture a guess as to when it would dissolve back into the ocean. Beneath his breath, he cursed the lack of sufficient atmospheric and oceanic sensors, feeling that if he had precise enough data, his models would be more effective at predicting the cyclone's behavior. Chaudhary was not blind to the larger challenges; the increasingly warmer temperatures of the Indian Ocean and other unseen effects of the warming planet were rendering storms more volatile, longer lasting and more dangerous. He feared that models and the assumptions upon which they were built would need to be jettisoned. While he was pressured to say so in front of the cameras, Chaudhri was not yet ready to admit when or if the storm would ever end.

The odd behavior of storms was not confined to the Indian Ocean. A year after Tej had finally subsided and Chaudhary had left the ABM, a hurricane in the Atlantic slammed into the Florida Panhandle and made its way up the Atlantic coast of the United States. Historically, such a storm might extend as far north as New England and then head out to sea where it would disintegrate, except in this case, the storm retained its coherence and velocity and, in fact, circled southward out into the Atlantic, then turned westward to, once again, impact the Caribbean and the United States. Only in crossing the United States did the storm subside, but not until states as far north as Ohio were hit by Category One-strength winds. Indeed, meteorologists were continuing to call Hannah a hurricane, even as it traversed the North American land mass. Chaudhri was called in to confer with US meteorologists, since he was now—whether he liked it or not—understood to be the world's leading expert on "long storms." One conclusion he drew was that hurricanes and cyclones were becoming bigger and inexhaustible to such an extent that anyone looking at the planet from space would be forced to conclude that the Earth was permanently encircled by a virtual "Red Spot."

The more he studied it—stalked it, really—the more Chaudhri began to ascribe behaviors to Tej. In his mind and in the journal he began to keep, he saw a personality in Tej. Every time he thought he had figured out its next move, the storm confounded Chaudhri s expectations. He began to take their cat and mouse adventure across the Indian Ocean personally, as if Tej were toying with him, making him look foolish. If he did not know better, he would have assigned Tej a kind of consciousness and intentionality, or perhaps something like a survival instinct. Was Tej alive? As a scientist, Chaudhri understood how absurd these notions were. The data simply did not warrant anything like these fanciful and absurd speculations. But then Chaudhri was beginning to wonder if he was, in fact, a scientist, or if he was transforming into something else.

Across its 215-day lifespan, the cyclone would always be known as Tej. But in his memoir/history of the event, he would call it Indra, King of the Divas in

Hinduism. Indra's historical associations had always been connected to the sky, weather, lightning and thunder and storms. This Indra, this was surely the king of all storms, with powers beyond any other before it. In the same way Indra killed the evil Vritra, this Indra devoured the evil Manu, or at least that was how Chaudhri recounted the meteorological event. In ascribing Indra with intent, with deliberate behavior, he was fashioning a new mythology, for he could think of no better way to tell the story of the cyclone that would not die. His parents never overtly expressed it to him, but he could tell they were pleased that their son had some remnant of Bharatiye culture in him. *The Epic of Indra* was published to great fanfare and was translated into a dozen languages, and provided a new framework for understanding long storms.

He no longer believed himself to be a scientist, or rather that science was no longer sufficient for understanding storms. He had become the historian, the anthropologist, the psychologist, the biographer of Indra. He had come to realize that the data had never been enough.

Key Futures Themes

- Climate Migration and Identity Fragmentation
- Extreme Weather Behavior
- Uninhabitable Urban Centers
- Weather Modification Technology
- Scientific Paradigm Collapse

Bibliography

Behar, Michael. 2005. Can We Stop Storms? *Popular Science* 267 (6): 17.

Cappucci, Matthew. 2023. Deadly Cyclone Freddy Has Become Earth's Longest-Lived Tropical Storm. *Washington Post*, 7 March 2023. https://www.washingtonpost.com/weather/2023/03/07/cyclone-freddy-indian-ocean-hurricane/.

Freddy: The Deadly Cyclone That Lasted More Than a Month. *BBC* Weather, 17 March 2023. https://www.bbc.com/news/world-africa-64978492.

Saaliq, Sheikh. 2023. Why India's Government Wants to Change the Country's Name to 'Bharat'. *AP News*, 5 September 2023. https://apnews.com/article/india-sanskrit-name-bharat-modi-g20-72782ba81aa67dcf7e197a98fec9b5f5.

Schlanger, Zoë. 2023. Hurricane Otis Was Too Fast for the Forecasters. *The Atlantic*, 25 October 2023. https://www.theatlantic.com/science/archive/2023/10/hurricane-otis-forecast-warming-oceans/675773/.

Shelton, Jim. 2022. Future Hurricanes Will Roam Over More of the Earth, Study Predicts. *YaleNews*, 3 January 2022. https://news.yale.edu/2022/01/03/future-hurricanes-will-roam-over-more-earth-study-predicts.

Shepherd, Marshall. 2018. Why Hurricanes Almost Never Form Near Or Cross The Equator. *Forbes*, 28 June 2018. https://www.forbes.com/sites/marshallshepherd/2018/06/28/why-hurricanes-almost-never-form-near-or-cross-the-equator/.

Zimmer, Katarina. 2023. The Secret Messages in Ancient Storms. *Nautilus*, 23 June 2023. https://nautil.us/the-secret-messages-in-ancient-storms-312906/.

Chapter 14
Saitō Miku: Supercentenarian

As Saitō Miku lay quietly on her bed, looking at the faces of her family and friends, she could confidently feel that she had no regrets in her life. No, she wasn't a pop influencer, no, she didn't contribute much to the community. No, she wasn't as reliable a spouse as she would have liked, but she would die in the knowledge that she lived her life forward, and she lived her life well. Hers was an otherwise unremarkable life, certainly not the kind that someone would write a biography about.

That she was born at all was an improbable event. Few of her parents' generation had children, and Saito's would wait until their late 30s before deciding to have her. The technology of the artificial placenta meant that women in their 40s and in some cases their 50s and even 60s could bear children. Saito would similarly have ambivalent feelings about parenthood. She would finally bear children and would raise her children and would love her children.

As a child, she received her first genetic screening, mandatory for all Japanese once they turned 3 years old. The procedure mapped the genetic code of each individual, looking especially for genetic anomalies, markers of disease that might manifest years later. Saito had only vague memories of the procedure. She remembered her mother taking her to a building, and that she waited with dozens of other children. As for the scan itself, she felt nothing or remembered feeling nothing.

In some cases, if a particular genetic disorder was discovered, a child might undergo gene therapy or even CRISPR replacement of the defective genes. The government estimated that some tens of thousands of cases that would have resulted in medical issues later in life were prevented as a result of this aggressive intervention. In fact, this was Saito's second screening. She had been tested while in utero. She had no genetic abnormalities, but for fetuses who did, the Japanese had pioneered a number of genetic interventions. These early interventions ensured that children born in Japan would have a life expectancy far greater than any other nation in the world.

D. Staley, *Anticipatory Biographies*, Anticipation Science 10,
https://doi.org/10.1007/978-3-032-08912-0_14

Saito would only come to understand later that she was born into a society that was being redesigned for longevity rather than GDP growth, the production and consumption of things. As a measure of prosperity, Japan had made the decision that quality of life, and especially longevity of life, would be the chief measure of the success of the economy and society. Of course, basic Maslow-level needs would have to be met, but these were viewed as necessary to help ensure long life. For almost a century, Japan had led the world in life expectancy. Her grandmother lived to 92, a statistically not unexpected lifespan. Her father would live to be 107. That she would live to be 121 was also not statistically unexpected.

Japanese society was reorganized around the principles of gerontonomics. This was a term invented by the economist Abe Hideyoshi. Writing in *The Economics of Longevity*, Abe asked the Japanese to restructure their economic priorities to focus on maximizing longevity for everyone. Instead of traditional metrics like GDP, wealth accumulation, or shareholder returns, Abe advocated for measuring success by how well a society extended and improved lives. This shift would reframe the idea of an "aging population" in developed nations as a positive indicator rather than a problem, as it had been framed for too long. Abe said that support systems for the elderly should be seen as a core purpose of the economy rather than as financial drains.

Abe argued that any decrease in life expectancy should be considered as serious as an economic downturn, prompting swift and decisive policy actions to tackle the root causes of the decline. Indeed, implementing the gerontonomic paradigm, moving it from the realm of economic theory to policy practice, occurred when Japan suffered an unexpected decline in its life-expectancy. Whether the result of the novel virus pandemic or some other factors, Japan's life expectancy had suddenly and unexpectedly plateaued and even began to decline slightly when her parents were in their late 40s. Japan's life expectancy still led the world, but the government and society at large were startled and unsettled. Abe's theoretical work, which included a lengthy list of policy interventions, was enacted. A Ministry of Gerontonomics was established, and soon this portfolio became one of the more powerful positions in Japanese politics.

Abe asserted that a gerontonomic economy would not neglect the needs of the young. Instead, it would prioritize the well-being of all ages by encouraging healthy habits and behaviors. The government would ensure that essential resources like healthcare and nutritious food were available to everyone, and physical activity would be integrated into daily life. Economic policies would promote longevity by incentivizing walking, sleep, and other healthy habits.

Abe even proposed using "miles walked per capita" as a new economic metric. Saito was like millions of Japanese who had downloaded a popular walking app, which measured the distance and time engaged in walking every day. No one was punished for not walking, but they were most certainly incentivized with reductions in their taxes during their first working life. Saito lived in a part of Tokyo that had undergone 15-minute city restructuring. She walked everywhere to her job, to the market, to her child's school, to her doctor. This was certainly the most expensive part of the gerontonomic restructuring of society, but perhaps the most effective.

Miles walked per capita increased steadily. No other country on Earth was so devoted to the health of its population.

Ensuring adequate sleep became an objective of economic policy, with employers incentivizing employees to get 8 hours of sleep each night. The mid-afternoon nap became a normal part of Japanese daily life. Saito was especially fond of the afternoon *hirune* and rarely missed a chance to leave work for her one-hour nap. She would occasionally think of her great-grandparents, of the generation of the "salarymen" who worked debilitatingly long hours. They probably would not recognize Japanese society today. Just as workers had historically advocated for shorter work hours, more sick time, or paid leave, some Japanese workers had demanded the right to have nap breaks incorporated into the workday.

Researchers had long understood that strong friendships and social connections also contributed to longevity, and the Japanese Ministry of Gerontonomics developed initiatives to address loneliness. This was not at all a problem for Saito, who throughout her life kept deep and long-lasting friendships. Indeed, her friends were more important to her than her husband, perhaps even her children. Government policy would focus not only on extending life but on improving the quality of life as well. In this framework, the emphasis was on ensuring a good, fulfilling life as much as on increasing its duration. The Ministry measured happiness, well-being, and overall quality of life; reports on these numbers were met with the kind of expectation that an earlier generation reserved for unemployment figures, the direction of interest rates or stock market process.

Saito's childhood was typical. Formal schooling was mandatory and still highly valued in Japanese society. Japanese leaders looked on in dismay as American education had disintegrated. In contrast, Japanese school children were significantly tracked. Students took tests starting as early as age 10 to determine which job or career path would define the first third of their life. An individual student's curriculum was tied to their test results and would even influence their placement in Japan's system of higher education. Saito tested into a medical chemistry track, although she was much more interested in music, theater and dance. Aside from music, these subjects were not a formal part of most school curricula. Students with these interests and aptitudes exercised them in clubs or in informal associations. Saito started up one of these groups, who would meet some evenings to sing and dance and play, all of which was performed for audiences on the feeds. Much more so than working in medical chemistry, Saito wanted to be an influencer, which she would do after her graduation from Nippon Life Science University and after starting her first job. She never had many subscribers. However, this did not stop her from devoting much of her free time to creating content, even if it was not remunerative. Singing and dancing gave her great joy. "Wasn't the purpose of life to be happy?" she rationalized.

Her day job was in plastic removal. She was a technician who helped filter microplastics from the body. Even before the government acted on the problem, Japanese society expressed alarm at the reports that microplastics had seeped not only into the environment but into the human body, even into the brain. Other problems loomed, of course, climate chaos most obviously. But opinion polls and parliamentary elections signaled over and over that the Japanese were concerned with this public health crisis.

Researchers developed a filtering process and Saito's first job was as a technician administering the treatment. This was similar to dialysis. The patient's blood was removed from the body, "cleansed" through an elaborate filtration system, then reintroduced back into the body. Removing microplastics from the brain was an obviously more difficult procedure, and it was only at the end of her first career that techniques for filtering cerebral fluid started to go through clinical trials. Most patients had the procedure every 10 years or so, the frequency of a colonoscopy, say. Saito had her first filtering when she was in high school, unaware as she was being injected that this would be her first career. Saito usually worked 10-hour shifts, 4 days a week. Because of the delicate nature of the procedure, it had never been fully automated, and so technicians like Saito were always in demand, for which she was grateful. But after more than 25 years of filtering bodies, she was more than ready for her first retirement.

During this stage of her working life, Saito might have been expected to meet a young man or woman, get married and have children. Unlike some countries with coercive, pro-natalist policies, the Japanese government had taken a laissez faire approach. Many couples, especially women, delayed childbirth if they decided to have kids at all. Nevertheless, even in the absence of an official policy, there remained deeply rooted gender assumptions and expectations. Women who were childless were frowned at, and were deemed selfish, unproductive, not contributing to the welfare of society. It must be said, of course, that these attitudes were formed mostly by Japanese men.

Saito's work schedule gave her ample time for socializing, and much of this time was spent with girlfriends making content. They sang and danced along to classics from AKB48 and Scandal and Takako Matsu, the kind of music her grandmother would have listened to. While she and her friends had followers, they never numbered more than a few thousand. Everyone understood that to really get ahead in Japanese society, you had to be an influencer with millions of followers. It was still the best way to get into the best universities, to secure the best jobs, to find the best romantic partners.

She dated in her early 20s, although she found most of the men immature and underwhelming. She contemplated for a while the idea of having children on her own, inseminating an artificial placenta. She paid no mind to the social pressures against this option. In the end, she met Ichiro Hachiro, and they would marry a year later. Ichiro followed Saito on her feed. In another time, he might have been labeled a stalker, but this was how many young Japanese couples hooked up. Now, had she been more popular, she might have attracted a better quality of husband. Ichiro was a quantum fusion harmonizer and proved to be a reliable partner for her. Whether or not she loved Ichiro was a question she asked herself throughout their relationship.

She was as attentive as any young Japanese mother. She had the services of a robotic au pair to help her raise her children, ostensibly to allow her to work, but she used this convenience to try and build her influencer career. Like most Japanese men, Ichiro played little role in raising the children. Her children liked watching their mother perform on the feeds to the old timey music, and she would often sing and dance with them to their own creations. Saito was very keen to raise her children in a house where music and play and theater were abundant. It must be said that she was not a faithful spouse, having affairs with men and women, which was hardly unexpected behavior for a young person of her generation.

After working at the filtering clinic, Saito took her first retirement at the legally mandated age of 45. She had several options to consider. Many young Japanese took the first few years of retirement to travel, and Saito visited Kyoto, Hawaii and Indonesia. When they went traveling, Saito and her friends frequented dance clubs where they were recognized as very minor celebrities. Some commentators had taken to calling this phase of life a "second childhood," and that was certainly how Saito lived it, enjoying reduced responsibilities and more control over her time. A new enterprise, the "playground" for 40- and 50-year olds, became commonplace across Tokyo and other Japanese cities. These were a combination bar, dance club, and jungle gym. Saito took up tennis and would take third place at her club's annual tournament.

This was perhaps the greatest, most challenging and costliest aspect of building a gerontonomic society. Via a series of complex and controversial laws, the very rhythms of life in Japan were redesigned. Saito's grandparents were expected to work until they were 75 then settle into retirement. Saito's generation now understood that work and retirement alternated throughout one's life, cyclical periods of work and leisure. Her children were grown and had moved out of the house, and so her responsibilities as a mother were now discharged. She would remain close to her adult children, but she now enjoyed her time off as they entered the workforce, reversing the roles they had played over the last 20 years.

Saito divorced Ichiro, a not unexpected development. For many couples who reached first retirement, either with no children or with grown children, divorce was quite common. Close to 57% of these marriages were dissolved. Saito engaged in a number of liaisons; this period of her life was one of sexual experimentation.

It was during her first retirement that she met Sasaki Mei, whom Saito would call the love of her life. The two never married but remained a couple until their 80s. Unlike many Japanese women, Saito decided against starting a second family, although there were at least a few Japanese couples that used the first retirement period to have another child using the artificial placenta. There emerged an interesting sociological phenomenon, where a 50-year-old woman would simultaneously be a grandmother and a mother of a newborn. They were called "double parents." Saito had no interest in being a parent again, and only halfheartedly looked forward to being a grandmother. She secretly hoped her children would not marry or have kids. If they were able to just enjoy life as she had, she would be pleased.

After a few years of travel, parties and finding a new partner, Saito decided to re-attend university. For anyone who wanted to advance in their career or who wanted a new career after retirement, re-entering university was a necessity. There were quite a few Japanese who eschewed quaternary education, content either to return to their previous jobs or take a position that didn't require an advanced degree. As part of the redesign of the rhythms of life, the Japanese had pioneered the development of quaternary education. These institutions catered to students in their 40s and 50s, prestigious universities as difficult to enter as those aimed at 20-year-olds. Saito took the standard entrance examinations and scored better than she did in her teens. She decided to pursue a perpendicular career path for the next phase of her working life. She would obtain a degree in biological design, completing a Bachelor's and Master's at the Tokyo University of Pharmacy. Her first career was as a clinical technician; for her second career, she would be a biochemical researcher.

At the age of 53 Saito began her second career at Jinsei, a synthetic biology company. Like many working adults at this stage of her life, Saito was a middle manager overseeing a team of researchers in Japan's world-beating pharmaceutical sector. Saito was not a bench scientist. These were usually younger colleagues, 20- and 30-year-olds, fresh from the top universities. Nor was she yet a designer, those who imagined and built the architecture of synthetic biological components. Perhaps if Saito had greater ambition, she might have ended her second career in such an executive position, but managing both people and automated processes was sufficient enough for her. It meant she was carrying out directives from those above her in the corporation, but she had the freedom to define her own hours and to be a part of a critical industry. Indeed, Saito found herself mentoring some of her younger charges, a position that the 20-year-old Saito could have scarcely imagined. Her colleagues found her to be an agreeable boss, if for no other reason that she seemed to shield them from the glare of the executives.

Her life with Sasaki Mei was more important to her than her career, although Sasaki's profession as a climate mitigation engineer often meant long hours spent apart, which strained their relationship. Saito had one grandchild, but Sasaki's child was unmarried and did not have children.

If she was to have any job at this point in her life, Saito was thrilled to be a part of the pharmaceutical industry. Because Japan had foregrounded life expectancy and longevity as anchors of social and economic policy, any industry that extended life had special privileges and prerogatives. After globalization gave way to what economists were calling "strategic capitalism," the Japanese government began a long-term strategy of directing resources and venture capital into those enterprises that worked to extend human life. "Innovation" in the Japanese economy meant, specifically, the technologies of prolonging human life.

Decades earlier, scientists had discovered that *Turritopsis dohrnii*, a species of jellyfish, had the unusual property of never aging, constantly reverting back to a younger stage of its life cycle. In theory, *Turritopsis dohrnii* never died of old age. It could be eaten or otherwise deprived of life, but absent any such catastrophe, the jellyfish did not die. Jinsei was the first enterprise to identify the specific gene sequence that afforded this property and to deliver it as a pharmaceutical. Rogue synthetic biologists had tried unsuccessfully to replicate this genetic pattern and to reproduce or otherwise splice it into human DNA. These unscrupulous entrepreneurs called their search "the Fountain of Youth," skirting any number of international accords aimed at thwarting such Moreau-ian efforts. They were never successful: legitimate scientists knew that the quest for genetically-engineered immortality was unlikely, even impossible, but not before one entrepreneur unleashed a genetically-altered teenager who mercifully died before his suffering could overwhelm him.

That would have seemed to have ended any such research into immortality, but Jinsei received official blessings to proceed, one, for the stringent protocols they followed, and two, because their stated goal was not immortality, but to slow the aging process, to add years to life that a patient might not otherwise have. There had long been companies that had developed an injection to extend the life of a dog. Indeed, today most pets live 20–30 years, largely the result of these injections. Jinsei developed the first injection that slowed the aging process in humans.

Saito's team developed the prototype and were working on the clinical trials. This process necessarily took years to study. Since the goal was to slow aging, this process would need to be observed over a minimum of 10 years. Side effects included organ overburdening in some patients, and in about 3% of test cases, evidence of cellular dysfunction was indicated. But otherwise, one injection was demonstrated to extend life by 11.4 years in men and 13.6 years in women.

Saito was a project manager, one of a dozen on the *Turritopsis dohrnii* project. Although she harbored no great ambitions to move up in the company, she was slightly miffed when an advanced AI agent was promoted ahead of her. Truth be told, Saito never got along with the bot. She thought the AI was too aggressive, too willing to cut corners, unconcerned with safety. The executives at Jinsei obviously didn't agree and promoted the AI agent to Director of the *Turritopsis dohrnii* project. Eventually, the AI would ascend to a vice president's role within the company.

Its safety and efficacy now proven, it was only to be determined when a patient would or should receive Kurage, as the drug was known. Clinical studies indicated that patients in their mid-50s could receive the treatment. When the government had given its authority, a large cohort of Japanese during the second career phase of life began receiving the shots. Because she had worked so closely on the project and understood the risks and benefits, Saito was one of the first to receive the injection. She would receive another when she turned 80.

Kurage was made available to any Japanese citizen who wanted it. The same could not be said for the overseas market. What was a birthright in Japan was a luxury of the super wealthy elsewhere. In America, especially, few states approved the drug for use by the general public. The price for an injection was made prohibitively high, meaning only a few could enjoy its benefits. Besides, Jinsei was very clear that the injection alone was insufficient to ensure a longer life. Diet, exercise, the kind of healthy living practiced by the Japanese along with the injection ensured the user at least another decade of life. Given their lifestyle choices, few Americans, even if they could afford it, could benefit.

Saito would work until her mid-70s, after which she would enjoy her second retirement. Like most second retirees, Saito would attend university. Very much like primary schooling, university attendance by 70- and 80-year-olds was compulsory if their social benefits were to be maintained. Unlike her tertiary or quaternary educational experiences, returning to university at this age was not about learning marketable skills or preparing for a career. Second retirees gave over these years engaging in rigorous academic study and physical activities, all with the goal of building cognitive strength. The science of aging was settled: keeping the brain plastic and supple required that it be exercised vigorously and regularly. This included participating in physical activities more strenuous than shuffleboard or tai chi.

Saito took yet another entrance examination and won admission to Keio University. Sasaki earned admission to Kyoto University, and this led to a rupture in their relationship. Saito had assumed that they would be enjoying second retirement together, taking classes and playing tennis. They very well could have done so, had Sasaki agreed to attend the lower ranked Keio University. But she declined and went off to Kyoto and slowly, their relationship atrophied. Because they never married, there was no divorce, although there was something of a complicated legal separation, largely around the dispensation and distribution of their common property.

And so, Saito set off for university by herself. But she needn't have worried too long as she fell in with a group of former content creators. Saito was the most "famous" among this group. Together, they worked their way through statistics, chemistry, philosophy, geology, French literature and anthropology. For those in second retirement, university looked very much like an old fashioned American liberal arts college. Saito and her fellow students were not taking these classes for cultural enrichment. They were graded and evaluated as any 20-year-old might be. Indeed, in her first semester Saito had difficulty with French literature. She had never been much of a reader—aside from technical articles. The courses in the sciences were easier for her, but even here she ran into some challenges. She assumed that she could sleepwalk through these classes, since she had spent two careers working in the sciences, but these classes included new research that challenged many of the assumptions she had been laboring under for the last 60 years. Further, the anthropology course revealed to her some of her own assumptions and prejudices, especially about Westerners. One goal of this education was to upend the worldview of those who were set in their ways.

Saito and the other second retirees were not segregated from the 20-year-old students. They sat in the same lecture halls, held discussions in the same seminar rooms, and partnered together in the same labs. Saito found this a little unnerving at first. When she was a young undergraduate, there were no 80-year-old women in her classes. About 20 years before she returned to university, the government had mandated that second retirees and young people would learn together, ending the practice of segregating the two groups on the same campus. Historically, old and young lived in separate spheres, rarely interacting with each other. To promote longevity, the Ministry of Gerontonomics felt that young and old should connect with each other on a daily basis. After her initial misgivings, Saito soon discovered that she liked learning with young people. She learned all about the currently popular musical forms, which content creators were most watched. (She was disappointed to learn that none of these young people had ever heard of her.) She even started dressing like her young schoolmates, none of whom objected when she dyed her hair orange. Saito was prepared to experiment with drugs of these students, but emogames were this generation's drug of choice, and so Saito immersed herself in romantic fantasies. She was especially attracted to Fujioka Haruto—a young man her granddaughter's age—although he did not return her affections. Such March–October romances were not unfamiliar but were largely giggled at by most young people. Besides, there were plenty of people her own age with whom she could hook up.

After 5 years, Saito was awarded her Bachelor's degree. She won no awards, nor had any distinctions, although she might have been described as a slightly above average student. For many elderly Japanese, this final stage of working life meant serving in a leadership capacity of some kind. A majority of the members of the Japanese parliament were people in their 80s and 90s, as were many executives, board directors, mayors, and other civic officials. Others were leaders of benefit corporations or nonprofits. Saito had little interest in politics and was probably too old to revive her influencer ambitions, but she was interested in nurturing the next generation of influencers. She became the headmistress of a school that taught content creation. It was really an after-school program, and Saito was nominally the headmistress. She did not oversee day-to-day operations. Like many in these roles, she was largely a figurehead, the deliverer of occasional addresses to the students, the gladhander who raised funds for the school, the attendee of civic lunches and other events. She also created content for the feeds extolling the virtues of the school, the closest she came to once again being an influencer.

All of these activities on behalf of the school took up less than 20 hours a week, leaving her time for her other pursuits. She reconnected with her only granddaughter during these years, and they would meet frequently for lunch and shopping excursions and emo-games. It was common for grandparents and grandchildren to form an emotional connection not shared between parents and children. A dutiful mother, Saito became the doting grandmother of an energetic and ambitious granddaughter.

After her breakup with Sasaki, Saito did not forge any other intimate connections, although there were opportunities. One of the instructors at the school—30 years her junior—flirted with her in ways that were not untoward but were still deemed inappropriate for an employee to engage in with a boss. Saito resided with nine other women in a multi-generational collective house. This arrangement was not unlike her dormitory situation at university. Indeed, two of her former roommates were part of this living collective that included young people, some her children's and her granddaughter's age. These living arrangements were encouraged by the government as another way to integrate the generations.

At age 100, at her third retirement, Saito was feted by her students and staff. But this was not a backward-looking celebration of life. Like her previous retirements, this was a moment that permitted one to enjoy *living*. Her children and grandchildren and a few close friends would travel with her to Jakarta, and Saito would travel to Paris for the first time in her life. She took up sculpture and painting, and even though her work was mediocre she still found occasion to have her work exhibited. Tennis was no longer an option for her, but pickleball was a suitable substitute, and she was just as competitive as she was at an earlier age. She and Natsuki Haru were doubles champions at their club for 3 years running.

A lifetime's preventative care meant that Saito was in relatively good health for a woman of 100. She had both knees replaced years before—almost as common and automatic a surgery as having a cavity filled—which allowed her to play pickleball for years into her third retirement. She had other maladies of someone of her advanced years, some hypertension, brittle bones, high cholesterol, but each was managed with pharmaceutical interventions.

Unfortunately, she had also developed immune system fatigue syndrome. Doctors had only recognized and diagnosed this affliction about a decade earlier. With more people living well into their one-hundreds—about 25% of the Japanese population—medical researchers had identified new diseases of old age. It was as if these afflictions existed only as theoretical potential until the population extended its life expectancy past previous limits. Thus, ISFS was an increasingly familiar malady experienced by woman of Saito's advanced years.

Doctors were only now prescribing treatments for the effects of ISFS. Saito experienced compromised pathogen responses, her body more susceptible to infection, even from typically nonpathogenic sources. When she did become ill with a minor infection, her recovery time was significantly prolonged. Persistent inflammation coursed throughout her body. One of the paradoxes of this disease was allergic hypersensitivity, so that while some immune responses were dampened, others became overactive. She discovered a sensitivity to soy that she had never experienced before in her life. Vaccines became less effective, exposing Saito to the ill effects of viruses that were of no concern to her when she was younger.

Indeed, it was a relatively benign flu virus that ultimately killed Saito, the kind of virus that barely registered in the public consciousness, vaccines making the flu nearly eradicated in Japan. But Saito's weary immune system could not fight off the virus, and she found herself hospitalized, struggling to breathe without assistance. At that moment, doctors summoned her family and friends and former coworkers to her bedside, a line forming outside her room as everyone celebrated the remarkably unremarkable life of Saito Miku.

Key Futures Themes

- Biotechnology and Health
- Economics and Policy (Gerontonomics)
- Urban Life and Lifestyle Design
- Work, Education and Life Rhythms
- Social Structures and Culture
- Technology and Governance

Bibliography

Anand, Paul. 2016. *Happiness Explained: What Human Flourishing Is and What We Can Do to Promote It*. Oxford: Oxford University Press.

El Kheir-Mataria, Wafa Abu, Omnia Mahmoud Abdelraheem, and Sungsoo Chun. 2025. Genetic, Socioecological, and Health Determinants of Extreme Longevity in Semi-Supercentenarians and Supercentenarians: Protocol for a Scoping Review. *JMIR Research Protocols* 14. https://doi.org/10.2196/63900. https://www.researchprotocols.org/2025/1/e63900.

Fengler, Wolfgang, Juan Caballero, and Vijeth Iyengar. 2024. The Age of the Longevity Economy. *Brookings Institution*, 29 January 2024. https://www.brookings.edu/articles/the-age-of-the-longevity-economy/.

Gratton, Lynda, and Andrew J. Scott. 2020. *The 100-Year Life: Living and Working in an Age of Longevity*. London: Bloomsbury.

Hong, Gee Hee, and Todd Schneider. 2020. Shrinkonomics: Lessons from Japan. *International Monetary Fund*, March 2020. https://www.imf.org/en/Publications/fandd/issues/2020/03/shrinkanomics-policy-lessons-from-japan-on-population-aging-schneider.

Moraes, Henrique Choer, and Mikael Wigell. 2020. The Emergence of Strategic Capitalism: Geoeconomics, Corporate Statecraft and the Repurposing of the Global Economy. *Finish Institute of International Affairs (FIIA) Working Paper* 117, September 2020. https://www.fiia.fi/wp-content/uploads/2020/09/wp117_the-emergence-of-strategic-capitalism_final30092020.pdf.

Moreno, Carlos. 2024. *The 15-Minute City: A Solution to Saving Our Time and Our Planet*. Hoboken, NJ: Wiley.

Muramatsu, Naoko, and Hiroko Akiyama. 2011. Japan: Super-Aging Society Preparing for the Future. *The Gerontologist* 51 (4): 425–432. https://doi.org/10.1093/geront/gnr067.

Nakatani, Hiroki. 2019. Population Aging in Japan: Policy Transformation, Sustainable Development Goals, Universal Health Coverage, and Social Determinates of Health. *Global Health & Medicine* 1 (1): 3–10. https://pmc.ncbi.nlm.nih.gov/articles/PMC7731274/.

Rich, Nathaniel. 2012. Can a Jellyfish Unlock the Secret of Immortality? *The New York Times*, 28 November 2012. https://www.nytimes.com/2012/12/02/magazine/can-a-jellyfish-unlock-the-secret-of-immortality.html.

Staley, David J. 2019. Superager University. In *Alternative Universities: Speculative Design for Innovation in Higher Education*. Baltimore: Johns Hopkins University Press.

Staley, David J. 2022. Gerontonomics at the Center of the Economy? *Columbus Underground*, 12 December 2022. https://columbusunderground.com/next-gerontonomics-at-the-center-of-the-economy-ds1/.

Chapter 15
Martin Solis: Jurist

Although he was a graduate of the prestigious Universidad San Francisco de Quito (USFQ), Martin Solis always maintained that his real education occurred at the Pacha Mama commune outside Quito. Pacha Mama was one of several communes to emerge in Ecuador after the Constitution of 2008 established the "rights of nature" as fundamental. "All persons, communities, peoples and nations can call upon public authorities to enforce the rights of nature," that Constitution announced. "To enforce and interpret these rights, the principles set forth in the Constitution shall be observed, as appropriate." Legal personhood was conferred upon the natural world, plants and animals and ecosystems. "The State shall give incentives to natural persons and legal entities and to communities to protect nature and to promote respect for all the elements comprising an ecosystem." Even though that constitution was superseded years later, the rights of nature continued to resonate and influence Ecuadorian jurisprudence and civic culture, enlivening a generation of young Ecuadorians and eventually spreading to other countries. Solis' parents were part of that first generation of students and activists who centered the care and protection of Pacha Mama. School curricula emphasized biology, ecology and the balance of human and natural worlds. Martin was nourished in this environment. Especially important to him was the idea that "nature" had rights that could be represented in a court of law. This also meant that these legal persons had responsibilities; as a legal scholar, Solis helped define the rights and responsibilities of nature, and would argue the first case of arbicide as a crime against humanity before the International Criminal Court.

The 2008 Constitution made specific reference to "Nature" as "Pacha Mama," saying the place "where life is reproduced and occurs, has the right to integral respect for its existence and for the maintenance and regeneration of its life cycles, structure, functions and evolutionary processes." Pacha Mama was an Earth goddess from Incan mythology, a fertility goddess long worshiped by the indigenous people of the Andes. The commune was organized around the worship of Pacha

D. Staley, *Anticipatory Biographies*, Anticipation Science 10,
https://doi.org/10.1007/978-3-032-08912-0_15

Mama, part of a general revival of indigenous religious practices and knowledge systems against "epistemicide," the destruction of indigenous knowledge perpetrated by the Global North.

The members of the commune were largely drawn from the undergraduate student population at USFQ, many of them biology or ecology majors, with some philosophy students—like Solis—included. They were deeply influenced by the theory of *planta sapiens*.

Once a fringe scientific idea, planta sapiens—that plants exhibit intelligence, perhaps even consciousness, despite not having a brain—had finally achieved mainstream status. Solis and his fellow communards felt that the planta sapiens idea took so long to gain adherents because it was first articulated at a Spanish university. Had it emerged from Oxford or Harvard or Stanford, planta sapiens would have become orthodoxy years earlier. For years, the planta sapiens paradigm remained an Iberian phenomenon, spreading to other Spanish speaking countries. For a country that had enshrined the rights of Nature, the theory of planta sapiens found a ready group of adherents in Ecuador.

The planta sapiens paradigm was built upon several observable facts about flora. Solis could plainly see that plants had the ability to differentiate brightness and color, could detect odors, and could orient themselves in space and time, with the ability to keep track of trends in humidity and temperature. This orientation in space and time gave plants the ability to anticipate and adjust their leaves to receive the sun before it arose. The communards had observed that plants could predict the appearance of pollinators based off previous experience, more than implying that plants had memories. More significantly, plants could communicate, sending each other electrochemical signals. The communards claimed that certain plants possessed a "vocabulary" of nearly 2000 "words." Of all the plants, Solis felt that trees were the most advanced, the most cognitively complex.

Taken together, Solis was coming to the conviction that plants exhibited a form of intelligence, not comparable to human intelligence, perhaps, but a plant intelligence nonetheless. That animals are intelligent had long been settled science; that there was a property called plant intelligence had finally been established by the scientific community. What took longer to establish was that this behavior was more than just intelligence. Evidence of communication among plants solidified the position that plants were intelligent; the communards would advance the proposition that the evidence of memories, of an understanding of their place in time and space, was proof of self-awareness among plants, that plants exhibit consciousness.

Although not yet consensus thought, a group of philosophers attached to the Pacha Mama commune argued that consciousness was a property of the universe like gravity, dark matter, electromagnetism. Consciousness pervades the world and is expressed in different degrees in different bodies. Human consciousness is different from animal consciousness is different from plant consciousness. This argument was easier to accept once artificial general intelligence (AGI) was finally achieved, and "artificial sentience" identified in some autonomous systems. No one could yet explain how AI achieved sentience—and indeed, a vocal minority of cognitive scientists and philosophers would not name AI behavior as sentience—only that consciousness was an emergent phenomenon, and that it could emerge from any complex system. If carbon-based entities could exhibit sentience (humans), why couldn't another carbon based entity (plants) do the same?

The members of the commune believed they were intimate with Pacha Mama. If consciousness was a property of the universe—found in all living things, not just human beings—and if plants especially exhibited a consciousness, then it must be that the consciousness pervading the universe *is* Pacha Mama.

The commune was made possible by a biotechnological device, the BioWreath, an interface that allowed communication with plants and trees. First developed in Denmark, the device linked a human to a plant, a device worn around the crown of the head that received the electrochemical pulses from a plant indicating whether it needed watering or if it were receiving too little sunlight or other such messages. Inasmuch as plants had a vocabulary, the BioWreath translated these words into a language humans could understand. The communards were identified by the floral wreaths that adorned their heads, a symbol that they were communicating with plants. When the plants indicated some sort of stress, the communards argued that their response—removing invasive insects, watering or feeding—was evidence of interspecies communication. What the communards could not do was initiate conversation, even on the order of "how are you doing today?" Solis in particular became interested in the problem of translating human language into a form the plants could understand, what he considered to be true communication.

The commune broke apart for the reason many of history's utopian communities have disintegrated: disagreements among the members, especially around foundational values. Since plants are sentient, argued a hardline group, we have no business eating them or otherwise using them for our benefit. Another faction argued that humans had to consume something. This group were vegetarian, although some consumed cell-grown meat, since the animal was not butchered. But for the committed, even this use of animals was forbidden. But if plants were as conscious as animals, then we should not consume them. The other faction was astounded at the implications of this logic: what do we eat, then? The faux-meat faction argued that lab-grown vegetation should be considered.

For his part, Solis wrestled with his conscience and his reason. Humans had to consume food. He was reluctant to place human sentience ahead of animal or plant sentience, but also saw the consequences of this (il)logic. He understood there was a radical philosophical movement that welcomed the end of humanity, and worked to hasten our demise, for humans had so destroyed the world it was better off without us. Solis did not subscribe to this philosophy, and saw the "no vegetable" approach as of a part of this movement. "We cannot act like plants and take nutrients directly from the sun and soil," Solis told his fellow communards. Some others devised a philosophy where permission should be sought from both animals and plants. This group described this as praying to Pacha Mama. If plants volunteered to be consumed by humans in order to sustain their life, that would be permissible. Solis realized the problematic consequences of the planta sapiens philosophy. He abandoned the commune but still maintained the idea of plant consciousness. He continued to dream of two-way communication between plants and humans.

Solis graduated with honors in philosophy and remained at USFQ to study law. After his law degree, he spent time in an environmental law firm, arguing cases where he represented the environment, represented plants and animals. In Ecuador, the environment, nature itself could be a party to any suit. His initial cases involved street widening projects, those that required trees and other flora to be cleared to make way for asphalt. Inasmuch as plants were legal persons in Ecuador, they had a right to representation, and for Solis this meant a right not to be killed. These cases were among the first to delineate the divergent interests between humans and plants. Rather than automatically and thoughtlessly deferring to human interests, Solis argued that, at minimum, the interests of plants should be accorded equal weight. In these cases, he asked how necessary was the destruction of plant life to benefit humans? The courts came to decide that the destruction of one tree or a small copse was legally justifiable. Destruction of a forest was beyond the pale. Determining the threshold between "a small number" of trees and "a large number" became the stuff of legal debate, and Solis' suits and other legal writings helped to clarify that threshold.

In a famous case, Solis made the argument that trees and other plants were not property. A logging company claimed that earlier decisions about how many trees counted as "too many" were irrelevant. The company owned the forest they were cutting down. Solis argued that a person could not be legally owned or possessed by another person. That is the very definition of slavery. Trees are legal persons—this was established law in Ecuador—and as such could not be treated as property.

The case had wide-ranging implications. Even when they weren't being cut down for lumber—a practice that had been declining worldwide—trees had nevertheless become capitalist objects, generators of value and wealth to their owners. In one widely read essay, Solis claimed that trees were "the new proletariat." For many companies, trees were more valuable alive than dead. The Weyerhaeuser Company becomes the first to transition to tree preservation rather than cultivation, not unlike the oil companies that transitioned into "energy" companies, away from fossil fuels. Trees were extra-efficient at removing CO_2 from the atmosphere, and so there were a growing number of firms who cultivated forests rather than harvest them. Indeed, biotechnology firms had been redesigning trees to more efficiently remove CO_2. There were companies that had used genetic engineering to manufacture trees with the ability to produce energy. One species of tree in particular was designed to produce a sap that, when refined, could fuel engines without harmful emissions. Forests of such trees became the new oil fields in some parts of the world. Trees had thereby transformed into a geostrategic resource. Defining their legal status was of no small consequence.

Although there was legal acceptance of the personhood of trees and other plants, their role in the capitalist economy meant that they were still treated as property. Solis felt that the law needed to clarify their rights and privileges. He set to work devising the legal argument that plants could not be property. He developed a novel legal argument: that when negotiating between human and plant interests, the "consent of the plant" should be sought out. A plant could be killed or manipulated to advance human interests, but only if the plant consented to this treatment by humans.

This argument rested on the assumption that the plant was conscious, of course, but also on the assumption that plant "vocabulary" was sufficiently advanced as to be able to express its intentions. Lawyers for arboreal companies countered that there was no evidence that plants had such intentions, and even if they did, they could not communicate them. Solis argued that the fault lies with us, that we had not yet developed the translation tools needed to be able to listen for their consent.

It was from this argument that Solis would develop a theory not only of the rights of trees but that destroying a tree is the equal to taking a human life, like a kind of manslaughter. He began to contemplate the idea of prosecution of someone who cuts down a tree. "What is the plant equivalent of manslaughter?" he asked in one essay published in *El Universo*. Although it was not raised in this essay, it was at this moment that Solis first started formulating the idea of arbicide: that cutting down a forest is like a genocide.

While the court was willing to accept the argument of the intelligence of plants, it was not ready to embrace the idea that plants or trees were not property. In her ruling, Judge Morena Ybarra feared that if plants were not to be disturbed that they could soon overrun human settlements, like sacred cows running amok in some Indian cities. Critics rejected Ybarra's decision as nothing more than a baldfaced attempt at maintaining the capitalist system: if trees were deemed "not property," then too many businesses would go under. In the end, Ybarra rejected the "consent of the plant" argument, which was the proximate reason Solis returned to university to develop the tools necessary to enable two-way communication with plants.

He left his law firm—going on what he called an extended sabbatical—and was admitted to Cornell's PhD program in environmental philosophy. In actuality, he designed his own program, a combination of bioengineering, cognitive science and linguistics. The BioWreath worn by the communards at Pacha Mama was a one-way communication system, translating the plant's electrochemical signals into a language humans could understand. Solis wanted to complete the circuit, to translate human language into electrochemical signals that the plants could understand.

It must be said that there was initial skepticism to this idea by the Environmental Philosophy faculty. Most were prepared to concede that communication was already two-way when the plant signaled "I need water" and the human watered the plant. Surely this meant the plant "understood" its message was received. Solis' research was twofold. First, to conclusively demonstrate that plants could indeed understand, could grasp the meaning of human action. He had no doubt about this, of course. Second, he wanted to redesign the BioWreath to be able to send messages to the plant, not simply receive them. The crux of this work would involve translating the thoughts of a human user into the electrochemical language understood by plants. Technologies for turning thoughts into actions were commonplace. There were many cognitive prosthetics for quadriplegics in the marketplace, and neural interface technology had been consumer grade for some time, especially for virtual gamers. Solis proposed designing a new BioWreath that would hack these existing technologies in order to send signals to plants.

He first wished to prove that plants were sending signals to humans, not exclusively to other plants that humans were merely intercepting. He claimed to have proved this when he noted new patterns in the electrochemical signals given off by test subjects. His argument was that these hitherto unidentified signals must be intended for humans, as they seem to have no effect on other plants. "These signals are meant for us," he would announce in his dissertation.

Working with the company who manufactured BioWreaths, Solis devised the mechanisms that would transform thoughts into signals that could be broadcast to plants. As more and more of plant vocabulary was understood, this turned out to be a relatively easy procedure, although the transmission equipment necessary to talk to plants was larger and bulkier than what could be elegantly contained in a single BioWreath. The prototype device was the size of an ice hockey goal, and so would not be as mobile. For purposes of his dissertation, Solis did not worry about this technical limitation; he would leave the miniaturization process for another time.

The crucial "aha" moment came when Solis demonstrated—although not to everyone's satisfaction—that he could hold a "conversation" with a plant. His demonstration involved a watercress with which he would initiate a conversation. He understood that any signal he would initially send would have to be at plant-level cognition. After a series of trials, he asked the plant "Turn your leaves toward me." To the unaided eye, the movement was imperceptible but cameras and measurement devices proved that the watercress turned its leaves in the direction of Solis' signals. Plants had been sending us signals: Solis had demonstrated that we could send signals to them.

Detractors maintained that even if the plant was responding to Solis' thoughts, this did not constitute "understanding" and certainly no kind of conversation. The plant reacted as a thermostat reacts to its environment, in that a change in temperature elicits a response by the thermostat. No one would ascribe "understanding" to this device. Perhaps Solis had constructed a cybernetic system, argued engineers with more sympathy for Solis' work. Others said that what Solis had created was something like a large language model from decades earlier. Solis' translated thoughts acted as a "prompt" for the plant to respond to. (The debate still rages today as to whether an LLM is intelligent, or indeed conscious.) Solis had no doubt that his experiment had proven the intelligence of plants. But in engaging in conversation with humans, the watercress had demonstrated self-awareness, consciousness and sentience. These conclusions were not included in his dissertation: he was awarded the PhD on the basis of the modifications to the BioWreath device that sends signals to the plants.

After the completion of his degree, Solis would work for BioWreath to refine the technology, specifically focusing on communication with trees, and secondarily with miniaturization. He also began to wonder if he might engage in more sophisticated conversation was with plants and trees beyond the "move your leaves" variety. In one experiment, Solis asked the tree equivalent of "how are you?" The first few trials produced no noticeable response from the grove of trees he was experimenting with. After repeated attempts, Solis thought he had detected the signal for "water" from the trees. He watered the trees in order to show his understanding. He repeated the question every day for the next few weeks, either receiving no response or a simple "water" request. (It was Solis who characterized the signal as a request.)

Then one day, the trees asked for "sunlight," suggesting theirs was not some sort of automated response.

Then a breakthrough. After asking "how are you?" the trees responded with a new signal. At first Solis could not translate it. Like Champollion, he wished for an arboreal Rosetta Stone to decipher this new word before he finally reasoned the trees were saying "We have no current needs."

Solis imagined deeper conversations with trees delving into subjects beyond the immediate description of their status. "We are at the lowest level of Maslow's hierarchy at this stage," Solis reported. He dreamed of one day discussing self-actualization with trees. He wondered if trees had any opinions about the state of the world. If they possessed a kind of collective memory, did this constitute a sense of historical consciousness? Did they contemplate death? Were they capable of poetry? Solis assumed that this higher consciousness must be found in the countless electrochemical signals that humans had not had yet to translate; that the tree vocabulary—the decipherment of which he helped to extend fourfold—was but the tip of a very deep iceberg. He was eager to plumb those depths.

Solis would join the faculty at Davos University as a visiting Fellow in Environmental Systems, where he would teach Environmental Ethics and Environmental Law for 3 years. Some of his most important articles in law journals came from living on the commune and "communicating" with trees. He used this platform to further share his radical philosophy that plants and trees were as conscious as animals, perhaps at a different scale, but their consciousness was no less important than humans'. He even ascribed sentience to trees, which became the basis for his argument that trees should be accorded the same rights (and responsibilities) as humans. While at Davos, Solis wrote a number of influential scholarly articles and policy briefs that challenged the prevailing orthodoxy of the animal rights movement. These theorists had long argued that animals deserved rights because, in the words of Tom Regan, they were "subjects-of -a-life" in a way that plants were not, meaning animals had a sense of awareness. Since his commune days, Solis was convinced that plants—and especially trees—were indeed self-aware and argued that the rights and privileges extended to animals should also be given to plants. He also linked the legal lattice that governed artificial intelligence systems to plants: that AI is not even a living system, and yet many such systems were assigned personhood. Plants, on the basis of being living entities, deserved the same treatment.

After a time on faculty at Davos University, he returned to Quito as an environmental prosecutor. He would mull a position as Environmental Minister in the Silva government, but was instead drawn to the International Criminal Court. Advocates had been clamoring for years to make ecocide an arrestable, criminal offense. It was long established that ecocide in wartime was a crime; these advocates wanted the statute to be extended to include peacetime. After almost a decade and a half of debate, the ICC included ecocide as an amendment to the Rome Statute, joining aggression, war crimes, genocide and crimes against humanity as crimes under their jurisdiction.

Solis wanted the same kind of international law that defined "crimes against humanity" to be extended to other living things. Not killing an individual animal or cutting down a single tree, but the decimation of an entire species or a forest should be given parallel weight as the murder of an entire ethnic group. Endangered species had long enjoyed protections: Solis sought to extend the doctrine to trees. The eradication of a forest should be defined as a crime against humanity, since trees belonged to all of humanity, not just to those within the political boundary the trees could be found.

Solis argued the first case of arbicide as a crime against humanity against the Brazilian president José Manuel Antônio Oliveira, a neo-Bolsanarist who felt particularly entitled to cut down the once-reviving Amazon rainforest. The arrest warrant read: "The pre–Trial Chamber of the International Criminal Court issued a warrant for the arrest of José Manuel Antônio Oliveira, in the context of the situation in the Amazon rainforest. Mr. Oliveira is allegedly responsible for the crime of arbicide under the ecocide provision of the Rome Statute, for the deliberate and negligent destruction of the natural habitat. There are reasonable grounds to believe that Mr. Oliveira bears individually criminal responsibility for the aforementioned crimes."

While Solis was certain he could convict Oliveira, other observers were less assured. Could Solis demonstrate that Oliveira bore the sole responsibility? The Brazilian president's speeches were clear: that Brazil needed to clear the rain forests in order to expand settlement, and that harvesting the wood would help fuel economic growth. Could Solis demonstrate that even if Oliveira had not personally directed the arbicide that he nevertheless failed to control those who actually felled the acres of trees detailed in the indictment?

Oliveira did not travel to The Hague, obviously, nor would any country extradite him. Oliveira did not even bother to maintain his innocence, instead questioning the legitimacy of the International Criminal Court itself. Oliveira was tried in absentia. Solis's argument in court was as eloquent and impassioned as any of his previous writings: that the government of Brazil and Mr. Oliveira in particular, had systematically and wantonly destroyed a living system whose right to exist was well-established and foundational. Solis did not resort to arguments grounded in the intelligence or sentience of the trees, staying within the narrow definitions of the statute.

Solis won the conviction, as large a victory of the plants' rights movement had ever seen. Oliveira would never be jailed and, indeed, the destruction of the rainforest continued unabated, although Oliveira would be deposed in a coup that effectively ended the arbicide. If the conviction had any effect, it was that nations were more circumspect about the treatment of the forests within their borders. Solis contemplated bringing similar charges against the president of Cameroon for its policy of deforestation. But after the Oliveira decision, the government quietly reversed its policy. Besides, some observers wondered if governments were the ones really responsible for arbicide, or whether it was the companies who claimed ownership.

International Criminal Court charges of arbicide were a mighty big hammer to swing and although they did not end the destruction of the natural world, they did signal a shift in planetary consciousness about the rights of plants.

Key Futures Themes

- Legal Innovations
- Consciousness
- Biotechnology
- Socio-Cultural Transformation
- Forests as Capital Assets and Geostrategic Resources

Bibliography

Basciano, Serafina. 2021. A Wearable That Helps to Understand the Needs of Plants. *Springwise*, 5 February 2021. https://springwise.com/sustainability-innovation/computing-tech/wearable-plant-communication/.

Calvo, Paco, and Natalie Lawrence. 2023. *Planta Sapiens: The New Science of Plant Intelligence*. New York: W. W. Norton & Company.

Constitution of the Republic of Ecuador. 2011. Political Database of the Americas, 31 January 2011. https://pdba.georgetown.edu/Constitutions/Ecuador/english08.html.

de Sousa Santos, Boaventura. 2014. *Epistemologies of the South: Justice Against Epistemicide*. London/New York: Routledge.

Farmer, Jared. 2022. The Ancient Wisdom Stored in Trees. *Nautilus*, 14 December 2022. https://nautil.us/the-ancient-wisdom-stored-in-trees-252713/.

Grandin, Temple. 2023. Can Plants Think? In *Planta Sapiens*, Paco Calvo Addresses Our 'Plant Blindness'. *The New York Times*, 23 June 2023. https://www.nytimes.com/2023/06/23/books/review/planta-sapiens-paco-calvo.html.

Hemsworth, Michael. 2021. The 'BioCollar' Helps Plant Parents Understand Greenery Needs. *Trendhunter*, 22 January 2021. https://www.trendhunter.com/trends/biocollar.

Popkin, Gabriel. 2023. For the First Time, Genetically Modified Trees Have Been Planted in a U.S. Forest. *The New York Times*, 16 February 2023. https://www.nytimes.com/2023/02/16/science/genetically-modified-trees-living-carbon.html.

Regan, Tom. 1983. *The Case for Animal Rights*. Berkeley: University of California Press.

Riccio, Gianluca. 2021. Biocollar, the Collar That Lets You Know the Needs of Your Plants. *Futuro Prossimo*, 24 January 2021. https://en.futuroprossimo.it/2021/01/biocollar-il-collare-che-ti-fa-conoscere-le-esigenze-delle-tue-piante/.

What are the Rights of Nature? Global Alliance for the Rights of Nature. https://www.garn.org/rights-of-nature/.

Wylie, Lesley. 2024. *The Poetics of Plants in Spanish American Literature*. Pittsburgh: University of Pittsburgh Press.

Chapter 16
George MacGowen: Dreamer

In the end, George Winston MacGowen only wanted to be alone with his thoughts.

MacGowen was an ambulance driver, or rather co-driver with an autonomous system. He travelled London streets 4 days a week in 12-hour shifts. In keeping with its long legal traditions, the European Union had heavily regulated the automation/innovation sector. Unlike in the US, companies were restricted in the kinds of jobs that could be automated, preserving the jobs of millions of Europeans and bypassing much of the social dislocation brought on by so many "unproductives." There was still some technological unemployment in the EU, make no mistake, but not at the levels reached in other parts of the world. The EU regulations were also based on the years of research that demonstrated that the most effective use of AI was in enhancing human abilities or in acting partnership with humans, that the symbiosis of humans and machines produced better results than either a human or a machine alone.

The ambulances had many more eyes than MacGowen, but only he was capable of observation, of understanding the context of the situation, of exercising judgment. Companies found that navigating the labyrinthine streets of London was still a difficult task for even the most advanced AI driving systems. Human drivers like MacGowan were still required because they understood the complexity of London streets and had the experience that machines could not yet muster. MacGowan had an unusually high spatial intelligence quotient, and so ambulance driver was an occupation clearly suited to his talents.

For this job, MacGowen wore an EEG headband, which for many jobs is a standard part of the uniform, like steel-toed boots or a hard hat for earlier generations of workers. At first, these headbands were employed as attention detectors, to make certain that long-haul truck drivers or others whose job required vigilant attention were in fact attending to their tasks. If a driver's mind began to wander or if he became dozy, the headband would send a mild shock to jolt the wearer. But as more jobs required an interface with an artificially intelligent system, the headband served

D. Staley, *Anticipatory Biographies*, Anticipation Science 10,
https://doi.org/10.1007/978-3-032-08912-0_16

as an efficient communications link between the two intelligences. Rather than pecking at a keyboard or even speaking aloud, a user needed only think, imagine, and this would be understood by the AI system. The BioWreath was an example of this kind of technology. After the Jonas Winkler debacle in the United States, regulators were very cautious about using the devices to directly manipulate human actions, emphasizing that the headbands facilitated communication.

His was an emotionally deadening job. His task was only to transport people, the sick, the wounded, the broken. He did not interact with the people he was transporting to hospital, and his interactions with first responders were minimal. Usually, he would arrive at the scene of a fire or an accident or the occasional murder and stand by as emergency personnel and the police would survey the situation, providing stabilizing first aid. As this was occurring, he would be contacting the nearest hospital, readying for the trip, imagining the route he would take, previsioning the fastest course. For its part, the machine would be conferring with real time maps of the city, identifying slowdowns, calculating the fastest way through the maze. When the patient was loaded, they began the negotiation, MacGowan surveying the scene as he thought the command "Forward." At the same time, MacGowan would extend his hands forward slowly to indicate the speed at which he wanted the vehicle to move.

The interior of driverless vehicles no longer contained a steering wheel or brakes or other levers to operate the craft. The machine was not actually reacting to the hand motions or to his feet extended forward when MacGowan wanted the ambulance to stop. These were kinetic actions that mimed what was occurring in the brain; in fact, the vehicle was receiving signals directly from the brain via the headband to move forward. Designers discovered that although the vehicles worked fine by thought control alone, human drivers found it difficult to sit still in the driver's seat and just think their directions. And so physical gestures were designed into the system.

Before he could pilot one of the vehicles, MacGowan went through extensive training. He recalled his first day behind the wheel at the test site in Surrey. He was instructed to empty his mind of distracting thoughts as he learned the hand signals for "Forward." The machine picked up emotional cues as well, or rather, emotions could disrupt the tether between human and vehicle. On that first day, MacGowan had learned to motion and think "Forward," but also had feelings of hesitancy and reticence. The vehicle moved forward a meter or so, then stopped, then started again. MacGowan learned to calm himself, and the machine learned to interpret McGowan's unique brainwave patterns, such that after a month of intensive training, the two were traversing the course in unison. A driverless vehicle was never distracted, an affliction of too many drivers before the advent of symbiotic transportation systems. The vehicle would in almost every case hew to the middle of the road and was exquisitely aware of its surroundings. If MacGowen were ever to have his mind wander the machine would compensate.

His training was considered complete when he had formed a relationship with his ambulance. There is no other way to describe it: the vehicle had tendencies, predilections, idiosyncrasies. It had the tendency to accelerate rapidly, even on a pedestrian lined street, which MacGowen learned to rein in. That description was not accidental: driving a symbiotic ambulance was very much like riding a horse. As part of his training, MacGowen had to "break" the vehicle, impose his will and intention on it. The machine had superior vision. The dozen cameras and half dozen sensors made the ambulance much more aware of its surroundings than MacGowen could ever hope to achieve. A not inconsequential part of his job was negotiating these two intelligences. Because of the analogy between riding a horse and operating a symbiotic vehicle, MacGowen and others like him—cab drivers, delivery drivers—were given the nickname "equestrians."

When he wasn't working, MacGowen spent much of his free time inside immersive games. It might seem odd that after a 12-hour shift MacGowen would choose to unwind by placing yet another headset around his temples. MacGowen never thought of it like that. He sought the emotional comfort and safety of immersive games, and didn't care much about how this experience was delivered to him.

Where other gamers experienced the thrill of violence, inhabiting the mind of a terrorist or a hitman or a soldier, MacGowen preferred games that soothed his fragile emotions. Critics complained that violent emo-games desensitized the experiencer from the consequences of violence. But manufacturers and their users said the thrill of the games was precisely because they provided sensations. It was the experience of the actual world that was desensitizing game players from violence. For his part, MacGowen never liked the violent experiences. He tried one such game once when he was a teenager, to fit in, to be in the boys' club. He did not participate in emo-game violence because there was already so much violence around him that he preferred to escape it. Reality was violent enough; emo-game violence was too hyperreal for him.

And so, his experience of games gravitated toward simulated love. Not sex—the pornography industry was the first to exploit emo-game technology—but rather affection, goodwill, beneficence, fraternity. These are the emotions he escaped into, that poured forth from him. It was a niche sector, to be sure, but MacGowen was one of a growing number of emo-game customers who sought to feel joy when the world outside was so joyless.

Tech companies had for decades been hoovering up user data as a way to feed their algorithms to create artificially intelligent systems. Startup companies were now mining users' emotional states to create the next generation of AI systems. Psychologists have long argued that conscious thoughts were only a small part of human cognition. The unconscious emotional states were far more influential, yet AI research had only concentrated on the logical, conscious brain. Any attempt to produce a machine with Artificial General Intelligence was never going to happen until it was capable of emotions, and so enterprising firms began to steal away talent from the few universities working on what was being called "artificial emotion." Large language models required mountains of human thoughts; to create successful AE would mean similarly mining the emotions of millions of users. These researchers were particularly interested in revealing the neural patterns of various emotional states. Immersive emo-games proved to be an excellent source of such emotional data, and MacGowen was under no illusion what was happening when he entered one of his immersive games.

He made money by receiving "royalties" on his data. There was a successful labor union/user's rights movement that began years earlier that pushed back against companies who used user data to, among other things, train AI systems. As users clicked and liked and otherwise engaged with the feeds, companies would hoover this up to feed their AI machines. The same machines that made people redundant now paid people for this data, for their interaction with media. And with each immersive game he entered, with each hit of dopamine he received, there was also a small stipend to augment his salary as an equestrian.

He remembered when he received his first EEG device. This is a big moment in any adolescent's life when parents could trust them. There were questions from some scientists about whether children had the emotional maturity to handle neuro-fiction, concerns his father, especially, did not seem to harbor. His first neurogame was a collection of children's fairy tales. Watching, experiencing one of these games was like watching an old-fashioned movie, except the story one was watching unfolded as a result of the watcher's emotional state. One game was *Snow White*, and the viewer reached a point where the heroine is about to receive the poisoned apple. Like a Choose Your Own Adventure book from a century earlier, the viewer's emotional state determined the next sequence of the story. If the viewer was frightened at the thought of what would happen to Snow White if she were to take the apple, their heightened anxiety would be picked up by the immersive story, and Snow White would politely but firmly refuse the apple. If the user's emotional state is one of curiosity, then Snow White takes the apple. All of this is seamless, the result of a new process that can operate thousands of scenarios, branching paths in a story, the resulting story is a symbiosis between director and viewer. Indeed, there are many Snow White stories as there are viewers to experience them.

Many of these games had emotional "circuit breakers" built into them—but only for underage viewers—that would refuse to unspool a story that became too violent or emotionally disquieting. That is, a viewer might have an emotional response that urged Snow White to violently kill the Crone.

There were no such circuit breakers in adult games, and too many psychopaths enjoyed watching scenes of cruelty and violence on the screen. The emo-game companies always countered that those scenes of violence only emerged because of the unconscious desires of the viewer: "Don't sue us for the depravity of the viewer," was their defense. There were demands that the authorities should be monitoring these games and revealing those whose emotional response tended toward violence and depravity. It caused a legal sensation when a viewer was arrested by Metropolitan Police for turning a soccer video game into an orgy of dismemberment. The police claimed that the viewer was a psychopath, and prosecutors did not accept the defense that "the game made me do it." One influencer made the claim on one of the feeds that what one does in the privacy of one's home is no one else's business. Because it was a fantasy, no one was actually dismembered, and thus no actual crime was committed.

The definition of playing a game had changed rather drastically. Whatever complaints earlier generations had about the deleterious effects of video games, players were at least physically engaged, moving a controller. Now playing a game involved having the scenes wash over the viewer. This was not passivity, adherents claimed, even as the game now bypassed conscious thought and action. Emotional responses, almost instinctual rather than deliberate, guided the action. Play was defined as an unconscious experience. Results from some clinical trials suggested that these games could be therapeutic, designed specifically to channel aggressive or antisocial behavior toward more bucolic states.

For his part, MacGowen's games never descended into violence or debauchery. His favorite emo-game were football matches where Tottenham Hotspur—his favorite club—wins the Champions League, a 5-0 final, with each goal more spectacular than the last. In the real world, his club had descended to the third tier of English football, the once proud club having never regained its former glory, except as experienced by MacGowen every time he played this game.

MacGowan still attended Spurs matches. When he was a boy, Spurs were the top of the Premier League and won a Double when he was 13 years old. As he grew older, the club started its slow descent down the English football pyramid, now languishing in the third tier for several seasons. Although he still attended games, he'd rather play the emo-game where Spurs were always victorious champions.

Sometimes, MacGowan's unconscious would allow some tension and drama to occur: Spurs down a goal late before they score a tying goal and then a miraculous goal to win in the sixth minute of stoppage time. McGowan would involuntarily allow his emotions to be so jangled by the possibility of a loss, if only to experience the thrill of the improbable victory. The emo-game made his enjoyment of the real-life Spurs much more tolerable. He was always optimistic each time he arrived at the stadium that the real-life Spurs will finally discover their form and rocket back up the table to be promoted back to the top. He was perhaps the only optimistic Spurs fan.

And then one day after returning home from a particularly tense day on the job and losing himself in an emo-game, Spurs lost. For the first time he could ever remember, from the opening whistle, Spurs lacked initiative and played without any urgency. Even after falling behind two goals after 20 minutes, MacGowan assumed that this would turn into one of those thrilling come-from-behind victories, those which had always guaranteed a maximum dopamine hit and would left him feeling euphoric. But not today. Spurs lost the emo-game four to one, and McGowan was despondent. The actual Spurs were dreadful to watch. He did not need this replicated in the emo-game simulacra.

He checked the game's settings as the result was becoming evident, but did not see anything amiss. He dismissed this as a glitch in the game—it was not uncommon—and thought nothing more of it. Indeed, 2 days later, Spurs won a decisive victory, and all seemed to return to normal. Then 2 weeks later, Spurs played another bafflingly poor game. Now MacGowan was ready to contact the manufacturer. He played these games as an escape, to experience joy. The whole point of playing games was to become intoxicated, to forget the world, to see only sunshine when all around him was really darkness. The customer service bot assured MacGowan that the system was operating properly and that the undesired outcome of the game was the result of "human emotions," that it was he, MacGowan, who had desired a poor result by Spurs. The company always maintained that emo-games were a mere reflection of the desires and emotional state of their players. "That's absurd!" he protested to the bot. "Why would I want, why would I desire Spurs to lose?!" "I have no answer for that, sir," the bot intoned, "but I will give you a credit for three free games for your trouble."

MacGowan might have overlooked the glitchy emo-game if there hadn't been an incident on the job. MacGowan was to transport a burn victim to a trauma center. This was hardly the first time he had seen third degree burns, but this time, uncontrollably, MacGowan began to sob. He looked away from the scene and attempted to concentrate on his task of piloting the vehicle. Even as the ambulance began its journey, MacGowan did not feel in control of the situation. The vehicle did most of the driving, but it failed to interpret a car speeding toward an intersection as unlikely to stop. The vehicle understood that there was a light there, and so assumed the vehicle would yield. In this situation, the human driver would step in, overriding a vehicle that had misinterpreted the situation. McGowan was not up to the task. His mind wandering, replaying the awful scene of the burn victim writhing in agony, McGowan began to cry again, and so missed the speeding vehicle that skimmed into the side of the ambulance. The ambulance had slowed sufficiently once it understood the other car was not stopping. McGowan's sadness turned into rage. He leapt from the car and tore open the door and dragged the other driver out into the street. "Are you mad?!" he screamed, "You didn't see my sirens?!" The other driver was cited for reckless driving, and the ambulance beckoned McGowan to get back so they might continue on to the trauma center, which they eventually did. McGowan and his ambulance had suffered these kinds of minor traffic accidents before, but in none of those cases had McGowan lost his temper or so verbally assaulted another driver. One might have excused McGowan his outburst, given the circumstances, but these outbursts became more commonplace, often targeting the vehicle itself, as in one instance when the machine accelerated too rapidly and McGowan became apoplectic. Ordinarily, all it took was a thought or a palms down gesture to corral the ambulance. But this time, he screamed at the machine.

McGowan was not playing emo-games much anymore. More times than not, the games turned violent, or at least uncivil, as characters would just as often bicker and scold each other as they would work cooperatively, the outcome McGowan had always preferred. There were now too many Spurs losses to make the game any kind of refuge for him. McGowan found himself sitting home alone in the dark or walking the neighborhood streets without purpose or destination. He discovered that he had lost his appetite, and then, just as suddenly, would have irrational cravings for curry, meat pies or Polish cabbage rolls.

McGowan had never been a deep sleeper, usually only getting 6 hours a night. Now he found himself alternating between periods of insomnia and oversleeping. Once after sleeping through the morning, he was late for a shift for the first time in his 5 years as an equestrian. Perhaps because of his chaotic sleep patterns, McGowan occasionally found himself tired on the job, sometimes without energy, which was detrimental to an ambulance driver, where he was expected and trained to be alert. But just as often he arrived for his shift elated, even saying “Good morning!” to the ambulance.

The emotional and psychological changes in McGowan transpired over the course of about 2 years. It might be claimed that the ambulance was “covering” for McGowan during one of his outbursts, or when he seemed sleepy or exhibited slower thinking, but it was absurd to conclude that the AI had any sort of “awareness” of the situation. It could identify patterns in MacGowan’s emotional state, a function he was unaware the machine possessed.

At no time had McGowan thought about his own death or contemplated suicide, despite being surrounded by death as part of his job. Only when McGowan’s mind wandered one evening—a passing uncontrolled thought of steering the ambulance into oncoming traffic—did the ambulance take action. It resisted MacGowan’s impulse to drive into traffic, and at the end of the shift, submitted a report to the dispatcher detailing this and other such incidents. The company was well aware of McGowan’s transgressions, as he had been disciplined two times already, but this was an extraordinary case. In filing its report, the ambulance registered its “alarm” at McGowan’s behavior. The ambulance proffered that McGowan had symptoms of depression based on its analysis of 27 instances over the last 2 years, starting with the traffic accident and McGowan’s rage.

It should be made clear that no autonomous vehicle had ever “diagnosed” a human driver before. Technicians were baffled that a vehicle’s after incident report would veer toward a psychological analysis of the driver. It simply wasn’t programmed for such an outcome. Scholars later postulated that McGowan and the vehicle had formed such an intimate cognitive bond that the vehicle’s sensing of MacGowan’s emotional and psychological state was an emergent feature of their complex interface. The company was not about to allow the vehicle to make the official diagnosis, and McGowan was removed from duty to undergo psychological testing by human doctors. The vehicle was also taken out of service. Given the symbiosis between vehicle and driver, one could not simply insert a new human. There would need to be months of training. But given the vehicle’s “awareness,” it was determined that it should be studied first to determine if awareness was the inevitable outcome of any AI system, even if it was not programmed as such.

MacGowan was confirmed to be suffering from depression, and the company placed him in the care of Bryce Hanley, a Cambridge professor who was developing a new therapy. Before prescribing a regime of pharmaceuticals, Hanley wanted MacGowan to undergo dream therapy. Hanley used a modified version of a “mind camera”—a now-common consumer item—to revive an ancient and, some said, discredited practice: dream interpretation as a form of therapy. Hanley was identified as a “new Freudian,” although he thought himself more of a “neo-Jungian,” especially since his practice centered on capturing dream images.

Found mostly in Japan and South Korea, the mind camera was a technology capable of depicting the mind’s eye of a user, in effect, visualizing thought. Early versions of the technology involved placing a viewer in an fMRI machine, scanning the brain to measure brain blood flow as a proxy for neural activity. By analyzing the brain's response to various visual stimuli, the technology could identify distinct neural patterns associated with specific images. A computer then interpreted these neural patterns to generate an approximation of the original image. This technology essentially discerned visual information directly from captured thought, turning what a user "sees" into a digital photograph.

The technology had progressed such that an EEG headband replaced the fMRI machine. And while there were certainly medical applications for the technology, it soon became commercialized such that young people took to wearing the headbands while they attended concerts or preened about the city or captured moments in the world around them. The feeds were littered with these often inane pictures. Critics complained that "there was no thought visualized here."

Hanley had modified the mind camera to specifically capture dream imagery. Hanley wanted McGowan to record his dreams over a two-week period. He would wear a headband at night when he slept, the recording would be transmitted to Handley's office. McGowan expressed his skepticism, stating that he'd slept irregularly and rarely remembered his dreams. "All the more reason to wear the device," Hanley counseled. "It will remember them for you."

Hanley's research was controversial, and not universally accepted by the scientific community. Derisively called "mind reading," researchers still only had theories as to why humans dream. Most researchers maintained that there was no purpose to dreaming, that dreams themselves were not meaningful, contending that any meaning we find in dreams is ex post facto. Hanley's research sought to prove that dreams provided access to the unconscious and that understanding the unconscious was key to understanding the mind.

Hanley was not only a Cambridge don with a scholarly interest in dream analysis. Unbeknownst to MacGowan, Hanley was the founder and chief technology officer of Oneiros, a company that turned "dreams into data." Deep in the fine print of a waiver MacGowan signed but did not read closely before beginning his treatment was language that said that the content of any dreams read for purposes of his therapy were the property of Oneiros and could be used any way they saw fit. Hanley would pile McGowan's dreams on top of those of scores of other patients, the totality being the data to feed a new technology being developed by Oneiros, the "artificial unconscious." The waiver made no provisions for dreamers to be compensated for their dreams, a violation of the EU's "Data is Labor" laws. Oneiros would later be cited and fined for their deception.

After two weeks, McGowan met with Hanley to watch and interpret the results. In practice, rewatching your own dreams allowed one time to reflect on them, to examine them at a critical distance, to play and replay segments as needed. Rather than asking patients to recall dreams from memory or to draw pictures of them after the fact—as Jung had done—the technology generated a very useful video facsimile of a dream. Hanley also found that users like McGowan, who otherwise did not remember their dreams, had greater recall filling in gaps. The device could only record the images, not the sounds, of a dream. Even if one were a particularly lucid dreamer, the technology could not produce the smells and tastes of a dream. If someone were speaking, that could not be captured by the device, but Hanley found that patients in about 37.4% of cases could reconstruct at least a portion of those sounds prompted by the video. The device had captured 27 of McGowan's dreams. Many were sexual fantasies or those where MacGowan was late for work and stuck in some foreign country. Some were nightmares. All would be analyzed, but two dreams caught Hanley's attention as worth further reflection.

In the dream, MacGowan found himself at the starting line of a Grand Prix race. At first, he was a spectator, hovering over the scene, but in the next instance he was a driver. The track twisted and turned through a surreal landscape, rising upward, suspended high above the ground like a floating city. While his competitors sat behind sleek race cars, MacGowan found himself in an old-fashioned car, like something from the 1930s, its glossy surface shimmering in magenta, a color that seemed to pulse and shift as if alive. At this stage, Hanley paused the recording and remarked that the old-fashioned automobile was significant, a return to a time when humans controlled automobiles, not the other way around. He also noted that the color magenta appeared throughout the two dreams in question.

Hanley restarted the video, and MacGowan's father appeared in the seat next to him. John MacGowan looked younger, like he did in old photographs. His father was speaking to him, but MacGowan could not hear what his father was saying. He could remember having the feeling that his father's words were comforting, telling him that everything was going to be fine. Hanley noted that any time "the Father" appeared in a dream was significant.

As the race began, the cars did not move in the usual way. Instead, they glided, almost hovered, and MacGowan realized that the track was not made of asphalt but of water, shimmering and translucent. His car bounced gently across the surface. The other racers now seemed far away, their vehicles leaving behind trails of magenta light.

The race then took a sharp turn through a tunnel made entirely of glass. On the other side, MacGowan was no longer in a car, but on foot, running through a forest where the trees were the same bright magenta color. His father was ahead of him, and MacGowan tried to catch up, but no matter how fast he ran John MacGowan remained just out of reach. "You are seeking your father's approval," Hanley concluded and then speculated that perhaps John MacGowan might have been disappointed with a son who was an ambulance driver. McGowan sat silently, nodding absently. His father was apprenticed as a biocoder and wanted to be a professional cricketer growing up. He had hopes of his son becoming a footballer but had given every indication that he was perfectly content with his son's job. That George McGowan never married did not particularly concern his father, though his mother, Josephine, had hoped that there might be grandchildren by now. All of this was to say that the idea that he was seeking his father's approval was bullocks.

MacGowan returned to the dream. The forest opened into a vast canyon, with cliffs on either side towering into the sky. John MacGowan stood on the edge, looking out over the void, his hands clasped behind his back. He turned and smiled at his son, but before MacGowan could say anything, the ground beneath him began to crumble. The magenta light around MacGowan dissipated and just as MacGowan started to fall, the dream ended. "The magenta," Henley pronounced, "is a color symbolic of joy and happiness. It pervades many of your dreams, which reflects your continued search for joy. But joy is elusive for you." This interpretation gave MacGowan pause for it had greater plausibility than the "father's approval" interpretation.

Hanley then played the second dream, where MacGowan found himself in a stark, sterile room bathed in a magenta glow. The walls were smooth and metallic, without any visible seams or openings. The only object in the room was a sleek, obsidian console in the center. Its screen flickered, emitting waves of magenta light that seemed to pulse.

John MacGowan stood next to him with an expression that was both familiar and distant. His father wore a simple white suit, the fabric glowing faintly in the magenta light. Without speaking, he gestured toward the console and MacGowan approached it. The screen then burst to life, displaying a stream of symbols, letters, and images that flew by too quickly to comprehend. Both placed their hands on the console, and instantly, the room disappeared. MacGowan was then floating in a vast expanse of data structures and flashing magenta symbols. MacGowan had a flash of remembrance. Seeing the video allowed him to recall the dream with a clarity he had never had before. In the dream, his thoughts were no longer just his own, they blended seamlessly with the console's data and with his father's memories. MacGowan now recalled his experiences, his emotions, his regrets, and his unspoken fears. It was overwhelming, a flood of consciousness that he could not control.

The console now felt alive, sentient, and MacGowan now recalled feeling as if it were watching him. Its presence was everywhere in this digital realm.

MacGowan was now having trouble recalling this moment in the dream, but he thought that he heard his father's voice, distorted, electronic, echoing through the space. "Can you recall what he was saying?" the doctor asked. MacGowan sat for a few minutes trying to retrieve the memory. At last, MacGowan says "We've gone too far." The magenta light began to flicker and fade, and John MacGowan's image dissolved into static.

Hanley said, "It is clear that 'we've gone too far' can only mean one thing: that your actions at work, the distractions, the mood swings, the lashing out, has reached a tipping point. I think we've made a breakthrough." McGowan nodded, said his thanks and promised to return in two more weeks after having had more of his dreams recorded.

As McGowan headed back to his apartment, he was lost in thought about what had transpired, not only his sessions with Hanley but also the last 2 years at work and at play. Hanley was right about one thing: joy did elude him, but not completely. He did indeed feel joy when immersed in certain emo-games. If joy eluded him, it was because he failed to feel it. Nothing should stop him from experiencing joy.

And then the epiphany: "I must detach," McGowan said aloud to his empty apartment. At that moment, he quit his job. He did not contact the ambulance service, he did not complete the appropriate paperwork. He just thought, "I quit." His next thought was to abandon London. "La Concha Beach" he thought and immediately went on a travel site to book a one-way ticket to Spain. He had no idea where that thought came from, and he didn't bother to analyze it. Indeed, he discovered that when he removed the headsets, he was full of thoughts, feelings, urges that had gone unlistened to for too long. At La Concha, he would sun himself and stroll lazily and eat good food and drink good wine, accompanied only by his thoughts.

Key Futures Themes

- Human–Machine Symbiosis
- Neurotechnology
- Emotion Economy
- Psychology and Mental Health
- Artificial Unconscious

Bibliography

Arrieta-Ibarra, Imanol, Leonard Goff, Diego Jiménez-Hernández, Jaron Lanier, and E. Glen Weyl. 2018. Should We Treat Data as Labor? Moving beyond 'Free'. *AEA Papers and Proceedings, Vol. 108, Papers and Proceedings of the One Hundred Thirtieth Annual Meeting of the American Economic Association*, 38–42.

Farahany, Nita A. 2023. *The Battle for Your Brain: Defending the Right to Think Freely in the Age of Neurotechnology*. New York: Macmillan.

Hutson, Mathew. 2018. This 'Mind-Reading' Algorithm Can Decode the Pictures in Your Head. *Science*, 10 January 2018. https://www.science.org/content/article/mind-reading-algorithm-can-decode-pictures-your-head.

Nguyen, Trinh, and Amany Elbanna. 2025. Understanding Human-AI Augmentation in the Workplace: A Review and a Future Research Agenda. *Information Systems Frontiers*. https://doi.org/10.1007/s10796-025-10591-5.

Chapter 17
Taniya Hughes: Tutor

When she was accepted to Spelman, Taniya Savannah Hughes saw vistas open before her, opportunities she never imagined as a child. She received a degree in linguistics and biology and creative writing, and while she had no definitive post-graduation plans, she ventured that she would end up working in biomanufacturing or possibly in state government. She was born and raised in Louisville, Kentucky and her education until that point had been peripatetic. Her father had been made redundant when his job as an electrician was replaced by a machine. Her mother was the pastor of a very small church. That she would be admitted to Spelman was an achievement, one she could not imagine growing up.

At a time when public education had been desiccated and teachers replaced by AI agents—the humans reduced to the role of "learning coordinators"—to have a human teacher for one's children was a mark of distinction and social class. Public, mass schooling is now AI-driven, with human teachers reduced to chaperones—and sports coaches.

American schools had been "unbundled," in the favorite phrase of innovators. Learning was separated out as its own enterprise, which few people actually engaged with—it was easier and better to teach children at home. But schools had long served a role as social capital incubators, and now this mission was also split off as a separate enterprise. Sports—the most important form of socialization—has been ceded to sporting clubs: many established high schools tried to stay in business redesigned as sports clubs. Indeed, there were some students who simply forewent schooling entirely to spend all of their time at sports clubs, their parents assenting to this claiming that the training and experience and connections made there were more valuable than what their kids could learn from an AI "teacher." For her part, Hughes was less interested in sports, but did like drama and music, and would attend clubs for these activities.

Her family scrimped and did without in order to send her to Anita Aguirre. Aguirre's was an institution in Louisville. The school was a single teacher who only

D. Staley, *Anticipatory Biographies*, Anticipation Science 10,
https://doi.org/10.1007/978-3-032-08912-0_17

accepted twelve students at a time. Aguirre's guaranteed that students who successfully navigated her curriculum would be admitted to whatever university they wished, and indeed had the record to prove it. Aguirre worked with students, individually and in twice weekly group seminars. She was a polymath, exercising students in math, philosophy, history, neuro-coding, an introductory level of knowledge of a broad array of subjects. Her students learned to write—they did not use Writers—to listen attentively, to speak confidently and knowledgeably. Taniya Hughes would never say whether she liked Aguirre's—her tutor meriting only brief mention in her memoirs—but it was more than obvious that had she not attended the school there was no chance she'd have been accepted to university. She would have had a very different life.

The admission to Spelman granted Hughes access to an elite network. Indeed, attending one of the few remaining elite institutions of higher education in the United States meant that attaining a degree all but guaranteed a career in research, government, business, consulting. Getting into one of these institutions was the achievement itself; once there, students studied whatever they wanted, if they studied at all. Hughes used the opportunity to explore her interests, which were broad and varied. Once the incredulity at being accepted to Spellman had subsided, and after 3 years in classes, Hughes began to wonder about her post-Spelman life.

As Hughes neared graduation, she was visited by Shamikah Woods, an alumna and influential Wall Street financier. Over lunch at a downtown restaurant in Atlanta, Woods—in a hushed voice—told Hughes that she had been selected to become a tutor for the Linville family.

Woods did not have to explain who the Linvilles were. Noah Linville was one of the automation innovators who used AI and robotics to upend the skilled trades. Generations of mostly young men were encouraged to learn carpentry or plumbing or construction or, like her father, electrical work, but these sectors employed few human workers today, 90% of the work having been automated. This was the fate of her father. Indeed, it was not much of an exaggeration to say that the Linville family had cost her father his livelihood and dignity.

Families like the Linvilles were "Escapists." Decades before, the ultra-wealthy purchased bunkers or had underground lairs built in strategically-defensible places. They feared the breakdown of society and sought escape from the catastrophic effects of climate change. For some this meant underground mansions in the desert, but because they were located within existing political jurisdictions, the residents were subject to laws and regulations and were otherwise still part of civil society. Some Escapists, therefore, built their compounds on the continental shelf, off the coasts, some even below the surface of the ocean. Residing in international waters, these compounds were constructed beyond the 12-mile territorial limit. These Escapists created their own microstates, like feudal barons, ruling their own watery manse.

But another group of Escapists wanted to be free of the boundaries of Earth entirely. The entrepreneurs of earlier in the century imagined colonizing Mars, bypassing national governments who were too sclerotic and who lacked the imagination and vision of humanity as a multiplanetary species. They had built up elaborate plans to terraform Mars, creating a Second Earth to supersede the decayed and dying planet they were leaving behind. It turns out that was the real driver of building rockets to Mars: to abandon the planet so many of the Escapists had worked to despoil.

The Linville family were the first generation of autonomous innovator billionaires to establish an Escapist compound on the Moon. Back when entrepreneurs were dreaming of colonizing Mars, they had built a transportation system to a launch base constructed on the moon. Rockets to Mars would be launched from here. It was cheaper and more efficient than launching from Earth, but sustaining interest in the project proved difficult, and gradually the Mars project was abandoned. The leftover base was purchased by Noah's father Mason Linville, who expanded it into a luxury compound. The Moon had not yet been carved up into national boundaries, and so the Linvilles claimed a kind of squatter's rights to the property. Like other escapists, the Linvilles claimed sovereignty over the land and ruled over it as their own private fiefdom. Noah Linville brought his wife to the Moon, and it was there that they had a family. Ameila was born there, and could be legally called the first Lunian, those born outside of the Earth entirely. She and the other children born on the Moon grew up knowing only tales of the Earth as told by her parents, her conversational AI and her tutors.

In withdrawing from society, wherever they might settle, the Escapists no longer sent their children to Harvard or indeed any elite school. Their wealth was so vast their children did not require the stamp of approval elite universities conferred. Their children would be educated "at home," groomed to take over the family business, which in effect meant managing the family's estate and the family's wealth, like a new aristocracy or royalty, minus the noblesse oblige.

The Escapists would hand-select the best of the best. Their agents would scour the elite universities of the world in search of tutors to educate their children. The agent would meet with the prospective tutor and present the standard offer. Hughes learned over the lunch in Atlanta that, should she accept, she would earn $500,000 a year plus accommodations, meals and free access to all of the amenities of the Linville Compound.

Hughes concluded the meeting with Woods by asking if she could take a few days to consider her decision. Woods agreed, but intimated that once the Linvilles had made their determination they would make it difficult to say no. Hughes was reluctant to accept and very nearly rejected the offer on the spot. The thought of working for the family that had done so much damage to the economy and to the dignity of so many people filled her with revulsion. Beyond that, the Escapists had a dodgy reputation. Conspiracy theories of life within the walls of the compounds swirled. There were stories of satanic sacrifices and Wicker Man-style cults. Like any cabal, so went the conspiracies, the Escapists were not truly withdrawn from society, but continued to direct efforts, puppeteers of the world's governments and corporations. Hughes never believed any of the more outlandish claims, but did harbor ethical concerns. If she accepted, would she now be an Escapist too? She wanted to use her education to solve problems—climate mitigation, tending to the "unproductive," using her knowledge to create solutions—and tutoring the children of the Escapists seemed like abandoning the Earth, especially if she were to venture to the compound on the Moon. As a Spelman graduate, she had any number of opportunities open to her, although even Hughes had to concede not at $500,000 a year. After a few days' deliberation, Taniya accepted the offer. She imagined she would do this for no more than 5 years, after which she would escape the Escapists.

Woods instructed Hughes to quietly book a flight for Santa Fe. She could pack three bags but was told that clothes and other such provisions would be available to her. When she arrived at the airport, she was to arrange a ride share but must request a specific driver. The driver would then deliver her to a location in the desert outside of Santa Fe, which turned out to be a private space port.

The day and time of the launch was never publicized; this was to avoid the demonstrations or other disruptions that would usually occur. Environmentalists, anarcho-communists and other anti-capitalists would attempt to disrupt a launch they knew was sending another billionaire to the moon. The fuel necessary to make the trip to the Moon was expensive and toxic to the already overheated environment. There were concerns that the Space Force of some country might try to shoot down the shuttle in transit; but, frankly, most nations were more concerned with their own strategic issues on Earth to divert attention and materiel to stopping a private junket to the Moon. Nevertheless, the Linvilles believed that precautions should be taken.

The voyage to the Moon was reminiscent of the luxurious ocean crossings of a previous era. The shuttle would dock at a lunar orbiting station, where Hughes would reside for two weeks before boarding a module that would alight on the Moon's surface. The station was in an elliptical orbit around the Moon, which meant that at times it was close to the Moon's surface, meaning the trip in the module was relatively brief. At the other end of the elliptical orbit, the station was close to Earth, meaning the trip via the private rocket was much shorter. The entire system required much less rocket fuel than earlier methods but also meant that the journey took five times longer than the time the Apollo astronauts needed.

Leaving Earth's orbit was a terrifying experience and at that moment, when the capsule shook with such ferocity that she was convinced every rivet would fly apart, Hughes regretted the decision to become a tutor. But once clear of the atmosphere, the trip to the orbiting station was smooth and uneventful. She still had to accustom herself to weightlessness—she struggled mightily to recall all of the tutorials she scrolled through while waiting at the spaceport. She might have been space sick a couple of times. They docked at the station a day later and now had to wait another fortnight or so for the station to complete its orbit near the moon. Those three weeks were taken up with dinner parties, dancing and other social occasions with the other arrivals to the Moon. These included military leaders, miners, government officials, entrepreneurs, researchers, technicians and other laborers, all with business to conduct on the Moon's surface.

Billionaires had once dreamed of escaping to Mars, but when that dream turned out to be more logistically complicated than anyone could afford, the Moon presented a closer and more obvious target of their Escapist fantasies. The challenge was to push aside the claims of national governments and commercial interests, who wished to mine the satellite. The one problem with settling on the Moon was the daily reminder of looking down on the planet below, of reflecting on its problems and bleak prospects, those problems in no small part created by the Escapists.

Hughes was surprised to discover there was a private army at the Linville Compound. Like those who wished to "create a state" in the ocean, the Compound was treated as sovereign territory, outside any nation-state, international organization or commercial interest. There was something like a Constitution governing the micro-state, although this was really a kind of family charter, as the compound was not so much a state as an extended clan. The Linville family, the Burnetts and the Clements had claimed this compound, which was originally built as a lunar base for missions to Mars. Hydroponics and other forms of artificial agriculture made the Compound self-sufficient up to a point, however the Escapists still needed occasional visits from Earth for supplies.

As she was escorted through the compound, the moment Hughes was dreading was finally upon her. She was introduced to Noah Linville, her benefactor, the personification of evil, the parasite who profited from the misery of people like her father. She readied herself, mostly by trying to rein in her feelings of resentment and anger.

The man she met was not the personification of evil but of acquiescence and docility. He was only 45 but looked considerably older, white hair, sullen face, gray pallor. He spoke absently, welcoming her to the Compound, but otherwise seeming blank and joyless. As she got to know the Linville family and the other members of the Compound, she found them emotionally emaciated. In escaping to the Moon, in removing themselves from society, they were small and pitiable. The conspiracy theories were all wrong: there was no satanic Bacchanalia here, only melancholy, sorrow and terrible isolation.

Noah Linville gave her little guidance on what his daughter's curriculum should be, only that she be "well educated." Hughes was given any materials she would need: lab equipment, holographic devices, biotechnological material. She will ask for books, then materials to make stages.

After she had settled into her suite—almost as big as the house she grew up in—Hughes finally met Amelia, her charge. She was escorted to Hughes suite and appeared bored and sullen, but not in the typical fashion of a 14-year-old girl. Her eyes were as vacant as her father's, she seemed neither interested nor disinterested in anything. Hughes attributed this to growing up in this environment, not just the physical environment, but being surrounded by joyless people surely influenced how she was raised. Hughes never learned why the previous tutor was let go, but wondered if it was because that person failed to connect with Amelia.

Amelia's oral communication skills were little more than orders barked at her Conversational AI. The "Voice in the Room" was also the source of her news and information about the world, and it has been significantly redacted by her parents, borrowing a technique from authoritarian regimes on Earth. The music, news stories, feeds Amelia has access to were carefully curated to avoid mention of the reality on Earth, presenting the Compound-approved version of Earth, all intended to convey to Amelia and the other children that Earth was such a hellhole that by comparison, the isolation of the Moon was infinitely preferable. The "Voice" was

Amelia's only companion, and she can be said to have formed an attachment to the conversational AI. Indeed, she had more of a relationship with the disembodied Voice as she did with her previous tutor. Hughes saw immediately that forming a bond with Amelia was going to be a challenge.

Hughes suggested they take a walk to have Amelia show her around the Compound. After it was seized by Noah's grandfather, the Linvilles set about expanding what had originally been the Marslink lunar base into a 200,000 sq ft compound that sprawled across the lunar surface. Walking its halls was an almost day-long trek for Hughes and Amelia, and they still did not make it to the tennis courts and fitness center. A semi-successful technology had created an Earth-like gravity inside the Compound, but Hughes still noticed that she "bounced"—she had no other word for the sensation—as she walked. Amelia took her to the entertainment wing and to the Grand Hall, the setting for magnificent parties that, over the years, had dwindled to the occasional get together. It was clear the Compound was built with the expectation that 1000 or so people would live here and that target might one day be met, Hughes thought. But today, only around 75 people rattled around this gilded cage. As she toured the Compound. Hughes carefully observed how these surroundings might serve as a third teacher for her pupil.

After their first excursion, Hughes and Amelia returned to the tutor's suite. Hughes was still unpacking, and girl noticed the books packed into one of her suitcases. "What are those?" Amelia inquired. Hughes was stunned to learn that Amelia had never seen a book before. Her parents didn't keep books around the compound—not one room of the 200,000 sq ft of this place was reserved for a library—and her parents also closely monitored what she accessed on the feeds. Amelia did not have access to reports of the Earth, no news, no entertainment, no sports. What Amelia knew of the Earth came only from stories from her parents and other adults at the compound, and these were mostly accounts of their harrowing escape from a dying planet.

Amelia pulled Hughes's copy of Zadie Smith's *White Teeth* from her bag and examined it as if it were an artifact from some lost civilization—which come to think of it, it might very well have been. "What's this?" Amelia inquired, and Hughes told her it was the story of how two friends from different upbringings attempt to negotiate those differences. "It's one of my favorites," Hughes said, and asked if Amelia wanted to read it. While Amelia most certainly could read, she had never read a book before and Hughes' first lesson as her tutor was to instruct her in how to use this venerable technology, how the words were arranged on the page, the order of the pages, the fact that it wasn't a kinetic device as she was accustomed to. "Let's read it together," Hughes suggested and for the next week the two of them sounded out the story. In fact, Hughes did most of the reading as Amelia was either reluctant to or incapable of reading aloud.

It turned out that Amelia liked stories and fiction, but her previous tutor discouraged her from reading these. Her parents, who made their fortunes as technologists, wanted Amelia to have a STEM-focused education, which their 14-year-old largely rejected. After they finished *White Teeth* and after they spent hours talking about the book and the characters and the meaning, Hughes suggested that they read more books together, only this time the tutor urged Amelia to do the reading. It was clear that Amelia had poor oracy abilities, and so the two began to work on Amelia's vocal expressiveness. Amelia encountered relatively few people in her life, and there were only a handful of kids her own age at the compound. Indeed, Hughes harbored concern about Amelia's socialization, inasmuch as there was a society here on the Moon.

After they had read aloud from half a dozen books, Hughes made her first requisition for real, physical books, which mystified Amelia's parents. Hughes lit upon the idea of acting out scenes and dialogue from the books. After a month or so of this technique, Hughes started asking Amelia about the motivations of the characters, then had her act out the part again. In acting as a director, Hughes felt that Amelia was exhibiting greater trust than their awkward first meeting. And indeed, Amelia's diction and expressiveness showed marked improvement after only a few months of this activity. Hughes had not prepared a pedagogical strategy, even during her layover on the orbiting station. Noah Linville had given her only vague direction as to the purpose of Amelia's education. Their educational program emerged spontaneously. Although she had not anticipated it, theatre, acting, direction emerged as the core of their private curriculum.

They expanded their repertoire. They read psychology, philosophy and literary criticism. And Hughes had Amelia transcribe these into literature, and then translate these into plays, for this forced Amelia to work on dialogue and descriptions of scenes. This was the first instance of Hughes having Amelia develop her writing. If she had occasion to write, she naturally used the Writer her parents provided. Amelia found the process of writing anything longer than a prompt felt odd and unnatural, but she soon developed the ability. Having now read and acted and directed together, Amelia was ready and eager to write. After translating literature into plays, Amelia began writing her own short stories and scenes and descriptions of her dreams. For it seemed that Amelia did, in fact, have dreams.

One day, Amelia remarked that when they were acting out a scene, the two of them usually remained seated. They had spent so much time working on expressiveness and diction that they forgot to move. "People move in real life!" Amelia exclaimed, and so the two of them worked on blocking, then choreography, concentrating on the movement of the body in space. At one stage, Hughes asked Amelia to stop reciting and just focus on her body, what it was doing, how it was gesticulating. "What is the body communicating?" she asked. "Is it saying the same thing the words are saying?" This was a revelation for Amelia, and for the next few weeks said nothing in Hughes' presence, communicating only through gesture, facial expression, body movement. They developed a kind of pidgin sign language between the two of them. It was only shortly thereafter that the two began to dance. Amelia woke Taniya one morning with the insight that she could dance. One of their plays told the story only through body movements. Amelia was delighted with her creativity and set out to prepare a small demonstration. She proudly acted without words to Hughes, her tutor refraining from telling her that she had invented ballet.

As the size and scope of their dramatic reading expanded outward, Amelia decided they needed to build a set, a real set, not just pillows and chairs propped up around Amelia room. Hughes secured an unused room. It turns out these were plentiful at the compound, and this became their theater. Up to this point, Hughes felt her own education had prepared her to tutor this burgeoning intellect, but when it came to making things, Taniya had little experience upon which to draw. Here was an instance where pupil instructed teacher. Amelia improvised techniques of architecture about how to shape space, to apprehend the properties of materials. There were many mistakes and missteps and, at first, Amelia was frustrated and ready to quit, but Hughes guided her with patience. "What did we learn?" she asked, when one structure collapsed. "Failure is an opportunity to learn," a lesson even Hughes had not grasped until this moment. The two of them hoarded a 3D printer to manufacture their set. Without planning it, Amelia was exploring the relationship between hand and mind.

"Costumes!" Amelia exclaimed one day, although producing their own costumes would require a specialized fabricator. None of the 3D printers at the Compound could handle fabric, so Taniya requisitioned a fabricator. Noah Linville had said that she could have access to anything, but this would mean several weeks before one could be delivered to the Compound. Hughes mused that some of the greatest geniuses in history—Da Vinci, Dali, Orson Welles, the Bauhaus—eventually worked on set design and costuming. Musical accompaniment proved to be a challenge, and so they had to rely on an AI music generator. But Amelia soon learned how to compose scores and how to balance music, movement and dialogue. The two of them had forged their own Black Mountain College here on the Sea of Tranquility.

Amelia felt comfortable enough with her performance skills that she and Hughes planned their first public performance. All of their work had occurred in their own private realm, both by choice and the fact that her parents showed so little interest in what they were doing. Since Amelia wasn't complaining to them, her parents assumed all was well. After much discussion, the pair decided to stage *Atlas Shrugged* for the compound community. The story was almost a religious text at the compound, especially among the male founders, even if the book was not much read anymore. Amelia and Hughes translated the book into a play and set to work building a stage, costumes, lighting.

At first, they had conceived this as a one woman show, but other children at the compound had developed an interest in what Amelia and Hughes were doing. Each had their own tutors, and each was dissatisfied with having to endure what they felt were pointless lessons. One boy, Christopher Burnett, approached Amelia and Hughes one afternoon as they were walking to their private theater, asking if he could join them. Amelia flatly said "No," whether to hoard Hughes to herself or from self-consciousness. Hughes was struck by how little interaction the young people of the compound had. She worried about their socialization, Amelia's especially. Aside from their time together, Amelia spent little time with other people. She would eat with her parents, spend time with her grandparents, occasionally goof around with some of the other young people at the compound, but otherwise had led a solitary life. Hughes could see this same behavior in other children she would meet, and so when Christopher Burnett asked if he could help build sets, Hughes took Amelia aside and asked her where the harm would be in including him and, indeed, other kids from the compound. At a minimum, they could stage *Atlas Shrugged* as a full ensemble. Amelia countered that the other kids lacked the acting and staging skills needed and would ruin the production. Hughes reminded her that at one stage she was similarly awkward and inarticulate. If they brought other kids into the production, Amelia could act as a teacher or mentor to them, imparting all she had learned. When presented like this, Amelia brightened and consented. The premiere of *Atlas Shrugged* would need to be delayed, since the play would need to be rewritten with more parts and the other children taught how to how to enunciate and project.

Six months after they were first approached by Chritopher Burnett, Hughes and Amelia opened *Atlas Shrugged* to an audience made up of the entire Compound community, the first such public gathering in many years. Amelia played the role of John Galt—in this version, she is Jonna Galt. There was much trepidation at performing publicly, but the play was a success, loved by all. The entire community was delighted with Amelia's interpretation of the sacred text. The other parents marveled at the confident young woman Amelia had become under Hughes's tutelage and the changes their own children exhibited and immediately terminated their tutors. Hughes was asked to form a school for all the children of the Compound, and she happily accepted.

In tutoring Amelia Linville, Hughes had developed a new pedagogical philosophy: education was integrative, education was a Gesamtkunstwerk, a total work of art. Upon her return to Earth, Hughes will form her own school. She will become the new Maria Montessori, minus the political illusions.

After the triumph of *Atlas Shrugged*, she was asked to form a salon for the adults, whose empty lives would now be filled with ideas, poetry, art and music. It was clear, however, that she was to stay clear from philosophy, ethics, current affairs, indeed anything that would ask her hosts to reflect on their situation, their condition, to consider the world they have abandoned.

Hughes took introductory psychology at Spellman, and so was by no means an expert, but she nevertheless diagnosed the people here at the Compound as suffering what she would term "withdrawal symptoms:" the vacant looks, the lack of initiative, despite the overwhelming material comforts that surrounded them. These were the effects of a collective that had withdrawn from society without really creating a new one to replace it. There were other people on the Moon, of course. Governments had established research stations across the expanse of the satellite, mining companies claimed vast areas, but the total number of people on the moon at any given time numbered in the thousands. It was reminiscent of what the Antarctic used to look like when it was just a collection of research stations, before the cities were established. As a sovereign territory, the Compound would occasionally send diplomats or emissaries to these other entities, but there was little other interaction. A key feature of withdrawal symptoms, according to Hughes, was the absolute certainty that the Escapists had "won," that they had survived the apocalypse they had helped unleash on Earth, and believed—truly believed—that they were thriving in this condition. Hughes briefly mused that she might publish a paper based on her observations of those with withdrawal symptoms, but then remembered that part of the agreement she signed when she took the tutoring position was that she could not write about, photograph, or otherwise publicize life at the Compound.

About the time Amelia turned eighteen, she approached her tutor in a hushed voice and confided her struggles to her. Chief among them, Amelia wanted to learn more about the Earth. For all of her life, the Earth was the boiling satellite that hovered above the moon. She knew only what her parents and grandparents had told her about it—not much—and the Voice only spoke vaguely about it. She knew that people on Earth were still forced to live on the surface, rather than below ground in a superior, environmentally-controlled environment. That people on Earth disliked work and were unproductive. Amelia understood that Hughes's tenure at the compound was reaching its conclusion. The Linvilles took the unprecedented step of offering her a second five-year contract to continue her school and to continue to mentor Amelia, but she had yet to commit to the renewal.

"You're not thinking of returning to Earth, are you?" Amelia asked incredulously. Hughes said that she was indeed thinking of a return, explaining that she wanted to solve problems, maybe not all of them, but at least one of them. She could not leave the planet to disintegrate. Amelia demanded lessons about the Earth, and their curriculum started to center around the "forbidden knowledge" of Earth, its history, its prospects. Only in the last year or so had Amelia even considered the Earth, and when Hughes intimated that she might be returning there, her interest grew.

"Take me with you," Amelia announced one day. "Take me back to Earth with you." Hughes was dumbfounded and more than a little concerned. "Your parents would never allow it. Besides, it would be a huge adjustment for you. If nothing else, the gravitational differences might be too much. You couldn't possibly cope." Amelia was adamant, and Hughes eventually acceded to her wishes. She would need to learn more about the Earth. It had many problems: it was dangerously warm, there was political conflict, many societies had yet to solve the problem of technological unemployment. It was at this moment that Hughes explained to Amelia why there were so many people without work on Earth. It was Amelia herself that made the connection to the source of her family's wealth, which only hardened her resolve to leave the Moon.

I wish I could say that the two hatched a daring escape under cloak of darkness to stow away on a shuttle, avoiding the security detail sent by Amelia's parents. But that is not how it unfolded. Although no member of the Compound had ever voluntarily left, and while her parents stamped their feet in protest, they finally agreed to their daughter's wishes. It seemed that in writing the Constitution for the Compound, no one had bothered to define the age of adulthood. That Amelia was eighteen now made no legal difference, the Constitution only saying that all members were free to choose their own life path. The age at which one could enjoy this freedom was never specified. Ameila wished to exercise the freedom to follow her own path.

She didn't know exactly what that path was and was hoping that Hughes would continue to mentor her upon their arrival. As Hughes had said, there were myriad problems on Earth. She only had to solve one. But which one?

And so, with little fanfare but no small amount of tears, Taniya Hughes and Amelia Linville boarded the shuttle that would carry them to the orbiting station, where they would spend their two weeks dreaming about how Amelia would bring welcomed change to the distressed planet. "Let's go" Amelia said, smiling at Hughes, as the ship undocked from the station, sending them drifting toward the Earth.

Key Futures Themes

- Education, Pedagogy and Learning
- Technological Unemployment
- Intergenerational Trauma
- Escapist and Secessionist Micro-States
- Social Capital
- Geopolitics of Space

Bibliography

Bates, Michael. 2015. *Principality of Sealand: Holding the Fort*. Principality of Sealand.

Bonner, Thomas Neville. 2002. *Iconoclast: Abraham Flexner and a Life in Learning*. Baltimore: Johns Hopkins University Press.

Marshall, Tim. 2023. *The Future of Geography: How the Competition in Space Will Change Our World*. New York: Scribner.

Rushkoff, Douglas. 2022. *Survival of the Richest: Escape Fantasies of the Tech Billionaires*. New York: W.W. Norton.

MIX
Papier aus verantwortungsvollen Quellen
Paper from responsible sources
FSC® C105338

If you have any concerns about our products,
you can contact us on
ProductSafety@springernature.com

In case Publisher is established outside the EU,
the EU authorized representative is:
Springer Nature Customer Service Center GmbH
Europaplatz 3, 69115 Heidelberg, Germany

Printed by Libri Plureos GmbH
in Hamburg, Germany